THIRD EDITION

Elementary
SOCIAL STUDIES

A PRACTICAL GUIDE

June R. Chapin
College of Notre Dame

Rosemary G. Messick
San Jose State University

Longman *Publishers USA*

**Elementary Social Studies:
A Practical Guide, Third Edition**

Longman, 10 Bank Street, White Plains, N.Y. 10606
Associated companies:
Longman Group Ltd., London
Longman Cheshire Pty., Melbourne
Longman Paul Pty., Auckland
Copp Clark Longman Ltd., Toronto

Senior acquisitions editor: Laura McKenna
Associate editor: Travis Lester
Production editor: Ann P. Kearns
Editorial Assistant: Matt Baker
Text design: Steven August Krastin
Text design adaptation and cover design: Celine Brandes
Text art: J&R Services, Fine Line Inc.
Production supervisor: Richard C. Bretan
Compositor: Digitype

Library of Congress Cataloging-in-Publication Data
Chapin, June R. Date.
    Elementary social studies : a practical guide / June R. Chapin,
Rosemary G. Messick. — 3rd ed.
       p.   cm.
Includes bibliographical references and index.
ISBN 0-8013-1568-9
1. Social sciences — Study and teaching (Elementary) — United
States. I. Messick, Rosemary G. II. Title.
LB1584.C47   1996
372.83 — dc20

95-17913
CIP

1 2 3 4 5 6 7 8 9 10-MA-9998979695

CONTENTS

PREFACE

We have made three assumptions in preparing the third edition of *Elementary Social Studies:* First, that you come to the professional sequence of your teacher preparation program with a general background in academic disciplines such as history, sociology, and anthropology that serve as a foundation for elementary social studies. Second, that you, like students in most professional programs, are scheduled for only a one-semester, one- to three-credit course in teaching social studies, or a core methods course in which social studies instruction is integrated. And third, that you have other courses in your program that expose you to learning theory, curriculum planning, the teaching of concepts and generalizations, and instructional technology.

Social studies instruction is a broad field that is becoming increasingly integrated with other content areas. To help you focus on important concerns, we have limited the scope of the text to topics that are *basic, specific,* and yet *critical* to teaching the social studies in the elementary years, kindergarten through eighth grade. Preparation of this edition has, however, made us realize that changes in current practice, in reform emphases, and in our society and schools require that we interweave new material that has now become *basic, specific,* and *critical* to this subject.

To conceptualize the core information on social studies education, we also present and analyze vignettes and provide additional textual exposition to enrich your knowledge about classroom instruction and curriculum in general. Chapter introductions and definitions of terms provide you with links to your other professional courses in the areas of curriculum and learning. Small group discussion topics, lesson plans, and other activities suggest instructional resources to pursue in your own teaching.

Some of the topics in this text are distinctive and new. They include discussions of the National Curriculum Standards in history, geography, civics and government, and the social studies (Chapters 1 and 5). Also included is new material on values or character education, considerations for process and content extensions that focus on culture learning, and numerous specific suggestions for teaching social studies skills such as developing cultural respect and understanding chronological time while using new technologies and the most recent assessment-oriented approaches to organizing evaluation in the social studies.

The small group and individual exercises integrated into all the chapters, if pursued as part of your class time, can position you to explore more thoroughly key issues that the text introduces. Time spent doing these exercises with your peers will certainly enrich your ability to think critically and reflectively about issues within social studies instruction. Lesson plans, unit outlines, and instructional resource lists throughout the text suggest activities you can try out as you participate in elementary classes and ideas you can build on as you plan more extended teaching sequences.

We continue to learn from the experiences of our own students, from classroom teachers with whom we work, and from our university colleagues throughout the country. Our reviewers, in particular, served an important role in improving and updating this text for the third edition:

Janet Elaine Alleman, Michigan State University
David M. Balzer, University of Toledo
Susan Bayard, Salem State College
Marlowe Berg, San Diego State University
Carl L. Harris, Sam Houston State University
Mary E. Hauser, Carroll College
Robert L. Leight, Lehigh University
Jean Luckowski, University of Montana
Gail McEachron-Hirsch, College of William and Mary
J. Sabrina Mims, California State University, Los Angeles
Nell C. Nicholson, Alabama A & M University
Ivory Phillips, Jackson State University
E. Wayne Ross, State University of New York, Binghamton
Sande Stratton, University of New Haven
W. Scott Thomson, East Carolina University
Scott Waters, Emporia State University

We are grateful for the valuable additions of all our colleagues to this text, although we alone are responsible for any errors.

Finally, between us, we have taught in the Midwest, Portugal, Spain, and Brazil and for many years in California. We have seen teachers make a positive difference in the lives of children and feel privileged to watch children gain opportunities through education. We believe that the social studies can help you make dreams a reality for children you teach, and we invite you to work with us toward that goal.

THE ELEMENTARY SOCIAL STUDIES CURRICULUM

In Chapter 1, we learn that the traditional social studies curriculum is being heavily criticized and that changes may come in the future. Specifically, we treat the following topics:

1/ Images of the Social Studies

2/ Why Teach the Social Studies?

3/ Goals and Standards

4/ Should We Teach Values, Moral Education, or Character Education?

5/ Definitions of the Social Studies

6/ National Curriculum Patterns

7/ Importance of Textbook Series

8/ Mounting Criticism: Scope and Sequence

IMAGES OF THE SOCIAL STUDIES

Welcome to the world of social studies! What do you remember about your elementary social studies program? If any of the following activities seem familiar, jot down on a piece of paper whether the memory is pleasant.

Clipping out items from a newspaper for Friday current events
Doing a research report on Daniel Boone from your school's encyclopedia
Finding out the latitude and longitude of a long list of cities
Learning about the Pilgrims at Thanksgiving
Visiting a site where your state's Native American tribes lived
Writing a contest essay on American government
Answering the questions at the end of a textbook chapter
Writing to foreign consuls and embassies for information about your assigned
    country
Reenacting pioneer life
Making a papier-mache globe
Writing a personal history book
Drawing neighborhood maps
Working on a committee that one person dominated
Learning about the immigrant groups from which you came

1.1   *SMALL GROUP WORK: WHAT WORKS BEST?*

Now add to this list the activities that you remember experiencing in elementary social studies. Try to include both pleasant and boring times. Compare with others in your class your list of what you liked and didn't like. Are there activities that everyone remembers enjoying? Are there other activities that everyone disliked? Your image of what elementary social studies is stems mainly from your own experiences. Can you now draw a simple picture or graphic that summarizes either positively or negatively your experiences as a social studies student? What one descriptive word best pulls together your image of the social studies?

1.2   *SMALL GROUP WORK: HOW IMPORTANT IS SOCIAL STUDIES?*

How do you rank the importance of social studies in the elementary curriculum? Look at the following list of traditional subjects taught in elementary school.

Health/physical education (PE)
Mathematics
Reading/Language Arts

Science
Social studies

Now rank these subjects, 1 through 5, in order of their importance to you. Share your list with other members of your class. Most elementary teachers and students rank social studies third or lower. If your ranking was within this range, what influenced your response?

Elementary teachers often have negative attitudes toward the social studies as a result of their own school experiences, perhaps because of the following:

Learning about social studies largely emphasized trivial facts.
The dominant instructional tool was the textbook.
Most social studies activities concentrated on large group recitation and lecture.
Emotional or affective objectives were not included as part of the curriculum.

Two other reasons may account, at least in part, for the less-than-enthusiastic attitude that many elementary teachers have toward the social studies: lack of preparation and lack of interest. Many of you have taken only a few social science or history courses in college. You may feel underqualified or reluctant to tackle the sometimes controversial subject matter of the social studies. Many of you may feel strongly that reading and math programs are basic in elementary education; however, a social studies program is also basic. In fact, a good social studies program can go far toward improving students' skills in other subjects, including reading, writing, and arithmetic.

A good social studies program can contribute to producing good citizens. The educational reform reports of the 1980s have reaffirmed the importance of the social studies in citizenship education. Children become adults and as citizens they must make thoughtful decisions. Our "Nation [is] at Risk"[1] unless we have the background and skills needed for that difficult task. In addition, effective citizenship depends on people's willingness or attitude to participate in our government. Attitudes toward authority and government are formed early, in the elementary grades; they do not wait until later in the middle school years to appear.

We believe in the *vital* importance of social studies instruction, both in providing students with basic skills they need to function in our society and in preparing students to become responsible, thoughtful, participating citizens. If we are successful in transmitting this belief to you, then social studies teaching at least in

---

[1]*A Nation at Risk: The Imperative for Educational Reform.* Prepared by the National Commission on Excellence in Education (Washington, D.C.: U.S. Department of Education, April 1983).

your classrooms may not suffer the neglect that otherwise often occurs at the primary level.

This text will help you find ways of teaching the social studies that you and your students will learn from and enjoy. Social studies *can* be taught creatively and thoughtfully. As a result of your efforts, students may find that social studies is their favorite subject. More important, through *your* social studies instruction, your students will acquire the necessary knowledge, skills, and values to participate as active citizens in our society.

WHY TEACH THE SOCIAL STUDIES?

There are good reasons for teaching the social studies in addition to its being a required and mandated test area. The social studies are about people. No other area of the curriculum is more concerned with human relations than the social studies, which is designed to help us understand ourselves as well as others—from our families and nearby neighbors to those who live halfway around the world. Each of us is concerned about self, family, and friends. The social studies, therefore, build on an area of inherently high interest.

Children studying the social studies today will have much of their lives in the twenty-first century. They will experience a world rapidly changing as knowledge dramatically expands. Their occupations and the skills they need to function in a modern, information based society may change rapidly as well. As teachers, we must always be conscious of how we can help our students live successfully in the coming years; we must prepare them *now* for the twenty-first century and not wait until it arrives. The social studies are uniquely suited for this preparation because they teach skills for living in and understanding our world, skills that will be vital in the next century.

In addition to *teaching* students about human relations, social studies plays an important role in *preparing* them to become active citizens. Students need to know their rights and their responsibilities as American citizens. They will have to make intelligent choices within the context of our democratic society about what kind of community and world they wish to inhabit. We want to encourage their concern about the quality of life in their community, in their nation, and in the world.

Understanding peace and justice poses an enormous challenge to all people. Students must not only incorporate basic American values such as equality, freedom, and respect for people and property, but they must also be able to put those values into action through effective participation in the classroom, school, community, nation, and world. A goal of the social studies (as well as of schooling in general) is to help students *reflect* on their own experiences and values. Effective social studies programs ensure that students will be informed and reflective when they begin to participate in both American culture and the global community.

Creative social studies instruction offers the possibility of producing humane individuals willing to help one another and to make the best of the world. All elementary teachers want their students to *know* things, but they also want to influence their students in what the students will become. Teachers want their students to be good people—caring, thoughtful, and humane rather than selfish and cynical. Therefore, an important goal of the social studies is to support the development of humane and thoughtful values in students who become informed and participating citizens.

The social studies curriculum is defined in terms of four major categories:

Knowledge
Skills
Values
Citizenship (often called social participation)

The *rationale* for elementary social studies is summarized in four major goals:

To acquire *knowledge* about human experiences in the past, present and future
To develop *skills* to process information
To develop appropriate democratic *values* and attitudes
To have opportunities for *social participation*

These four goals are not separate and discrete; rather, they are intertwined and overlapping (see Figure 1.1). You may find that in frameworks for certain states, two goals are combined into one sentence. Each word in a goal statement is significant as each word may be translated to mean several years of student learning. Social participation may be regarded as a democratic value, or the goal may be called "skill attainment and social participation." The knowledge goal can be referred to as "knowledge and cultural understanding" or "democratic understanding and civic values." Values may sometimes be called *civic* values to differentiate them from *personal* values. But regardless of how the goals are combined or written, together they form the basic objectives of a social studies program.

Frequently, the process of learning has emotional values attached to it. Did you *hate* math in school? Did you *love* music? For example, when students study pollution, they usually acquire opinions or attitudes about it. Emotional concerns such as racism in the community can have a striking impact on both subject area and students' skill development. Certain skills like writing or thinking may be taught in school, but there is no guarantee that students will make use of them. Unless students have a commitment to, a need for, or a willingness to use the skills they have learned, those skills will be of little value either to the students or to society. All this underlines the connections among the four main goals of a so-

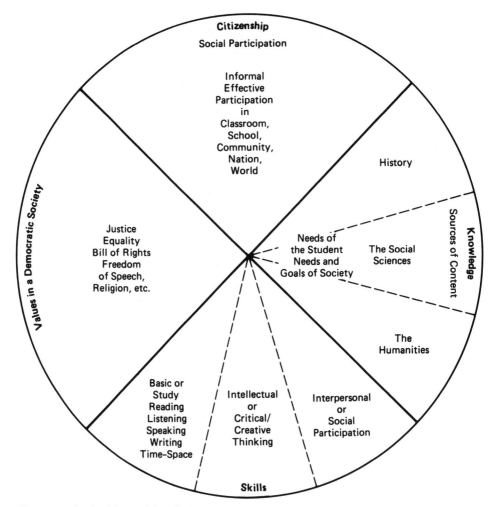

Figure 1.1 Goals of the social studies

cial studies education; although we may speak of each one separately, we must not forget their inherent interrelationships.

GOALS AND STANDARDS

Compared to previous years, the public now worries more about how well American public schools are performing. Calls for changing the system through educational reform continue to be widely heard in the 1990s. Each state is taking steps to respond to public demands to improve the schools. Your career in education will be partly shaped by policies still being formulated that aim to prepare more children to face the challenges of increased economic competition. Keeping up with this national debate is part of our professional obligation. Probably the most important events in this controversial political debate have been the following:

1983   *A Nation at Risk*
        Reported that there was a crisis in public education.
1984–   Competency exams introduced.
        Many states required prospective teachers as well as
            students to achieve a certain level of competency.
1989   Six National Education Goals (1–6 below) adopted by the nation's
            fifty governors with then Governor Bill Clinton as chair of the
            group.
1991   Adoption by President Bush of these six national educational
            goals, *Goals 2000*, for accomplishment by the year 2000.
1994   President Bill Clinton signed *Goals 2000*: Educate America Act,
            which added the last two goals for a total of eight voluntary
            goals. These apply to all children and young people.
        Many professional groups published their guidelines for high-quality
            social studies programs for use throughout the United States.

1. All children will start school ready to learn
2. High school graduation rate will be at least 90 percent.
3. At the fourth, eighth, and twelfth grades, students will demonstrate competency in English, mathematics, science, foreign languages, arts, history, geography, civics, and government; they will be prepared for responsible citizenship and productive employment.
4. U.S. students will be first in the world in sciences and mathematics achievement.
5. Every adult American will be literate, will be able to compete in the global economy, and will be a responsible citizen.
6. Schools will be free of drugs and violence.
7. Funds for improved teacher education and professional development will be allocated.
8. Parental participation will be encouraged in the schools.

You already know that *goals* are the overarching aims or desired outcomes of education. Goals are not achieved in one day, one week, or even one year. Goals like good health or good citizenship are pursued by individuals for decades and in a certain sense are never completely achieved. Another term used in the national educational discussion is *standards*. A standard is used in education to measure a student's level of performance. In addition, it is used to define achievement goals—what students should know and be able to do. Think of the word *curriculum* in front of standards—curriculum standards—to get a more precise sense of the usage of the term. Of course, there also can also be standards for teachers, schools, and state and local education agencies. Congress and other interested governmental, civic, and professional groups hope that high standards for all students based on national goals will be catalysts for change and a stimulus for improving education. The U.S. Department of Education believes that all children need high standards and that national goals will be the means of putting excellence in education. They contend that with varying local standards, too many students get a watered-down curriculum at the present time and that most local and state reforms have not made dramatic improvement in students' achievement. In contrast, in national educational systems like those of Japan and France, high expectations are the norm for all students, and examinations are administered annually to test students' mastery.

Not everyone agrees with the emphasis on the particular national goals listed above, or with the assessment that there is really a "crisis" and if so, the degree of the crisis in American education. Many educators disagreed with the pronouncement that all American public schools are failures, pointing to international reports on the reading skills of American children and other strengths of American public education. However, the U.S. achievement in international testing is much more mixed than is widely known. Our students have been world class in some subjects at certain ages. In the early 1990s, U.S. nine-year-olds ranked among the world's best in reading (second place) and science (third place) out of thirty-one nations. U.S. thirteen- and fourteen-year-olds have done well in reading and literature. But U.S. students have usually ranked last or near last in mathematics and, among older students, anywhere from the middle to the bottom in science.

Geography results have also been mixed. U.S. thirteen-year-olds ranked fifth out of nine countries in a 1991 comparison, but eighteen- to twenty-four-year-olds ranked last in a 1988 Gallup survey.

Some critics think too much emphasis was placed on meeting industry/business goals of being competitive in a global economy while such goals as social cooperation and physical education were neglected. Others feel that the American schools are being blamed and made the scapegoat for the mistakes of business executives.

Note that history, geography, economics, civics, and government were singled out in *Goals 2000* as being important enough to be tested in the fourth, eighth, and twelfth grades. However, not everyone approved of this emphasis. Reflecting the division and controversy within the field of social studies, some did not like the neglect of other academic fields such as anthropology and sociology. In addition, it appeared that social studies testing in the eighth and twelfth grades would be separated into the disciplines of history, geography, civics, and government without reflecting the integration of these areas, the other social science disciplines, and other subject fields. This separation was partly in response to the intensive lobbying on the federal level of groups like the National Geographic Society, who insisted that Americans were almost illiterate or severely deficient in a particular subject area. But this decision meant that there would be separate standards for history, geography, economics, civics, and government and not a single integrated social studies format. Critics such as the National Council for the Social Studies felt that emphasis on separate subjects would not promote integration of the social studies curriculum.

The standards movement's immediate impact on the social studies is Goal 3— all students should leave grades four, eight, and twelve competent in history, geography, economics, civics, and government. Goal 3 and Goal 5 also stressed that all students should be prepared to exercise the rights and responsibilities of citizenship. In response to these national goals, five professional groups composed of nationally recognized experts developed curriculum standards based on the national goals, which then can become the basis for content, student performance, and evaluation. These standards provide a concrete measure for the public to use in judging whether students are meeting the achievement standards. Details of the four separate subject curriculum standards are found in Chapter 5. However, for K–4, the groups agreed on an integrated approach and have cooperated with each other in their standards.

The National Council for the Social Studies (NCSS) was the only group in favor of an integrated social studies approach versus a single subject approach for the eighth and twelfth grades. Their standards used the following ten thematic curriculum strands based on the major concepts of the social sciences and history: culture (anthropology); time, continuity, and change (history); people, places, and environments (geography); individual development and identity (psychology); individuals, groups, and institutions (sociology); power, authority, and governance (political science); production, distribution, and consumption (economics); and three more broadly based themes: (1) science, technology, and society; (2) global connections; and (3) civic ideals and practices. The National Council for the Social Studies felt left out of the process that led to national standards as they received no outside funding that the history, geography, economics, and civics/government projects had to work with to develop standards. Furthermore, the National Council for the Social Studies standards may have limited impact since the disciplines named in Goals 2000 did not explicitly include the term *social studies* but used terms like *history* and *geography*.

What is the significance of the national goals and standards to you? In the past, the federal government has played a very minor role in our system of decentralized state and local American school systems. However, the public's lack of confidence in the public schools has intensified the desire for greater accountability for the schools, and this concern has led to the creation of national educational standards. In effect, many citizens feel that local standards are not high enough and that competency examinations at both the state and local levels have not been successful in moving the educational system toward excellence.

It is difficult to predict with certainty the effect the national standards will have on the American public schools. Critics have said that elementary teachers will need a truck to carry all the national standards in the social studies field as well as the standards in the other curriculum areas such as mathematics, language arts, and science. Elementary teachers face a huge task if they are to become knowledgeable about all the new curriculum standards, let alone decide what changes to make in their instruction.

Ultimately, teachers like you will be the final decision makers in the classroom. It is teachers who can improve the quality of social studies in the elementary school. The national curriculum standards may well have a profound effect as teachers and school districts examine what they presently teach and decide whether they should make changes. The standards should not be thought of as fixed mandates but rather as a framework for teachers and the public/community to use as they examine what they think is most important in the education of elementary school-age children.

The tests based on these national standards will probably be designed by individual states or possibly even a group of states. If so, the impact of the national goals may vary from state to state. The national standards will also influence textbook publishers, who will align their texts to meet the standards; this influence already is evident in many of the new mathematics textbooks. Also influencing curriculum decisions will be the amount of funding that the federal, state, and local governments give to retrain teachers and reallocate resources for testing as well as any perceived threats to the states that they could risk losing federal funds unless their state curricula reflect the national goals.

1.3   *ON YOUR OWN: DO YOU FAVOR TESTING BASED ON STANDARDS?*

Do you think testing should be required in the elementary school in history, geography, economics, and civics and government? Jot down your reasons for your point of view. Learn whether your state or local district presently mandates any testing in the social studies.

SHOULD WE TEACH VALUES, MORAL EDUCATION, OR CHARACTER EDUCATION?

The morals of young people are a very present concern among much of the electorate as the public sees increases in local juvenile crime, substance abuse, and suicides. All these issues have led many to demand that the schools do more about teaching values or, as it sometimes is called, moral or character education.

Many books and articles have been written exploring the reasons some children appear unable to tell right from wrong. Supporters of having schools take a more prominent role in character education often cite statistics on the number of troubled families in our society and quote from studies on the influence of a media that stresses violence and materialism. Many fear that there is a breakdown in our traditional values and that the schools are failing to provide moral education as they once did. They argue that the family and the church appear to have failed or become ineffective in teaching moral values to the young and consequently, there is a critical need for the schools to take a more important role in such instructions. However, efforts to promote the teaching of values in schools also spark a heated debate. Some conservatives feel that character education is an attempt to spread political correctness and undermine parental authority. Meanwhile, liberals fear that the character education movement may be a backdoor effort to mix religion with public education. Teachers, on the other hand, often approve of the teaching of values as a successful way to reduce discipline problems.

Of course, moral education is not new. In nineteenth-century American public schools, textbooks frequently stressed morals (describing what happens to wicked children or extolling the virtue of being honest like George Washington). Using poetry, biography, patriotic and religious ceremonies, and Bible readings, teachers felt free to tell or preach to children about what was right or wrong. Teachers talked seriously about character development and the importance of adhering to moral principles. This type of education presumed general agreement among the community, the church, and the school on the right values to teach.

In the last thirty or more years, many educators have become more neutral about teaching values in a society where people hold different beliefs. They are worried that parents may criticize them for imposing their own values on students. Court decisions against Bible reading in the schools and a greater variety of religious and ethical systems in our society have made schools more cautious about the teaching of values. The most important exceptions to the decline in moral education have been drug and sex education, both of which have been thorny curriculum areas for some school districts. Critics of drug and sex education state that the programs have not been effective because they have not been strong and forceful enough in teaching specific values.

Although the term *moral education* became unfashionable, schools always have taught values through textbooks, teachers, and school rules. Values are presented by the way teachers treat students and the way students are allowed to treat teachers and each other. There is a hidden curriculum of what is right and wrong even when questions of right and wrong do not come up directly in the classroom. Every classroom has rules that embody values. "Children should put or store their possessions in certain places in the room." "Raise your hand if you wish to speak."

Teaching values often became restricted to teaching broad, general civic values such as justice and public responsibilities—voting, obeying the law, paying taxes, and serving on a jury. These values have a high level of acceptance by almost all members of the community. The primary organization in the field of social studies, the National Council for the Social Studies, has listed democratic beliefs and values they believe are relevant to education.[2] Look over this list. Are there any values that you would feel uncomfortable teaching? Are there any values you feel are omitted?

DEMOCRATIC BELIEFS AND VALUES

A. Rights of the Individual

Right to life
Right to liberty
Right to dignity
Right to security
Right to equality of opportunity
Right to justice
Right to privacy
Right to private ownership of property

B. Freedoms of the Individual

Freedom to participate in the political process
Freedom of worship
Freedom of thought
Freedom of conscience
Freedom of assembly
Freedom of inquiry
Freedom of expression

C. Responsibilities of the Individual

To respect human life
To respect the rights of others
To be tolerant
To be honest
To be compassionate
To demonstrate self-control
To participate in the democratic process
To work for the common good
To respect the property of others

---

[2]John Jarolimek, Chair, NCSS Task Force on Scope and Sequence, "Social Studies for Citizens of a Strong and Free Nation," in *Social Curriculum Planning Resources* (Washington, D.C.: National Council for the Social Studies, 1990), 31–32.

D. Beliefs Concerning Societal Conditions and Governmental Responsibilities

Societies need laws that are accepted by the majority of the people.
Dissenting minorities are protected.
Government is elected by the people.
Government respects and protects individual rights.
Government respects and protects individual freedoms.
Government guarantees civil liberties.
Government works for the common good.

Few educators or parents would dispute the inclusion of any of these values in the classroom, but more controversial issues and "personal" values often elicit different reactions. It was reported in 1992 that teachers in the Los Angeles area schools were forbidden to discuss the Rodney King trial in their classes. The rationale for this edict was to prevent outbursts of violence. Was the issue too hot to be discussed? Should students have discussed the morality of the Persian Gulf War as the surrounding political and military events were unfolding? What if a student believes drugs should be legalized? Can that student write an editorial or try to persuade his or her classmates about the value of this point of view? Should that student be allowed to wear a T-shirt with a message advocating drug legalization? You can see that both teachers and community members might react to different concerns, such as classroom management or free speech rights. More discussion on guidelines for the teaching of controversial issues is found in Chapter 5.

Even though moral education has generally received little attention by educators (see Table 1.1), Nel Noddings and many other have advocated that more attention be given in the schools to developing caring individuals who have a knowledge of self and a moral recognition that they can do both evil and good. According to Noddings, restructured schools need to teach students not to harm each other.[3] Lawrence Kohlberg sought to help students develop more complex reasoning patterns based on a higher set of values. Kohlberg called for students to discuss the *reasons* for their value choices, not merely to share with others, but to foster change in the students' stages of moral reasoning. His main method was to present artificial moral dilemmas (should you steal a drug to help some family member, should you tattle on a friend who has stolen a sweater in a department store, etc.). Students then would take positions (such as whether you should tell on a friend) followed by group discussion and relatively structured argumentation in a Socratic dialogue format.[4] Carol Gilligan criticized Kohlberg for omitting a feminine perspective. She believed that females had a different but equally valid way of arriving at moral

---

[3]Nel Noddings, *The Challenge to Care in Schools* (New York: Teachers College Press, 1992).
[4]Lawrence Kohlberg, "Moral Education in the Schools: A Developmental View," *School Review*, 74, no. 1 (Spring 1966): 1–30.

TABLE 1.1   APPROACHES TO MAJOR VALUES EDUCATION

Approaches	Purposes	Methods
Caring (Noddings)	Care for self Care for others	Modeling, dialogue, practice, and confirmation
Moral Development (Kohlberg)	Students to develop higher set of values	Moral dilemmas, small group discussion, teacher in devil's advocate role
Values Clarification (Simon et al.)	Students to become aware of their own values Students to identify values of others	Variety of methods Self-analysis exercises
Social Action	Students have opportunities for social action based on their values	Projects in schools and in community
Indoctrination	Changes values of students in desired direction	Variety of methods Selected data provided
Analysis	Students use logical thinking to decide values issues	Rational discussion Research

NOTE: Difficulties arise on where to place such programs as substance abuse approaches like the "Just Say No" programs, which stress self-esteem and drug-free behavior. Some would classify these programs as indoctrination while others would put them in the analysis approach since they may use medical research as a data source. There is also a similar problem with many of the character education approaches.

decisions.[5] Critics of this approach have argued that the moral dilemmas were not realistic and not the problems that most students presently face in everyday life.

However, the most severe criticism about values education in the schools was directed against Sidney Simon and his colleagues, who advocated a nonjudgmental approach called *values clarification.* These authors wanted to help students become aware of and to identify their own values and those of others. They wanted students to communicate honestly with others about their own values even if their beliefs might be supportive of using drugs or other socially "unaccepted" values. Simon's methods included using both rational thinking and emotional awareness to allow students to examine their personal feelings, values, and behavior. Often these exercises were contrived situations (deciding who should be chosen to stay in a fallout shelter, making your own obituary) and self-analysis exercises (writing about two ideal days, jotting down twenty things you love to do). While critics raged against the values clarification approach for not teaching "good" values and allowing any value system to be acceptable, teachers purchased his handbooks of values clarification exercises by the hundreds of thousands and most students enjoyed working with the "fun" exercises.[6]

[5]Carol Gilligan, *In a Different Voice: Psychological Theory* (Cambridge, Mass.: Harvard University Press, 1982).

[6]Sidney B. Simon, Leland W. Howe, and Howard Kirschenbaum, *Values Clarification* (New York: Hart, 1972).

Critics of the values clarification approach were also concerned about invasion of privacy issues as students talked about their own personal behavior. Some parents also felt that the schools were teaching the wrong values or not correcting students who had "bad" values; many were horrified at Simon's conception of values as relative rather than absolute.

In addition, the few teachers who implemented *social action*—changing or reforming the community—also were criticized when students were encouraged to take social action based on their values. Usually no one complained if the students cleaned up the local park, and student campaigns to protect the faraway whales usually did not engender much controversy. Citizens were upset, however, when the students began a public information campaign about a local factory that was polluting the environment or when students tried to protect local endangered species like the spotted owl in an area with an economy dependent on logging.

All these approaches to values education—caring, Kohlberg's moral development, Simon's values clarification approach, and social action—raise the question of whether the values education classes in the schools really work (Table 1.1). If you teach students to think and reason about important values, do they *behave* according to their reasoned values? Does formal teaching about values always translate into action? Measuring the effectiveness of any values education approach in the schools has always been difficult. What do you count? A reduction in the number of student referrals or suspensions? The number of children who report more smiling faces?

Your values influence how you teach. Your definition of the social studies, citizenship education, treatment of controversial issues, and culture education springs from your position on values and the way they should be explored in the classroom. Are democratic values and how these values relate to living in a democracy central to teaching social studies? You will decide whether you want to formally teach values, moral education, or character development.

1.4 *ON YOUR OWN: WHAT ARE THE SOURCES OF YOUR VALUES?*

What do you think have been the main sources of your values? How do you think your values may affect your teaching?

DEFINITIONS OF THE SOCIAL STUDIES

Although we have listed four main goals, educators do not always agree on either the *definition* or *content* for the field of social studies. In fact, some people would like to title textbooks like this one *History/Social Science Elementary Teaching* instead of using the term *social studies*. Indeed, there are separate textbooks and journals for the teaching of history or other specific social science subject areas although these are generally more popular with high school teachers. In contrast to the separate subject approach, the National Council for the Social Studies (NCSS) has adopted in 1992 the following formal definition of the social studies.[7]

> Social studies is the integrated study of the social sciences and humanities to promote civic competence. Within the school program, social studies provides coordinated, systematic study drawing upon such disciplines as anthropology, archaeology, economics, geography, history, law, philosophy, political science, psychology, religion, and sociology, as well as appropriate content from the humanities, mathematics, and natural sciences. The primary purpose of social studies is to help young people develop the ability to make informed and reasoned decisions for the public good as citizens of a culturally diverse, democratic society in an interdependent world.

Note that this NCSS definition does not use a separate history/social science subject approach. The NCSS point of view stresses that citizens must be involved in civic affairs and that these civic issues, such as health care and crime, are multidisciplinary in nature. In other words, you need knowledge from several disciplines, not just one social science, to think intelligently about an issue, and generally it is best to try to integrate the curriculum rather than to teach history or other academic fields separately.

Traditionally, social studies draws content from seven disciplines: history, geography, economics, political science, sociology, anthropology, and psychology (see Table 1.2). The key ideas and concepts of these fields are found in Chapter 5 where the details about the specific standards for history, geography, economics, civics, and government are given. Note that the academic fields of sociology, anthropology, and psychology have not produced standards for the schools and therefore these three subject areas will probably not receive the same public attention as history, geography, civics, and (eventually) economics in designing and shaping the curriculum. All these fields have discipline-specific standards that have been produced or are being formulated at this writing. While there are some key ideas, concepts, and skills common to all the social sciences, there is also a different perspective and knowledge stressed by each of these four academic subject areas. How these various standards are to be integrated in the curriculum is a matter of great concern since fragmentation could occur. Content overlaps with other themes and topics in English and the sciences must also be addressed. Historically, whether history/social sciences should be taught separately or integrated has always been a major issue in the teaching of the social studies. Although we listed four widely accepted main goals at the beginning of this chapter, educators do not always agree on what specific *content* should be included in the social studies.

---

[7]Task Force of the National Council for the Social Studies, *Curriculum Standards for Social Studies* Bulletin 89 (Washington, D.C.: National Council for the Social Studies, 1994):3.

TABLE 1.2 DISCIPLINES OF THE SOCIAL SCIENCES

The Past	*The Present*	*The Future*
History	Geography	Future science
Geography	The social sciences:	Where and how might people
Anthropology	Economics	live in the future?
Archaeology	Political Science	
How did our world/nation/community	Sociology	
come to be the way it is?	Anthropology	
	Psychology	
	Where and how do people	
	live now?	

1.5 *ON YOUR OWN: CONTENT FOR THE SOCIAL STUDIES*

What do *you* think the social studies should include? Write down the topics you would expect to teach. Would you include subjects such as career education, consumer education, substance-abuse education, child-abuse education, law-related education, sex-equity education, AIDS education, multicultural/diversity education, or environmental education?

Although definitions of the social studies may vary, the definition that *you* accept is important. Every elementary teacher should be able to define his or her objectives in teaching the social studies, as well as his or her own decisions about its content.

Robert Barr, a social studies educator, and his colleagues defined three main social studies traditions, shown in the following list.[8] Note that all the approaches emphasize the broad goal of citizenship education but differ on how to achieve this goal. Concrete examples are given to illustrate the differences of each.

Citizenship Transmission: A Society-Centered Approach

Purpose—Citizenship is best promoted by inculcating right values as a framework for making decisions.

Method—Transmission: Concepts and values are transmitted by such techniques as textbook, recitation, lecture, question-and-answer sessions, and structured problem-solving exercises.

Content—Content is selected by an authority and interpreted by the teacher, and has the function of illustrating values, beliefs, and attitudes.

---

[8]Robert D. Barr, James L. Barth, and S. Samuel Shermis, *Defining the Social Studies*, Bulletin 51 (Washington, D.C.: National Council for the Social Studies, 1977).

Social Studies Taught as Social Science

Purpose—Citizenship is best promoted by decision making based on mastery of social science concepts, processes, and problems.

Method—Discovery: Each of the social sciences has its own method of gathering and verifying knowledge. Students must discover and apply the method that is appropriate to each social science.

Content—Proper content is the structure, concepts, problems, and processes of both the separate and the integrated social science disciplines.

Social Studies Taught as Reflective Inquiry

Purpose—Citizenship is best promoted through a process of inquiry in which knowledge is derived from what citizens need to know to make decisions and solve problems.

Method—Reflective Inquiry: Decision making is structured and disciplined through a reflective inquiry process that aims at identifying problems and responding to conflicts by means of testing insights.

Content—Analysis of individual citizen's values yields needs and interests. These, in turn, form the basis for student self-selection of problems that constitute the content for reflection.

Citizenship Transmission

What do you think the tradition of social studies taught as citizenship transmission means? Every nation or societal group brings up its children to reflect its own values and culture. Primitive groups as well as the most advanced technological societies attempt to socialize their children. For example, the French want their children to appreciate French culture; members of various religious groups want their children to practice their religious beliefs.

In the United States, children must also be prepared to live in our common culture. They must understand our unique American heritage and our political and economic systems. In addition, they must speak English and participate in community life. Many institutions in our society, including the family and the media, contribute to our children's knowledge about mainstream culture. Our schools also play an important role in this process of teaching about our shared political and social values.

Some social studies authorities like James Shaver argue that the school *must* instill in students a commitment to democratic values. These basic values, called "the American creed," cement the nation together; they include, among other things, due process of law, respect for others, free access to information, freedom of choice (including multiculturalism), and respect for the value of rational thought. According to Shaver, it is crucial that social studies instruction be based on democratic values and that students accept the basic values of our society as fundamental and not debatable.[9]

But this position does not mean that the teacher has the right to indoctrinate students in every area. *Indoctrination* is the shaping of people's minds by providing information without permitting them to question or examine the information being transmitted. Often the purpose of indoctrination is to make citizens subject to those in power or to influence individuals to accept a dictated solution to a problem. Indoctrination can also be considered a value approach similar to those already discussed such as moral development or values clarification (Table 1.1).

As teachers, we are guilty of using indoctrination if we base our presentations on biased or incomplete data or if we do not allow students to question ideas offered as solutions to problems. Sometimes a teacher's motivation in such a case may be understandable or even admirable. He or she may not want students to express certain "wrong" ideas or opinions. For example, assume that Ms. Cherez wants the students in her class to collect funds for starving children in Africa. She may want to show a film or pictures demonstrating this great need. Ms. Cherez certainly does not want to receive comments from students suggesting that, according to their parents, donated money would be wasted because it would not get to the starving people or because developing nations should solve their own problems. If Ms. Cherez manipulates the discussion to prevent alternative opinions and comments, she is guilty of indoctrination—even if she feels it is indoctrination for a good cause.

However, the citizenship-transmission model of social studies often contains elements of indoctrination. One goal is to instill in students the basic American values and not simply an understanding of those values themselves. In this process of cultural transmission, the teacher will emphasize the positive nature of our society's democratic values.

Many authorities want to teach children to be patriotic and to love their country. They want all students to know about our historical traditions, our nation's great achievements, and our uniquely high ideals. How can this goal be achieved? Traditional methods include beginning the school day with the Pledge of Allegiance, singing patriotic songs, and retelling legends and myths (e.g., George Washington never told a lie). Celebrating birthdays of our presidents or outstanding citizens also makes children aware of the heroes and heroines of our nation's history. In these activities, the teacher is not simply using a textbook or a prepared curriculum guide but is also socializing for the desired value. Good literature or films can be used as well to invoke in students positive feelings about their heritage.

As students get older, however, they must begin to explore how the basic values of our nation should be interpreted to help sovle the problems facing our society. The goal must be to promote a "good" society.

---

[9]James P. Shaver, "Commitment to Values and the Study of Social Problems in Citizenship Education," *Social Education* 49 (March 1985): 194–197.

According to the citizenship-transmission tradition, social studies education has two main purposes: to instill in students a basic commitment to the values of our society and to help students develop an ability to *apply* those values to the issues facing our nation. Note that a vital component of our basic values is the application of rationality and critical thinking, or inquiry, especially among older children (see Table 1.1).

Social Science/History

The social science/history model is a knowledge-centered approach. This model became popular in the 1960s, when a wide variety of new social studies curriculum projects were funded by various government agencies. Curriculum planners wanted students to understand how social scientists did their work and to grasp the major concepts of each social science discipline. For example, there were anthropology projects in which students were given actual artifacts from a particular culture and were instructed to study the objects and guess their purposes. In the study of history, students were taught the difference between primary and secondary sources. They might, for example, be provided with conflicting eyewitness reports of what happened on Lexington Green at the start of the American Revolution and be asked to compare these reports with the textbook description.

Social studies textbooks in the 1960s began to include more short selections from original source documents so that students might learn more about how historians actually go about writing history. Sociological Resources (the American Sociology Association's project for the Social Studies) designed inductive exercises in which students gathered data and then were led to form hypotheses from a more critical point of view. Students might be asked to complete sentences like the following: "Parents are _____." "Rich people are _____." Russians are _____." Police are _____." Typically, students filled in the blanks with glib generalizations, often based on inadequate information, limited experience, and prejudiced views. After gathering data on the topics covered, they were made aware of their errors and assumptions. The goal of this kind of exercise was to show students how easily we all jump to conclusions, rather than to treat general statements as hypotheses to be tested. These exercises also demonstrated how sociologists obtain data on stereotypes.

In some cases, the new curriculum projects focused on a single subject area—such as economics or anthropology—but in many cases they used an interdisciplinary approach such as Asian studies. On the whole, the new social studies curriculum projects included more sociology and anthropology than did more traditional approaches. But in the 1970s, many questioned whether these new curriculum projects with their emphases on the structure of the social sciences were relevant. In numerous cases, students had difficulty with the reading and conceptual levels of these projects.

Reflective Inquiry

The social studies, when taught as reflective inquiry, emphasize the importance of motivating students to think. The teacher helps students use logical thinking and scientific investigation to decide on issues and values. One difficulty with this approach is the lack of a clear definition for *inquiry* or *reflective inquiry*. In general, with the *inquiry* approach, students engage in the process of discovering and thinking for themselves, weighing pros and cons, and interpreting the facts. Students are taught not merely to absorb or memorize materials but to evaluate them critically.

Reflective inquiry or analysis can be considered a value approach when students are helped to use rational, analytical processes in interrelating and conceptualizing their values (Table 1.1). The methods used for this value approach might include discussions requiring students to cite evidence, other analyses, and research to back their statements. For example, in a discussion of proposed health care plans, students might have to research the topic carefully, citing analogous cases and coming up with data to support their positions.

There are many formats for reflective inquiry. Some view it simply as answering the questions under an illustration in the textbook. For others, it involves the use of case studies that place individuals in dilemmas (e.g., whether or not to support the American Revolution) or force them to examine questions (e.g., what should happen to individuals who have broken a particular law). The new law-related education projects often use this format. In general, this approach is more open-ended than the more traditional social-studies-as-citizenship-transmission approach.

Two Other Approaches: A Child-Centered Approach and a Reform Approach

Two approaches in addition to those outlined previously are sometimes used in social studies education. The child-centered approach suggests that the purpose of social studies and other subjects should be student centered and directed toward personal development. The focus is on development of the student's unique potential by allowing for the fullest pursuit of creativity, personal integrity, love of learning, and self-fulfillment. Children should feel that they are competent and capable of making choices and that they can influence their own behavior as well as that of others. This child-centered approach, which concentrates more on the individual than on the needs of society, encourages children to gain an understanding of their own needs and to work with others to achieve their goals. This approach is sometimes followed by teachers in private schools.

Social studies as informed social criticism, or critical theory, is another way to examine social studies education. This approach, which is based on Marxism, calls for giving students the opportunity to analyze critically the ideological base of their schools and of our society. You would not likely find this approach used in standard teacher-training programs or in school districts, but it has adherents at the graduate university level and can be found in the literature on social science education.

Your Choice

Which of these five approaches do you prefer for teaching elementary social studies? Which model do you think reflects the most common practice in schools today? These questions may be difficult to answer because most teachers use some combination of all three mainstream approaches. They choose from various positions depending on the topic being taught. They do some indoctrination, especially of American values and patriotism, while also encouraging students to think about social policy issues. They teach one unit on a problem in the community using an inquiry approach and the next unit on local government using a traditional citizenship-transmission approach. Monday's lesson might be on making economic or consumer choices, whereas Tuesday's lesson might return to a structured textbook reading with questions at the end of the chapter.

Probably the approach that is *least* used of the three main traditions is social studies as social science. This approach is difficult to implement unless a teacher is willing to do a great deal of preparation and gathering of materials. Most elementary textbooks include material from all social sciences but do not devote much time to explaining the methods used by various social scientists and historians.

You can see now that definitions of social studies content will vary depending on the value system or philosophical orientation of the teacher or curriculum planner. The *citizenship* or *cultural heritage approach* tends to emphasize American history and our nation's high ideals and achievements. The *social science approach* uses content from the various social science disciplines and history with a view to understanding the major concepts and the respective methods of gathering data. The *reflective-inquiry approach* can use almost any content as long as it encourages thinking on the part of students.

1.6 *ON YOUR OWN: MAKE A CHOICE*

Do you now have a tentative definition of the social studies? Which approach do you think is best for the children? List the strengths and weaknesses of each model on a piece of paper. Which model do you think you would use most often in an elementary classroom?

1.7 *SMALL GROUP WORK: PARENT SURVEY*

Interview three parents and then three adults who do not have children in the schools. Ask them to define the social studies. Ask what they think the social studies should do for children. Bring your responses to class. What concerns does the public have about social studies education?

The public may be more concerned than some elementary teachers about which curriculum is implemented in elementary social studies classrooms. In fact, court cases indicate that many parents are very worried about the values and curriculum approaches schools are using. Controversies over the adoption of social studies textbooks by districts confirm this indication. Some critics of the schools seem to fear that an approach bordering on Marxism, undermining our whole society, is being taught. They are calling for a return to the basic citizenship-transmission approach.

NATIONAL CURRICULUM PATTERNS

The United States has thousands of local school districts. Although each one is autonomous and can organize a curriculum to suit its own needs and meet state requirements, a national social studies curriculum exists. There are two reasons for this. First is the dominant role that textbooks have had in social studies instruction. In fifth- and eighth-grade classrooms across the nation, you will find United States history being taught from books published by only a handful of large companies. Eight or ten publishers probably control about 90 percent of the textbook market, which ensures a certain similarity in course offerings throughout the nation.

A second reason for the national curriculum is that most educators follow guidelines produced by the National Council for the Social Studies as well as by their own states. Some state guidelines are very broad, requiring only that history, geography, and the social sciences be taught in some manner from kindergarten though twelfth grade. The trend recently, however, has been toward more state control and guidance, particularly since the reform movements of the early 1980s. Some states require all students to be tested in the social studies before they can graduate. Some state frameworks, such as California's, already provide topics in considerable detail for each grade level. Statewide testing tends to make teachers follow the state frameworks more carefully, since students may suffer if the content taught does not match what is being tested.

State frameworks in turn influence textbook publishers, who want as broad a market as possible. In particular, the state frameworks of the largest states, particularly California and Texas, help to determine what focus textbooks have. For these interrelated reasons, we see a certain amount of uniformity in elementary social studies programs throughout the nation.

In 1980 Project SPAN (Social Studies: Priorities, Practices, and Needs, funded by the National Science Foundation) found the following social studies curriculum pattern in most United States schools:

Grade	**Topics**
Kindergarten/Grade 1	Self, Family, School
Grade 2	Neighborhoods

Grade 3	Communities
Grade 4	State History, Geographic Regions
Grade 5	U.S. History, Culture, and Geography
Grade 6	World Cultures, History, and Geography
Grade 7	World Cultures, History, and Geography
Grade 8	U.S. History
Grade 9	Civics
Grade 10	World History
Grade 11	U.S. History
Grade 12	American Government/Problems of Democracy

The National Council for the Social Studies Task Force on Scope and Sequence (1983) recommended the following topics. This was the last time that the National Council for the Social Studies recommended the traditional curriculum pattern.

Grade   Topics

Grade	Topics
K	Awareness of self in a social setting
1	The individual in primary social groups: Understanding school and family life
2	Meeting basic needs in nearby social groups: The neighborhood
3	Sharing earth-space with others: The community
4	Human life in varied environments: The region
5	People of the Americas: The United States and its close neighbors
6	People and cultures: The Eastern Hemisphere
7	A changing world of many nations: A global view
8	Building a strong and free nation: The United States
9	Systems that make a democratic society work: Law, justice, and economics
10	Origins of major cultures: A world history
11	The maturing of America: U.S. history
12	One-year course selection (issues and problems of modern society, introduction to social sciences, arts in human societies, international arts studies, elective)

Is this the pattern that you followed when you were in school? The basic structure of social studies content at both elementary and secondary levels has changed little during the past fifty years, but a careful reading of the above lists reveals some problems in the traditional social studies curriculum.

Notice first that U.S. history is taught at three grade levels. Too often, all three courses are surveys, covering repeatedly everything from Columbus to the latest space shot. There is little differentiation of content and minimal attempt to build from one course to the next.

How did this come about? It happened partially for historical reasons. In the early years of this country, children attended school for only a few years. Because it was important to teach children U.S. history before they ended their school careers, American history was taught in the fifth grade. Then, as more children remained in upper elementary school, the course was taught again in the eighth grade, just before students left school to go to work. Finally, as more students continued on through high school, educators again wanted to make sure that they remembered their U.S. history. So history was repeated in the eleventh grade.

Concerns about patriotism continue to favor the inclusion of the U.S. history in elementary and secondary schools. It would be unpopular for a local district or a state framework committee to suggest dropping a U.S. history course—how unpatriotic or un-American! Thus the impact of tradition and patriotic concerns have led to the entrenchment of three separate U.S. history courses.

Notice also the problem area in the sixth and seventh grades. Both grades cover the same broad topics, but there is little agreement about what the content should be at these levels. In some schools, ancient civilization is taught in the sixth grade; in others, this topic is found at the seventh-grade level. Thus, world history/ world cultures also has a similar problem of duplication as U.S. history courses. Usually the high school course covers everything again, from early human history to the latest world crisis.

Some social studies educators believe that the primary-grade topics are not sufficiently differentiated. One study by Marion Rice of the University of Georgia (1966) showed that second graders' knowledge of content before instruction ranged from 33 to 84 percent: In other words, in some classrooms students knew one-third to virtually all the material *before* it was taught. Topics are stressed in the first, second, and third grades without the new material being introduced or higher levels of thinking being required.[10]

But perhaps the heaviest criticism of primary social studies content focuses on the "holiday curriculum." In many schools, holidays like Thanksgiving, Christmas, Presidents' Day, Valentine's Day, Easter, and Mother's Day dictate what is covered in the primary social studies program. These holidays do offer the opportunity to explain much about our cultural heritage, but reliance on them suggests that many teachers feel more comfortable teaching these topics than ones that require more thoughtful preparation.

The holiday curriculum, however, need not be narrow. Holidays can be used as springboards for teaching about cultural diversity by showing how they are celebrated (or not celebrated) in this country and throughout the world. In many cases, though, holiday activities are simply repeated grade after grade, with little attention paid to learning beyond entertainment. Valuable social studies time is wasted. Furthermore, teachers are not always sensitive to the feelings of children from different backgrounds who may be offended or excluded by the holiday focus. In the same manner, children may not understand why particular religious holidays are not mentioned or are celebrated in ways unrelated to their religious

---

[10]Marion J. Rice, *Educational Stimulation in the Social Studies: Analysis and Interpretation of Research* (Athens: Research and Development Center in Educational Stimulation, University of Georgia, 1966).

meanings. The separation of church and state in the United States means that children may *learn* about different religions but religious beliefs may not be practiced in the classroom.

As you can see, there *is* a national social studies curriculum pattern. But your state's pattern may vary from this model in several ways. Each state generally requires that its own state history be taught at the fourth-grade level. Check on what your state recommends for the sixth- and seventh-grade levels as well. Information about social studies content guidelines can be obtained from your state department of education. Your state may also have *legal requirements*—observance of holidays, positive and accurate portrayal of the roles of women and minority groups, or the protection and conservation of the environment—that dictate to some extent what will be taught in the social studies.

New York State has made some changes from the national pattern, as shown in the following list:

Grade	Topics
K	Self and Others
1	Self, Family, School
2	Communities (U.S.A.)
3	World Communities
4	Local History and Government in the Context of American History
5	United States/Canada/Latin America (especially Geographic, Economic)
6	Western Europe/Eastern Europe/Middle East
7 and 8	U.S. and State History (Foundations of Government)
9 and 10	Global Studies (by region)/The World Today
11	U.S. History and Government (Chronological)
12	Economics/Participation in Government

1.8 *ON YOUR OWN: YOUR STATE CURRICULUM*

How does your state or local curriculum compare with that of New York? Do you like the more global emphasis in the New York social studies framework? How do you think participation in government could be implemented in the twelfth grade?

IMPORTANCE OF TEXTBOOK SERIES

The adoption of textbooks has had a great influence on what is taught in elementary social studies. If you compare a new social studies textbook series to the one you had in elementary school, you will notice that modern-day textbooks are much more colorful and attractive.

There are other differences as well. Almost all textbook series now show pictures of a wide diversity of ethnic, racial, and religious groups, in response to demands to eliminate racism and sexism in our society. The portrayal of the elderly and the handicapped demonstrates an interest in presenting a more realistic view of American life. The primary social studies textbooks on the family now move beyond a traditional two-parent family; an illustration may show a mother remarrying with her two children looking on or a family headed by a mother, father, or grandparent.

Generally, the large publishers offer a series (often called a *basal series*) of textbooks covering kindergarten through grade six or seven. For the kindergarten level, some publishers issue only a teacher's manual; more frequently, kindergarten-level texts are small booklets containing attractive pictures with little vocabulary. A teacher's guide is essential to the use of these kindergarten booklets.

Even if you follow a basal series closely, you will have some choices about what you teach. One choice occurs at the fourth-grade level, where state history and geography are generally taught. The major publishers issue specially prepared state textbooks for large states, and regional books are available for smaller states. Smaller publishing firms may also offer state history textbooks.

The next choice occurs at the sixth- and seventh-grade levels. Because there is no standard curriculum pattern at these levels, publishers often offer two or more textbooks that can be used for either grade, thus providing a wide and varying range of topics—the Eastern Hemisphere, the Western Hemisphere, or the world, for example.

Far more supplementary material coordinated with the textbooks is available now than ever before. Publishers have recognized that elementary teachers are busy planners with responsibilities for many subject areas and activities. Along with the traditional student textbook and teacher's manual, the major publishers are now likely to include a student workbook containing exercises to supplement the textbook, tests for chapter and unit review, and in some cases additional resources for the teacher (such as posters for the classroom). Generally, this is all packaged attractively in one large binder. It is likely that future textbook series will also include computer software to supplement each unit. Teachers expect assistance from the publisher and would be reluctant now to adopt a series that did not have these aids.

Some critics argue that the basal social studies textbooks are very similar. This concern may stem from the similarity of titles; the word *family*, for example, shows up frequently at the first-grade level. But a careful examination of the textbooks will show considerable differences. Some textbook series are better for slower learners. Others emphasize global education. Still others, although they bear recent copyright dates, really have changed very little from those of twenty years ago. Map skills are found in all textbooks, but some series also emphasize reading skills, information-finding skills, and thinking skills.

1.9   ON YOUR OWN: COMPARE THE SERIES

At a curriculum library, examine three different social studies textbook series at one particular grade level. Note carefully what content is covered in the textbook. Also, look at the teacher's guide for suggestions on how to teach the program. How are the series similar? How are they different?

Educators complain about overreliance on the textbook. Often it has been the only instructional tool used, and this limitation has resulted in narrow, restricted programs. Applied creatively, however, the textbook can be a very valuable resource. It is important for teachers and committees concerned with the selection of textbooks to look very carefully at the possible choices. There are many differences among the textbook series. The wide range of activities suggested in a teacher's guide may make a social studies textbook series unique. Teachers stuck with unsuitable textbooks for their classes work at a disadvantage in trying to provide a good social studies program.

MOUNTING CRITICISM: SCOPE AND SEQUENCE

Almost all the textbooks use what is often called the *expanding communities pattern*, the *expanding horizons* or the *widening world scope and sequence model*. All three terms are used interchangeably. *Scope* refers to the list of topics covered in a program. *Sequence* is the order in which these topics are covered. Usually, the two words are used together to indicate what is being taught, whether in the social studies or in any other area of the curriculum.

Scope and sequence issues are important. You need to know when students are ready for certain difficult concepts, like time or chronology. Most primary students have great difficulty trying to imagine what life was like 2,000 years ago. They may think that we have always had television, airplanes, and cars. The eras B.C. and A.D. pose conceptual difficulty for most primary students. Determining at what grade level you might successfully try to teach time concepts is a scope and sequence issue.

The traditional scope and sequence pattern for the elementary grades—the expanding communities—is based on a consideration of the developmental needs of the child. Children usually learn better about real things and life around them than about abstract topics that they cannot see or feel. Therefore, the expanding communities concept begins with where children are when they enter school. The focus in the primary grades is first the family and then the school, the neighborhood, the larger neighborhood (city and county), the state, the region, and finally the nation and the world (Figure 1.2).

This pattern of expanding communities made a lot of sense years ago. But at present, with mass media, and especially television, children are exposed to events

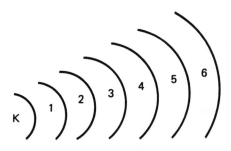

Key:

K Self and Others   4 Regions
1 Families   5 United States and Canada
2 Communities   6 World
3 Cities

Figure 1.2 The expanding horizons curriculum. *Source:* Reprinted from *Defining the Social Studies*, Bulletin 51 by Robert D. Barr, James L. Barth, and S. Samuel Shermis, with permission of the National Council for the Social Studies.

and issues taking place far from their homes. Children also travel more. Primary-grade children are aware of international and domestic crises, wars, terrorism, and pollution problems.

It may seem as though all the social studies textbooks are following the expanding community concept for scope and sequence, especially if you scan chapter titles. But a more careful examination often demonstrates that even in the first grade, information about families includes families in Israel and Zambia. A second-grade textbook on neighbors may focus on groups in the United States and also in other parts of the world. A topic such as where food comes from is more likely to expand into farming in other lands, since the United States gets an increasing number of products, including food, from other parts of the world.

So the traditional scope and sequence pattern of expanding communities found at most elementary grades is being supplemented by topics outside the child's immediate environment, but not all educators are satisfied with this arrangement. Many want to break away even further from the traditional scope and sequence patterns.

Critics who reject the expanding community pattern often argue that even very young children are aware of events beyond their immediate local environment. Critics also charge that there is no research base to support the expanding community pattern.

The 1980s were years of concern about the social studies curriculum as well as general reforms in other curriculum areas. The National Council for the Social Studies issued a position paper on the importance of early childhood and elementary social studies stressing three main goals: knowledge, skills, and attitudes.

However, this report did not make specific recommendations for content at different grade levels.[11]

Pressure does appear to be building to change both the content and grade placement of the traditional social studies curriculum that has been taught for decades. Different scope and sequence alternatives intended to produce a better social studies curriculum have been proposed.

One alternative pattern is the *spiral* curriculum advocated by Hilda Taba (see Figure 1.3). In this model, basic concepts and processes from the social sciences such as interdependence or cultural change are taught each year on a higher level of abstraction. For example, first-grade students might learn how families depend on one another for natural resources and manufactured goods. By the fourth grade, they might study the first pioneer families that settled in their state. The spiral curriculum is found in one or two textbook series. Care must be taken in using this pattern to ensure that the books are truly moving to higher levels and not just repeating topics such as "community workers" or "food." The spiral curriculum can be used to support the rationale to keep repeating U.S. history three times—each time it is taught at a more complex and more meaningful level.

In a special issue of *Social Education* in 1986, several social studies experts gave their suggestions for alternative scope and sequence patterns.[12] The proposals illustrated a great diversity of opinion, with some differing radically from the typical pattern of expanding communities.

Matthew Downey, a historian, would like the fourth grade to focus on early peoples of the world and on primitive cultures that exist today, the fifth grade to study classical and medieval civilizations, and the sixth grade to focus on U.S. history with an emphasis on the early period of building a new nation. In the seventh grade the content would be world history and early modern and industrial eras; in the eighth grade, U.S. history would focus on the years 1789 to 1914. As you can guess, the eleventh grade would study U.S. history in the twentieth century.

Downey is trying to bring a chronological coherence to the curriculum and also to improve the teaching of U.S. history by dividing the three offerings into specific periods. For years, authorities have recommended that something be done to distinguish the three U.S. history courses from one another. More radical is Downey's emphasis on history in the elementary school. In his curriculum, history is the dominant subject from the fourth grade on, and students learn both world and U.S. history. This emphasis on history reflects a trend that has some public support.

In the same issue of *Social Education*, Shirley Engle and Anna Ochoa proposed a curriculum for democratic citizenship. They suggested moving away from the memorization of facts in the social sciences and history and focusing instead

---

[11]*Social Education* 53 (January 1989), "Social Studies for Early Childhood and Elementary School Children—Preparing for the 21st Century," 14–23.

[12]*Social Education* 50 (November–December 1986), special issue on alternative scope and sequence patterns.

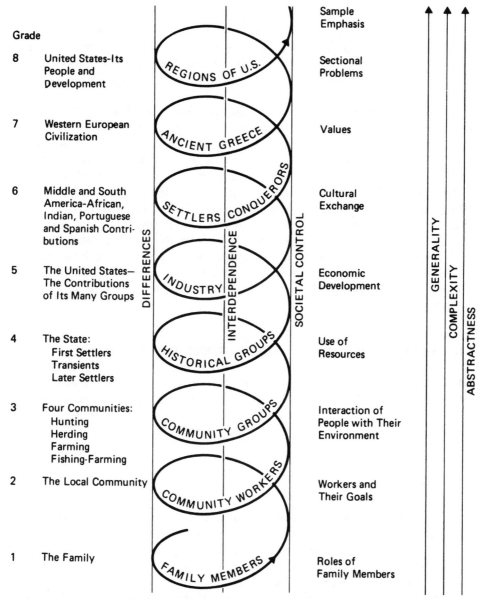

Figure 1.3 The spiral of concept development. Source: "The Spiral Development of Three Key Concepts" (Fig. 1). From *A Teacher's Handbook to Elementary Social Studies, Second Edition*, by Taba, et al., Copyright © 1971 by Addison-Wesley Publishing Company. Reprinted by permission.

on the study of problems—past and present—as the best way to prepare citizens in a democracy. For example, environmental concerns and international problems such as terrorism would be appropriate choices for study.

Other proposals include greater emphasis on global education within the social studies and on the basic idea that the content taught be current, accurate, and comprehensive. All these proposals suggest that there is not a consensus on scope and sequence in the elementary social studies curriculum. This issue probably will not be settled for some time, even at the local level. We can expect further debate in the coming years.

No matter what material you eventually teach, we would like to point out two important concerns: gender bias and the increasing number of different ethnic or racial minorities in many urban public schools. We must continually try to ensure that our social studies curriculum, as well as all school experiences, include women and minorities. Teachers who wish to improve student attitudes in these two areas should not limit themselves to a special unit taught once a year devoted to African-American history, for example. The infusion of all assignments and materials with an antibias, pro-justice concern will have more impact than a once-a-year unit. In addition, you need to be very conscious of your own teaching behavior. Whom do you call on to answer questions? Who gets the hard-thinking questions? Far too often, teachers fall into patterns such as reinforcing boys to the detriment of girls and of not expecting high achievement from children of certain ethnic and racial groups.

1.10 *SMALL GROUP WORK: CHECK WHERE YOU STAND*

Do you think any changes should be made in what is taught (topics) and when it is taught (specific grade levels)? Should there be a greater emphasis on certain topics? Do you think the expanding community pattern is the best way to organize the elementary social studies curriculum?

SUMMARY

A good social studies program should help students become informed citizens capable of making good decisions. Advocates of National Goals and national standards encourage teachers and schools to strive for higher achievement and citizenship goals. The traditional social studies curriculum has been faulted by students, teachers, and reform reports as not being adequate to fulfill the goals of citizenship. The typical expanding community pattern that has been the basis of national curriculum patterns is presently under criticism. Other alternative scope and sequence patterns are being suggested, many of which emphasize more history and geography in the elementary social studies curriculum. Together, these trends are pushing educators to make the social studies in the primary grades more challenging, with a greater number and depth of concepts and an inclusion of more content than what has traditionally been taught.

SUGGESTED READINGS

Barr, Robert. D.; Barth, James L.; and Shermis, S. Samuel. *Defining the Social Studies*. Bulletin 51. Washington, D.C.: National Council for the Social Studies, 1977.

Bennett, William J., ed. *The Book of Virtues*. New York: Simon & Schuster, 1993. Hundreds of stories to help children understand and develop character. An example of building character education approach. Other advocates of the character education movement are the following: Kilpatrick, William. *Why Johnny Can't Tell Right from Wrong*. New York: Simon & Schuster, 1992; Lickona, Thomas. *Educating for Character*. New York: Bantam, 1991; Wynne, Edward, and Ryan, Kevin. *Reclaiming Our Schools: A Handbook on Teaching Character, Academics, and Discipline*. New York: Macmillan, 1993.

Cuban, Larry. "History of Teaching in Social Studies." In James P. Shaver, ed., *Handbook of Research on Social Studies Teaching and Learning*, pp. 197–209. New York: Macmillan, 1991. Summary of history of social studies teaching.

Jenness, David. *Making Sense of Social Studies*. New York: Macmillan, 1990. A publication of the National Commission on Social Studies in the Schools.

Kaltsounis, Theodore, "Democracy's Challenge as the Foundation for Social Studies." *Theory & Research in Social Education* 22, no. 2 (Spring, 1994): 176–193. Democracy and democratic citizen education should be the logical foundation on which to structure the social studies program. Previous models of democratic education have failed.

Kirschenbaum, Howard. *100 Ways to Enhance Values and Morality in Schools and Youth Settings*. Needham Heights, Mass: Allyn & Bacon, 1995. Traditional methods for inculcating and modeling as well as the values clarification approach.

National Commission on Social Studies in the Schools. *Charting a Course: Social Studies for the 21st Century*. New York: National Commission on Social Studies in the Schools, November, 1989. Rejection of expanding communities pattern by four organizations.

Noddings, Nel. *The Challenge to Care in Schools*. New York: Teachers College Press, 1992. Alternative approaches to education organized around the theme of care.

The three journals of social studies that teachers should become familiar with are *Social Education, Social Studies and the Young Learner*, and *The Social Studies*. In addition, publications like *Learning* and *Instructor* may also have social studies materials.

Social Education 48 (April 1984), special issue with responses to preliminary report of Task Force on Scope and Sequence.

Social Education 50 (November–December 1986), special issue on alternative scope and sequence patterns.

Social Education 49 (May 1985), special issue, "The New Criticism: Alternative Views of Social Education."

Social Education 49 (March 1985), article by S. Samuel Shermis and James L. Barth followed by response of James Shaver on indoctrination in the social studies.

Social Education 54 and 55 (November–December 1990 and January 1991), special issues devoted to pros and cons of *Charting a Course: Social Studies for the 21st Century.*

Task Force of the National Council for the Social Studies. *Curriculum Standards for Social Studies.* Bulletin 89. Washington, D.C. National Council for the Social Studies, 1994. NCSS's curriculum standards.

PLANNING for SOCIAL STUDIES INSTRUCTION

The importance of planning for effective social studies teaching is emphasized in this chapter. Planning is organized into several steps including the unit approach, resource units, and lesson plans.

1/ Planning

2/ Goals, Long-Range Planning, and Instructional Objectives

3/ Resources for Planning

4/ Units

5/ Lesson Plans

6/ Organizing and Scheduling

PLANNING

The teacher is the key to what the social studies program will be in any classroom. As a teacher, you will make many decisions: What units will I include during the year? How will I teach tomorrow's lesson on the roles of the family? In general, the more decisions you can make during *planning*, the better prepared you will be. Your alternative is to make decisions on the spot, with a classroom full of students waiting for your instructions.

How do you go about planning? First, assemble all available planning tools and resources. They include the following:

State and/or district curriculum guide(s)
Your adopted textbook, the teacher's guide, and ancillary materials
Media catalogues for your district and county
Recommendations from your school media specialist (usually your librarian)
    for stories, trade books, and reference books
Ideas from other teachers in your building
Parent resources
Community resources

Once your resources are assembled, you are able to begin making choices. Choose units and activities for which you have appropriate materials and which you think will interest your students. It is equally important that you choose a program that interests *you*. Any lack of interest on your part will surely be conveyed to your students. Finally, prepare your plans in detail. Write down not only the names of the units you wish to cover but also the specific topics you plan to include and, if possible, some thoughts about how you will teach them.

Should you, as a beginning teacher, try to create original lesson plans or should you use plans designed by "experts" (e.g., textbook authors and curriculum designers)? Some local districts mandate that all teachers cover given units according to specific instructional modes—often the popular Madeline Hunter direct instructional model (see Chapter 3 for more detail.) Other districts give teachers complete freedom to choose content *and* method of instruction. Most districts occupy a middle ground: They outline the general content areas to be taught but allow flexibility for teachers to achieve content goals in any manner they wish.

Most beginners would panic at the thought of total freedom and move quickly to see how they could adapt an existing textbook program or other curriculum projects. Many experts would approve of this decision, arguing that often teachers, especially beginners, can best select and modify existing materials and ideas rather than try to create entirely new programs. This alternative makes better use of teacher time and is more likely to bring success. Developing an innovative social studies program on your own is difficult, and it ignores time-tested resources already available, including the teacher next door.

"Borrowing" creatively also provides for flexibility in your social studies program. Why, after all, do experienced teachers continue to attend conferences, workshops, and courses if not to get new ideas from other experts? Good teachers are continually modifying their programs, always on the alert for new and useful suggestions. In borrowing, however, you need to be certain that the new ideas and materials you adopt help you to achieve your desired objectives and that their appeal is not simply their newness.

2.1 *SMALL GROUP WORK: YOUR CONCEPT OF PLANNING*

Concept maps are useful ways of organizing ideas. Jot down the words "teacher planning" in the center of a sheet of paper. Think of the various subtopics such as "lesson" or "books." Now try drawing the relationships you see among the topics. Compare your concept map of teacher planning with the maps of others in your class.

Sometimes elementary schoolteachers resist planning because they are so busy with immediate responsibilities—filling out forms, grading papers, checking homework. Planning is often a low-priority task. But there is an important psychological benefit to planning and especially to working out and writing down daily lesson plans: confidence. With a plan in front of you, you feel organized and prepared to face the class. A plan a day keeps disaster away! Planning can often help you anticipate management problems in the classroom, and it enables you to have better control of the situation.

Sometimes a new teacher will say, "I did a lot of planning for a lesson on our local transportation system, and the whole thing fell flat. But the next day I walked in 'cold' and taught a terrific lesson on neighborhoods. So why plan?" This can happen. Planned lessons do not always go as well as expected. Instead of abandoning planning, however, you should go over an unsuccessful lesson at the end of the day, when you are less emotionally involved. At what points did it go off track? Were the students bored? Unable to keep up? Confused? What actually was wrong with the lesson? Make notes on your lesson plan to help you with future planning.

Even if a lesson *is* successful, you should critique your written plan. What would have made the lesson better? Write down proposed changes so that you won't forget them. Having in writing both the original plan and your notes on how to improve it will provide you with an ever-expanding resource file in years to come.

Some teachers argue that planning encourages rigidity. Having a written plan, they suggest, prevents teachers from taking advantage of unexpected instructional opportunities. Serendipity is always welcome! Your lesson plan, however, is meant to be a guide, not a prison sentence. Always be ready to bend it to take advantage of student interest or some recent and unanticipated event.

You may find that you have no choice about writing out lesson plans. Some school districts and/or principals require teachers to submit lesson plans for the coming week throughout the year. Frequently, administrators ask only for brief statements of topics and textbook pages to be covered. Most plans written for administrators show very little detail. The fact that a lesson plan must be submitted, however, acts as an incentive for many elementary teachers to plan ahead, if only to list the subject areas they will cover in a given week. Writing in topics under subject-area headings—science, social studies, math—may suggest areas of potential integration: How can language arts or science work with this week's social studies lesson?

There are often differences between what is listed on the plan handed in to an administrator and what actually goes on in the classroom. Some differences are inevitable, since lesson plans should always allow for flexibility. In a few cases, subjects are listed that are never taught. Frequently, this happens because the teacher does no planning in depth and therefore has no real plan to implement.

Successful planning needs to be detailed enough to help you organize what actually happens in the classroom. It is inaccurate to suggest that only drudges and drones plan; planning is a vital and basic skill for all effective teachers. Research indicates that teachers who plan are more likely to be satisfied with their teaching and are more likely to remain in the teaching profession. Poorly planned activities are frustrating to both teacher and students; valuable time wasted can never be recovered.

2.2 ON YOUR OWN: UNDERSTANDING YOUR FAVORITE TEACHERS

Jot down what you remember most vividly about your favorite elementary teacher. Do you remember what he or she taught you about social studies? Do you think that your teacher planned? What characteristics suggest his or her planning or the lack of it?

GOALS, LONG-RANGE PLANNING, AND INSTRUCTIONAL OBJECTIVES

Goals

Goals are broad statements of desired outcomes. In education, they provide the pillars for setting up learning experiences. Goals do not define specific achievements to be attained within a specific period; a goal is not necessarily to be reached in an hour, a day, or even a year. Rather, goals are frequently defined in terms of enhancement or of providing foundations. We work on some goals such as improving our reading skills throughout our schooling—even throughout our lives.

Each school district usually has a list of its own goals, which often include some of the following:

Education should provide a basis for good citizenship.
Education should provide a basis for vocational choice.
Education should provide the best of our cultural heritage.
Education should provide each student with a command of fundamental skills such as reading, writing, arithmetic, information finding, problem solving, and computer literacy.
Education should develop each student's ability to think clearly.
Education should develop each student's unique potential.

Other goals may have to do with ethical character, health, or personal behavior. Generally, school-district goals reflect the broad desires of the community. In many districts, parents have helped significantly in defining the district's goals.

Promoting good citizenship, which is often found on district lists of educational goals, is also generally listed as a goal for social studies education. The social studies program does not have sole responsibility for teaching citizenship skills; other areas of the curriculum also contribute. But an elementary social studies program should be designed to do as much as possible to move students toward effective citizenship participation (see Chapter 6). As an elementary teacher, you will plan the entire day for your students. In looking over the day's program, you will want to be alert to those activities that best promote both broad educational goals and specific goals of the social studies.

In Chapter 1, we mentioned the four basic social studies goals:

1. To acquire knowledge about human experiences in the past, present, and future
2. To develop skills to process information
3. To develop appropriate democratic values and attitudes
4. To have opportunities for citizenship education

These goals provide the framework for planning in the social studies and also fit easily into the general goals of many school districts. Since they are so broadly stated, however, almost any social studies activity you propose to teach could be listed under at least one of them. Goals are useful in defining broad objectives but they lack the specificity necessary for effective day-to-day teaching.

Long-Range Planning

Most elementary teachers begin social studies planning by roughing out an outline of the entire, year-long curriculum. Given the number of weeks in the school year, how will you divide the subject matter normally covered in, say, the second grade?

What would make reasonable, manageable sections? You must make some decisions: Will you select only certain units from the textbook, or will you try to cover all of them? Will you use the district's curriculum guidelines, or will some of your units be from specific curriculum packages—an economic simulation, perhaps? Once you begin to make these basic determinations—what you will cover and how much time you will devote to each topic—you can focus your attention on the individual chunks of time, frequently called *units*. Long-range planning is vital because there is usually far more content (and resource material) available than there is time to teach it. Your first step is to examine what must be taught, according to state or local mandate, at your particular grade level. Usually, grade-level mandates are broad. What other criteria could you use for selecting topics for a year-long curriculum? You should consider all of the following:

The adopted textbook
Tradition (e.g., last year's units in your school)
State-mandated tests
What other teachers in your building are doing
District guides
Personal teaching style/strengths
Resources (resource, books, media, speakers, etc.)
Suggestions from parents
Potential management problems
Need for efficient use of time in planning and developing materials
Student needs (children's ability, etc.)
Social studies experts' recommendations and standards
Your philosophy of education

We include the adopted textbook as a prime resource for instructional planning, acknowledging and agreeing with the criticisms leveled at "textbook-centered" teaching. In our view, a good program needs structure and topical direction. Most textbooks provide this. Taking advantage of the content outline, activities suggested, and enrichment ideas need not condemn you to a rigid chapter-by-chapter, lesson-by-lesson coverage. Instead of thinking of the text as a novel to be read from beginning to end, we need to see the text as a tool to help us conceptualize and speed up our long-range planning. If you use the textbook as your main guide in long-range curriculum planning, you should typically follow these steps:

1. Skim the text, looking at broad unit titles. Decide which ones you will use. (The author's recommendations about how much time a unit will typically take may be helpful.)
2. Examine the teacher's guide. Look for activities for you and your students.
3. Find other activities to supplement the text. The teacher's guide may suggest some; the publisher may also provide other materials, like worksheets.

4. Decide whether you will use the tests supplied by the publisher for evaluation.

Because a major part of your long-range planning will be done early in the school year or even before it begins, you probably won't know your students' full range of talents and abilities. Once you begin to learn more about your students, you may need to modify the learning activities in your year-long curriculum to fit your classroom, where student abilities may range from those of special education students to the gifted. Some teachers also involve students in planning what is to be learned.

Instructional Objectives

Whereas a *goal* is a broad statement of purpose, an *instructional objective* (or behavioral objective) is a specific accomplishment that you want your students to achieve in a specific period. The terms *instructional objectives, behavioral objectives,* or *terminal objectives* are often used interchangeably. A well-written objective specifies the level of acceptable performance and the conditions under which a student must perform. Many teacher-training institutions advise their students to use Bloom's taxonomy (see Chapter 10) for writing objectives in the cognitive domain.

You are no doubt familiar with the general process of curriculum planning. Typically, there are three main questions to answer:

1. What are your objectives?
2. What learning experiences will be used to achieve the desired objectives?
3. What evaluation procedures will be used to determine whether the objectives have been achieved?

You have probably learned a formula for writing the three parts of an instructional objective. The first part is to pinpoint an exact verb such as the "The student will (insert an action verb, such as *write, say, construct*) (insert content, such as *three major roles of a parent*)." An appropriate instructional objective might be this: "Students will draw a picture of *their* own family." The second part of the objective should include any restrictions on time, equipment, or aid. For instance, you might write, "*Given an outline map of Europe*, the student will list the names of all major rivers shown." The third and last part is to let students know the criteria for an acceptable performance. Must the names be spelled correctly, with proper capitalization? Will a student be considered successful if he or she can identify eight out of ten rivers shown?

Instructional objectives, often called simply objectives, may be broad or narrow. You may set a few broad social studies objectives for the year, narrower ones for each unit, and specific objectives for each day's lesson. This division into long-range and short-term, broad and narrow objectives is a reflection of how teachers typically plan a curriculum.

What is your opinion of the instructional objective approach? There are signs in teachers' lounges that say "Stamp Out Instructional Objectives." Because of the time necessary to write them out, many teachers strongly resist having to translate broad long-range objectives into more specific ones. In making a choice for yourself, think about the following issues:

1. *Is specifying objectives worthwhile for elementary teachers?* Teachers, even those who have been trained to write out instructional objectives, frequently think first about learning activities or materials and only then about a suitable purpose or objective. Some teachers believe they are using instructional objectives but write them so vaguely that the objectives are virtually useless; others write them at the lowest level of factual information, using content such as memorization of state capitals. Advocates of instructional objectives believe that some of the negative feelings about their use stem from misuse. They believe that much of the instruction in education is aimless because teachers fail to define objectives clearly. What do you think?

2. *Do your students need to know what the instructional objectives are to ensure their achieving the desired behavioral change?* If you assign a worksheet, do you need to explain the instructional objective to the students in order for them to understand what they are gaining? There is some research indicating that this does help students to achieve.[1] What about objectives in the affective domain — for example, improved citizenship or respect for people of various ethnic or racial groups? Do students need to be told what your objectives are in any of these areas?

3. *Do students have to know what an adequate performance level is?* Part of the problem in teaching important social studies skills like small group participation or writing and presenting a report is that students do not always know what a good paper or a good discussion is. Often they do not receive corrective feedback about how to improve. Do you think students should be told in the beginning what constitutes acceptable performance? Can you think of ways to clarify what is adequate student performance?

In thinking about objectives, you face the questions not only of defining important content in the social studies but also of how you should go about teaching and evaluating students to determine whether they are in fact achieving your objectives. But many objectives written by teachers are not precise. Instructional objectives in the affective or value domain are particularly difficult to write and measure. However, *any* effort you make to think about and plan your teaching objectives is probably better than no effort. Since teachers often have difficulty writing objectives, many publishers now provide in their teacher's guides objec-

---

[1]Jere E. Brophy, Mary Rohrkemper, Habim Rashid, and Michael Goldberger, "Relationships between Teachers' Presentation of Classroom Tasks and Student Engagement in Those Tasks," *Journal of Educational Psychology* 75, no. 4 (August 1983): 544–552.

tives for each unit and for each lesson. Often these aids are helpful for teachers to target more clearly their direction and their purpose. Other teachers, professional journals, and instructional objectives exchanges can also offer assistance to teachers in writing objectives. In the future, computer banks of objectives will probably become more widespread.

2.3   *ON YOUR OWN: EXPLORING POINTS OF VIEW*

Administrators and teachers often view instructional objectives in a different manner. List three reasons explaining why administrators more than teachers might favor the instructional objectives approach.

RESOURCES FOR PLANNING

In thinking about objectives, can you identify any factors unique to the field of social studies that should be considered in planning? Students' families, the community, and other resources may help you with better planning of your social studies program.

Parent and Family Resources

Because the social studies are about people, members of the students' families can often be used as resources. A grandmother may be able to tell what it was like to live on a farm fifty years ago. A parent may be able to describe his or her job when the class is studying community workers or the job market. There may be artifacts from different nations in the homes of students that would be of interest to the class. Many teachers find that these resources add sparkle to the class. Use special events such as open house and media presentations by the class to talk to and ask for help from parents. Try writing notes or newsletters to parents outlining what is going to be covered in the coming social studies unit and asking if they can help in any way.

Community Resources

The community is the neighborhood beyond just family. There are two important community resources: field trips and guest speakers. Use the community as a resource for field trips, especially if the students are able to walk to see something such as the local bakery or police station. If this is not feasible, resource people from the community (e.g., probation officers or park rangers) can come to the classroom. Community resources can also include free local newspapers or materials from the local bank or other community institutions.

In addition, students can serve the community in projects ranging from helping senior citizens to cleaning up local parks. Community service provides a bridge between students and the community and can be an important resource in building toward the goal of citizenship. (See Chapter 6.) Be certain to clear such projects with your school principal.

Media and Inexpensive Resources

You need to look carefully at the videos, filmstrips, photographs, slides, television series, and so on that can be obtained in your district. Typically, the sooner your order is placed, the better will be your chance of securing the items as other teachers also may want to use these resources. These media, especially with visual components, can add meaning to otherwise abstract ideas that a teacher's voice cannot provide. New technology such as laser discs will also become more available, adding an additional resource to enrich your teaching. (See Chapter 9.)

Free or inexpensive posters and other materials may be obtained from the consulates of foreign nations in large U.S. cities. Order the materials as early in the school year as possible to allow time for shipment, and make arrangements well in advance for speakers, especially those on tight schedules, such as government officials.

Current Events/Current Affairs

The social studies are unique among elementary-school subjects because they deal with events that are continually happening in the local community and the wider world that have an impact on students and their families. Often these events are directly relevant to what you are trying to achieve in your social studies program. The goal of encouraging social participation in community affairs should lead you to consider how current events can be used to enrich the social studies program.

Weekly papers, prepared by publishers at the appropriate reading levels for students in different grades, can be helpful. But in real life, newspapers and magazines are not as neatly balanced and objective, and students eventually need to become familiar with regular news reports. In addition, students living in an environment dominated by television must understand what the news reporters on television are talking about. Discussions on television are often incomplete. Students need more background to understand the issues. Also, television news is frequently weak on analysis. Teachers must teach students to understand how all elements of the mass media are important and how the students can analyze the messages that are being given.

All these elements make the social studies unique among subject areas and should be part of your consideration in planning. See Chapter 5 for more detail on teaching current events/current affairs.

UNITS

A *unit* is the unifying structure around which lessons are prepared. Basically it is time allocated to teaching a major subdivision in the year's course. The unit is a plan that organizes a sequential progression of lessons related in theme, topic, issue, or problem. Typically, a social studies unit covers the main concepts of a particular subject area. In addition, the unit has provisions for teaching skills, values, and, if possible, social participation.

Why do experts recommend teaching in units? It is better to introduce a unit, have a progression of lessons to develop a theme, and conclude with an activity than to teach isolated lessons. Students learn less if on Monday they have a map exercise on latitude and longitude, on Tuesday they have a value exercise on twenty things they love to do, on Wednesday they visit their local fire department, on Thursday they read their social studies textbook on Native American tribes in the northeastern part of the United States, and on Friday they study current events. Each lesson may be worthwhile by itself, but the lessons do not build sequentially. A unit should tie skills and knowledge together under a theme so that learning is not isolated and fragmented. Learning is more likely to take place when topics are not fragmented or isolated. We can characterize the many different types of units as textbook units, commercial units, and teacher-prepared units.

Textbook units are found in most texts in use today. Almost all social studies textbooks are organized by major units such as *Africa Today* or *The New Nation Faces Many Problems.* There are usually several big units in the book and under each unit are several chapters. Then, within each chapter are several daily lessons. The publishers generally predict or project a given time for how long a unit will last and offer many suggestions for teaching or enriching the unit. Probably the greatest advantage to using the units in the textbook is that they reduce the amount of planning a teacher needs to do, especially if the teacher's background in the content is not strong or current. However, we should use textbooks with caution. Some students may not be able to read the textbook, or they may find the concepts are described too briefly, making the ideas seem artificial and abstract. Often the textbook's lessons and chapters are written in a repetitive format, requiring students to read and answer questions posed by the textbook. The students' reaction: boring, boring, boring. With few hands-on experiences or discussion of the topics, the social studies program is listless.

Textbook units cannot accomplish every aspect of planning for us. Specifically, they may cause us to make the following instructional errors:

- Teacher makes all the decisions on what will be learned and when
- All students must learn the same body of knowledge despite individual differences
- Students do not always know why they have the assignment
- Texts may encourage fragmented connections with other subject areas

- Texts may encourage the teachers to ask lower-level factual questions based only on the textbook
- Texts may not focus on changes and problems in the students' own community
- Students will see social studies as just facts and figures from a textbook

Commercial units are similar to textbook units but are prepared by a specific group. For example, the Anti-Defamation League has prepared workbook units with the objective of reducing bias and discrimination in our society. Funding from private sources in different geographical areas was used to produce locally specific workbooks; thus the workbook for the Los Angeles area was completely different from the one produced in the Philadelphia area. This method then allowed the teacher-authors of the workbook to include lessons that better reflected the student population and the needs of their regions. In other words, compared to national textbooks, commercial units can often be tailored to state and local differences. Units on state history often fall into this category. Many commercial units, however, have only one set for all the country.

Often these commercial units are designed by teachers or consultants who are trying to meet a special curriculum need or a desire of the sponsoring group to get their point of view into the classroom. For example, changes in population and new state curriculum directions may suddenly ask sixth-grade teachers to cover Islam, a topic that has rapidly achieved high interest and importance. Many experienced teachers would feel unprepared to teach a unit on Islam or other unfamiliar topics. They are often willing to pay or have the district pay for a unit that can specifically help them to include a topic new to them in their program. Buying commercial units is common in the teaching of novels, especially classics such as *The Adventures of Tom Sawyer* and *Little House on the Prairie*. One company, Novel Units, has over three hundred titles, each available with vocabulary words, comprehension questions, and activities. If a teacher is trying to integrate literature with a social studies unit on the American antebellum period, he or she may be eager to buy a unit that summarizes a novel's chapters, gives good evaluation questions, and shows how to integrate the novel into a social studies unit. Groups such as those trying to introduce more economic education into the curriculum may find one of the easiest ways to do so is to produce a unit that teachers can immediately implement.

Commercial units, often free, are also produced by associations or companies with the goal of exposing students indirectly to the organization's ideas. Organizations ranging from the Dairy Council to the National Association of Newspaper Editors and the National Rifle Association produce units and free or inexpensive instructional materials. For example, Procter & Gamble for years has produced social studies units on ecology, the economy, and advertising. These free materials may include reproducible lessons, teaching tips for each lesson, and colorful posters. A teacher, of course, needs to be aware that a given company may be introducing subtle bias into the unit and should carefully alert students to the source of the data.

Teachers can develop or adopt from a variety of resources to organize their own units. Unlike the typical textbook or commercial units, *teacher-prepared units* can be based on the concepts/generalizations/themes generated by the social sciences. For example, economics focuses on how individuals and groups use the resources available to them. Therefore, both individuals and groups make economic decisions every day. Using this major economic generalization, a teacher can ask primary students to keep track of what they spend their money on during a given time period. Then they can classify which expenditures were for goods and which ones were for services. Which is the largest category? Children often see their parents paying by check or money when they buy goods, but they seldom see them pay for the dentist, and they are even less likely to realize that their families pay indirectly through taxes for public services such as those given by teachers or other people in the schools. Children can be asked to list people who provide services that are paid for by taxes. Shifting from services to goods, students can classify the materials that were used to produce the goods they purchased, such as candy bars, or the tools that workers used to deliver services. For example, what resources are needed to make candy or bread? Another resource is time. How are students spending their time when they are out of school? What choices are they making? What are the implications of their research? What do the data reveal about themselves and their community? This one economic generalization can lead to a variety of interesting lessons focused on the children's lives while also helping the children make sense of the complex world in which they live. Most textbook or commercial units would not be as focused on the lives of the students and their communities as would be possible with a teacher-made unit.

Teachers can experience several advantages from making their own units:

- Having a sense of ownership and pride in the unit if it is successful
- Integrating the curriculum easily across subject areas because the teacher knows what will be taught during the rest of the day
- Individualizing the unit to match students' abilities
- Using the teacher's own talents and experiences
- Using local community resources

Interdisciplinary Thematic Units

Combining student sources and integrating skills and content are the hallmarks of the newer approach to unit teaching known as *interdisciplinary thematic units*. (See Chapter 4 for a primary application.) Interdisciplinary units typically try to combine science, reading/language arts, and literature with social studies content. If possible, music, art, and other areas are also added as content to the unit. In an integrative social studies teaching unit, reading/language arts and mathematics should not be seen as an end in themselves but should become tools students use to study the major social studies content. Thus, some skill development in these subjects flows from the tools needed in the unit, lending an organic or more natural sequence to instruction.

How are thematic units put together? Let us look at a possible primary grade topic: transportation. The major theme or generalization is that transportation is moving people or things from one place to another.

Sometimes changing the theme into a question makes planning easier. What kinds of transportation exist in the world today? By brainstorming ideas that fit this broad question, you will develop a list of concepts, definitions, and questions relating to the theme. Some possibilities might be these:

Animals that provide transportation
People power, such as walking
Machines that provide transportation
Transportation on land, air, and water? Different kinds? Classification.
Why it is important to have good transportation?
Safety—Roads and highways—Traffic rules and signs
What is a vehicle? A wheeled vehicle?
What makes a vehicle run or go?
Trucks
Trains

The next step is to look over these ideas. Which ones seem logically connected with each other? Drawing these connections on a large sheet of paper using the technique of schematic webbing helps us visualize ways topics can be linked and sequenced. Once the topics or questions are diagrammed, the next step is to focus on what objectives you wish to achieve from the unit. They might be as follows:

1. Students will identify examples of transportation on land, air, and water. (a content objective)
2. Students will create a graph of the different types of transportation their family uses within a week. (a skill objective)
3. Students will give reasons why it is important to have a transportation system in their community. (content and appreciation objective)

Once the objectives are sketched, the next task is to think of all the learning activities and resources that would help develop each objective. Trade books, songs, tapes, and records need to be surveyed as a first step. Then you could list other resources and activities:

- Possible guest speakers such as female pilots and bus drivers
- Taking class surveys of different transportation used by students

- Field trips to airports and truck depots to see these systems in operation
- Observation and discussion of correct ways of crossing streets
- Figuring out distances to school
- Getting lost, or the value of helpful maps

You can add a lot more. The difficulty usually comes in deciding when to stop and select the ideas you will use.

This type of unit would have the usual introductory activities as well as a final culmination activity. The learning activities and resources come from a variety of different academic areas. With no artificial divisions between time periods in the classroom, students can put together and reconstruct their own ideas more easily. Students can express their ideas through dramatization, writing, projects, visual arts, or music. Assessment and evaluation could include portfolios of student-produced projects and anecdotal records as well as paper-and-pencil tests.

What are some sources of themes? Besides traditional themes like transportation, the Westward Movement, and the environment from content areas, they could be biographical, local events, local history, world events, or family history. Teachers have successfully used such themes as Egyptian mummies, architecture of a given community, or a book like *Sarah Plain and Tall*. Themes could be selected by the teacher or could emerge from the experiences and current needs of students.

Good interdisciplinary thematic units have many advantages. Students are more likely to see the connections among the various curriculum areas. In many cases, social studies is the most logical area for integration of a theme. Although reading/language arts as well as art and drama are often easily incorporated into a interdisciplinary thematic unit, sometimes there may be drawbacks. At certain times it is artificial to try to integrate many subject areas into a theme. Most teachers have found the most difficulty with trying to move math into larger thematic units.

Beginners often ask how long a unit should last. There is no fixed answer to this question, but younger students probably profit more from shorter units, perhaps a few weeks, and older students gain more from units that are longer, up to six weeks. If the unit goes on too long, students may lose interest. Some teachers, however, find that students beg for more after interesting units, such as the economic simulation called *Mini-Society*, which lasts a full six weeks. The ideal time depends both on the age of the students and the material being taught.

Units may vary in length depending on how many other areas of the curriculum are included in them. A social studies unit that incorporates art, music, literature, and science usually lasts longer than one that includes no other disciplines. In planning a unit, try to incorporate as many relevant curriculum areas and skills as possible.

Travel Day to Hawaii

The following unit is planned to last one week and is prepared for the primary grades. It could be used following New York State guidelines that focus in the second grade on communities of the United States. Usually, such a unit has a broad objective and specific daily objectives. Although it might be inappropriate to use verbs such as *know*, *value*, and *understand* in behavioral objectives for individual lessons, such words are appropriate at the beginning of a unit where they provide overall guidance and organization to the instructional process.

UNIT GOALS

1. Students will understand the geography, history, and traditional culture of Hawaii.
2. Students will identify different types of transportation.

DAY 1

Objectives: Students will distinguish an island from a land mass.
Students will describe their experiences about Hawaii.
Students will draw the Hawaiian Islands.

1. Introduce the vocabulary term *island*. Brainstorm with the class: What is an island? Have the children look at a map of the United States and find a state that is a group of islands.
2. Discuss the history of Hawaii. Share past experiences of children or their parents who have visited there.
3. Tell the children that the class will go on a "pretend" trip to Hawaii in five days. Discuss different modes of transportation.
4. Draw the islands on brown butcher paper and label them according to shape. Have the children pin up the product on the bulletin board with a blue background for water.

DAY 2

Objectives: Students will differentiate the various types of transportation.
Students will calculate distances from their state to Hawaii.

1. Brainstorm with the children as to the different ways the class could travel to Hawaii (airplane, ship, sailboat, etc.).
2. Design an airplane ticket. Include the date, time of departure, and so on.

DAY 3

Objective: Students will describe the traditional cultures/history of Hawaii.

1. Read "Palm Tree" from *Young Folks Hawaiian Time*.
2. Discuss the term *luau*, as well as foods usually eaten, dances, and so on.
3. Have children make drawings of Hawaiian traditions for a mural.
4. Learn the hula from a community member.

DAY 4

Objective: Students will depict the sequence of a volcano.

1. Brainstorm the term *volcano*. Discuss how volcanoes formed the islands.
2. Have the children divide paper into four squares. Illustrate an eruption of a volcano in sequence.

DAY 5

Objective: Students will simulate a travel day in Hawaii. This lesson plan is part of a full day's activity: a "pretend" in-classroom flight to another state. Hawaii is used as an example in this lesson, but other states or nations could be used as well. This travel day combines all subjects in a *fun* educational setting. The following is an example of such a day.

MORNING LESSON

1. "Takeoff"
   a. Collect children-made airplane tickets at the door.
   b. Review the flight route (ocean to be flown over, etc.).
2. Math-Macaroni Leis
   a. Design a simple count pattern (two reds, one yellow, and repeat) with dyed macaroni and construction-paper flowers. Save for the luau.
3. Language/Letter-Writing Skills
   a. Write and design a postcard to a friend or family member. Discuss how to address a postcard, the purpose of a stamp, and how to use descriptive language.
4. Reading/Vocabulary Skills
   a. Share "Hawaiian Alphabet" from *Young Folks Hawaiian Time*.
   b. Complete a worksheet on Hawaiian terms.
   c. Write in alphabetical order.

continued

SAMPLE UNIT PLAN 2.1 (CONT.)

5. Science: Parts of Flowers
   a. Label a hibiscus flower. Discuss the climate needed for it to grow and the stages of plant growth in general.
6. Art and Music
   a. Learn the hula and Hawaiian folk tales.
   b. Design a scrapbook of the day's events. Draw scenes of Hawaii with brief written descriptions.
7. Social Studies: Culture and Foods of Hawaii
   a. Finish with a luau in Hawaii. Poi, coconut, and pineapple juice are a few suggested foods to share. The children should eat with their fingers.
   b. "Reboard" for the return flight home.

Elizabeth A. Gelbart reported about this unit, which she had designed at a social studies conference. In addition to the previous outline, Ms. Gelbert provided ten pages describing in more detail worksheets with topics such as "A Hawaiian Volcano Erupts."[2]

2.4   *ON YOUR OWN: ANALYZE THE UNIT*

In the Sample Unit Plan 2.1, is the theme and content appropriate for the age group? Are there provisions for teaching skills and values? Are there a variety of activities for the children? Is there integration with other subject areas of the curriculum? Do you think the class would enjoy the unit? Is there a progression of experiences and activities that leads to a cumulation in the unit?

Sample Unit Plan 2.1 has many strengths; many classes would learn from and enjoy it, especially the final day's culmination activity. But there is one serious concern: Is the unit reinforcing stereotypes about Hawaii? Will students learn about the large city of Honolulu with its wide diversity of people? Will students find out about the problems Hawaii is facing today as its land usage changes? The unit focuses on the tourist world of Hawaii. Attractive as that may be, it is not the whole picture. Note that the basic plan of this unit could be used for other nations or even states within the United States, but a teacher must be certain that students understand there is more to a region than the tourist view.

---

[2]Elizabeth A. Gelbart, "Travel Day to Hawaii." Presented at the California Council for the Social Studies Conference (Los Angeles, 1986).

SAMPLE UNIT PLAN 2.2

Living in Hawaii

Now let us examine carefully another unit on Hawaii prepared for primary grades.

UNIT GOALS

1. Students will understand the geography, history, and traditional culture of Hawaii (same objective as first unit, "Travel to Hawaii").

2. Students will describe how contemporary life in Hawaii differs from their own and how it is the same (different objective compared to first unit).

DAY 1

Objectives: Students describe their images and experiences concerning Hawaii.

Students formulate questions to answer about what it would be like to live in Hawaii.

Students locate Hawaii on a globe and relate it to their location.

1. Ask what the students think of when they hear about the state of Hawaii. Explore individual experiences. Locate Hawaii on the globe as well as the community of the class. Ask students to describe how it would be to live on one of the Hawaiian islands.

2. Ask students to imagine they were going to move to Hawaii. Ask "What would you like to know about Hawaii?" and record questions.

3. Read *Hawaii in Words and Pictures* (Dennis B. Fradin, Children's Press, 1980) to find possible answers. Discuss where and what children do to play, what homes are like, how life is the same or different.

4. Have students draw individual pictures of their images of Hawaii to place in their Hawaiian unit folder.

DAY 2

Objective: Students describe how islands are formed.

1. Share student drawings from Day 1, clustering them in subgroups such as food, homes, and play; display on a Hawaiian Life unit bulletin board under "First Images."

2. Have students write captions cooperatively telling the essence of

continued

each cluster. Ask students to cross-check these images with their initial questions as a bridge to formulating questions differently or to asking other questions.

3. Ask students questions on how islands are formed. Using pictures, video, or encyclopedia visuals plus lava and coral samples, lead presentation of volcanic island formation. Introduce vocabulary — *volcano, lava, eruption, erosion, coral,* etc. — in explanation; review and copy for Hawaiian dictionary page of unit folder.

4. If available, present science lesson on volcano eruptions including model eruption.

5. Show aerial photographs of actual inhabited islands to show varying water depth around the islands.

DAY 3

Objective: Students recount how the islands came to be populated by a non-Western voyage of discovery.

1. Were there always people, plants, and animals on the new islands? Hypothesize how the islands came to be populated. Use globe, encyclopedia, and library resources to visualize the story of how the islands were colonized by Polynesians.

2. If possible, show video of a 1992–1993 voyage that replicated original voyages of Hawaiian settlement that began in South Pacific islands. Count out on calendar sheets the length of this voyage. What did the travelers eat? Where did they sleep? Mark the route on a globe. Have students draw their version of Polynesian discoverers for unit folders and write what their picture tells.

DAY 4

Objectives: Students contrast traditional Hawaiian life with living in Hawaii today.
Students contrast their own lifestyles with those of contemporary students living in Hawaii.

1. Students share pictures and stories. Teacher asks what students think children in Hawaii do to remember the early days of Hawaii.

2. Teacher shares sections of books on Hawaii that describe and/or picture ways of maintaining traditional cultural practices such as hula, canoe teams, net fishing, fish farming, weaving from palm and banana leaves, making flower leis. Teacher directs viewing and listening of video and tape materials, such as annual hula contest

broadcast on Hawaiian television, or uses promotional materials from local travel agent and recording of Hawaiian music.

3. Resource person teaches students short hula, speaking first in English, then in Hawaiian.

4. Teacher shows pictures and or video of people living in a city in Hawaii (John Penisten, *Honolulu*, New York: Macmillan Child Group, 1990). Students discuss how Hawaii has changed since people first came to the islands; how it would be to live there now; how living there would be the same as or different from where they live.

5. Teacher provides newspaper or magazine articles of native Hawaiian descendants marching for sovereignty. Discuss what that might mean. What would be good/bad about recognizing Hawaiian land rights?

6. Students draw pictures of Hawaii "today and yesterday" with explanatory captions for display on the unit bulletin board.

Day 5

Objectives: Continued from Day 4.

1. Students take turns presenting "today and yesterday" pictures.

2. Teacher leads students to review initial questions and make conclusions about what they have learned for a cooperative chart story for bulletin board display.

3. Teacher plans with students what they could do to share their unit with another class.

4. After practice, students give a presentation on the unit to another class, using bulletin boards, video segments, map displays, hula performance, and oral presentations.

2.5 ON YOUR OWN: COMPARING THE UNIT

Using the same questions found in 2.4, Analyze the Unit, analyze and compare the unit "Living in Hawaii" with "Travel Day to Hawaii." Notice that although the subject matter for both is Hawaii, there is a great difference in what students will learn, the skills they use and develop, and the attitudes or appreciations that they may acquire as a result of the unit. What are the strong points of the unit "Living in Hawaii"?

Comparison of the two units certainly shows the variety and creativity that can be developed with the same topic. Both units encourage an integration with other areas of the curriculum and use skills and content from a variety of subject areas. Both also try to make the activities interesting and meaningful for students. By comparison, both can make connections with previous units.

Both units have the power to expand student knowledge. Compared to the first unit, "Living in Hawaii" goes beyond tourist stereotypes and pushes students beyond their first, and probably inaccurate, images of Hawaii. Students will use higher-level thinking skills as they compare traditional Hawaii, contemporary Hawaii, and their own way of life. They will probably appreciate more the daring and brave Polynesians who made the trip to Hawaii and have more respect for their culture. The emphasis on the native culture and its history probably also reinforces a more multicultural view of world history. The unit also introduces the idea that Hawaii is more than a holiday paradise; real people live there facing real problems.

Is there any weakness in the unit "Living in Hawaii"? Could you easily implement the unit? There may not be a weakness in the unit itself but any teacher trying it might feel unfamiliar with some of the content and worry about the difficulty of getting the materials and resources to make it successful. Living months in Hawaii might be the solution to successful implementation of this unit! This point illustrates the importance of the knowledge and background that a teacher brings to a theme. Try to build on your own strengths; during your vacations as well as during the year, round up as many resources as possible for current and forthcoming units. Increasing use of computer networks should make access to teaching materials easier (see Chapter 9).

SAMPLE UNIT PLAN 2.3

Understanding Prejudice

The following excerpts are from another unit developed by the San Mateo Elementary School District (San Mateo, California) that emphasizes the affective (emotional) domain. This unit is designed for the sixth grade and is intended to last almost four weeks. Notice the difficulties in writing objectives in the affective domain.

UNIT OBJECTIVE:

The students will demonstrate an acceptance of human differences while engaged in activities in the classroom and in other situations.

Specific Unit Objectives:

1. The students will define prejudice and give examples.

2. The students will distinguish between dislike and prejudice.

3. The students will recognize stereotyping, including male and female roles.

4. The students will recognize prejudgment against persons who are handicapped, either physically or mentally.

5. The students will understand the physical differences of ethnic minorities.

6. The students will describe differences related to socioeconomic, religious, and emotional factors.

LESSON: THE STRANGER

Objectives: Students will define prejudice and give examples of it.

Procedure: Ask a visitor to come to the room dressed entirely in paper bags. The visitor comes in and sits down with no introduction or other attention directed toward him or her. After the visitor has spent about fifteen minutes in the room, he or she leaves and a discussion follows.

Possible questions: What did you think about the stranger when he or she first came into the room? Who can tell us about the stranger? (Record answers since they may bring out fears and stereotypes.) How did you feel with a stranger in the room? Would someone tell us about a time when you were a stranger in a group of new people? How did you feel? What did you think of the other people? Why? How do you react to words such as *the homeless* and words describing other groups?

LESSON: STEREOTYPING

Objective: Students will be able to give an example of stereotyping.

Procedure: Review the meaning of prejudice. Ask the students how they think children learn prejudice. Then do the following:

Instruct the students to close their eyes and imagine a Native American. Have them draw their idea on paper. Show some of the pictures to the class. Next show them some pictures of Native Americans without feathers, war paint, and so on. Ask them where they learned about American Indians.

continued

SAMPLE UNIT PLAN 2.3 (CONT.)

Discuss with the students how they might expect a typical person of another race, nationality, and so on to look. Discuss why they might expect these things because of stereotypes. Ask if stereotypes are good to have. Ask if stereotypes can make us treat people unfairly.

LESSON: STEREOTYPED ATTITUDES

Objective: Students will recognize and give examples of stereotyping attitudes.

Procedure: Discuss with the class the opinion of some people that most children are terrible. Have them give examples of things they have heard people say about their age group.

Then ask the students what they think about these things. Are they fair? Why? Why do some people feel that way? Do the children have reason to be upset?

Point out that ideas are formed by our experiences, but we should try not to group all people by the actions of a few. Ask students to write a description of a teacher. When they have finished, read the descriptions and explain that all teachers are not exactly alike simply because they are teachers.

2.6   ON YOUR OWN: MORE UNIT EVALUATION

Look at the questions in Exercise 2.3. What are the strengths of the sample unit plan "Understanding Prejudice"? From the lessons provided, do you see any weaknesses in this unit? What skills might a teacher need to make this unit work properly?

Elements of a Unit

What does a unit contain? The following elements are typically found in a unit:

Unit title.

Description of the grade level, target student population, and general rationale for the unit.

Goals or major objective(s) for the unit.

Series of lesson plans, normally, each with the objective and purpose. The lesson plan should give enough detail on procedures so that the teaching strategies and activities are clear. Worksheets and similar handouts should be included.

List of resources. This could include a list of resource people, media, library books, and so on.

Evaluation. Tests and other evaluation procedures should be included.

No set format exists for writing units. Some teachers prefer to divide a page into three columns—the first one for objectives, the middle one for teaching procedures, and the third one for materials. Others like to put each lesson plan on a separate page so they can eliminate or modify the lesson plans more easily.

What is the difference between units (sometimes called teaching units) and resource units? *Resource units* are units designed (e.g., by the Census Bureau to help teachers teach about the census) for use by a great many teachers. Districts may design a resource unit for a given topic. Usually, resource units contain more ideas and activities than any one teacher can use.

SAMPLE UNIT PLAN 2.4

Food

The following resource unit, designed to promote global education, is from the *Indiana in the World* Teaching Activities Packet:

ACTIVITIES

The pupils may:

Draw a two-column chart.

Head one column "Animals" and one "Plants." List in the columns the foods students eat that come from plants and animals.

Make a list of their favorite foods.

Make a collage of their favorite foods.

Make a list of junk foods.

From a list of favorite foods, categorize the foods according to the six groups of the nutritional pyramid, identifying those that qualify as junk foods.

Discuss the nutritional value of the food they eat.

List and discuss health problems that can be prevented through adequate nutrition.

Describe and discuss their individual family eating patterns and compare them with those of other members of the class.

---

continued

SAMPLE UNIT PLAN 2.4 (CONT.)

Divide into groups, each group choosing a foreign country; research and list the foods of their chosen country.

Find pictures and make a picture chart of the foods of their chosen country.

Discuss the eating utensils of a country (e.g., chopsticks in the Orient).

Visit a supermarket that features foods of many countries. List the foods that are featured from the country they are studying.

Take a field trip to a restaurant featuring food of a chosen country.

Research and make a picture story chart on the influence religion may have on the diet of a country.

Plan a balanced diet from the foods of their chosen country.

List five or more foods eaten by people of other countries. State the countries (e.g., octopus, Italy).

Research and report on the history of some foods eaten in the United States.

List some of the foods eaten in the United States that were brought here from other countries. Name the countries.

Find pictures of children suffering from malnutrition in other countries.

Research and report on the diseases prevalent in these countries because of malnutrition.

Write two story paragraphs, one explaining plankton and the other hydroponics.

2.7 ON YOUR OWN: WHAT ARE THE STRENGTHS OF THESE ACTIVITIES?

In many cases, teachers incorporate the ideas from resource units or guides into their own teaching. Do you think any of these ideas on foods are helpful? Might you incorporate them into your own unit?

What are some special considerations that teachers should be aware of in designing and implementing units in the social studies? One is *variety*. Look at your lesson plans. Are you using the same techniques (e.g., worksheets) every day? Are you showing three videos three days in a row? Is content emphasized without consideration of the importance of skills, values, and citizenship education?

To spot these problems more easily, some teachers like to jot down in broad

TABLE 2.1   LESSON PLANS FOR THE WEEK—SOCIAL STUDIES

Monday	Tuesday	Wednesday	Thursday	Friday
Introduction of community images	Map of community	Telephone book used to locate businesses	Librarian to visit	Post office counter used

outline what they are doing throughout the course of a week (see Table 2.1). Seeing a whole week's schedule often points out the need for more variety in teaching strategies and more attention to skills and values.

After you have completed a unit, evaluate it from your students' point of view. What was their favorite activity? What did they like least about the unit? Most important, what did they learn from it?

LESSON PLANS

A *lesson plan* is an outline of what you expect to teach in a given day's lesson. (See the daily plans in Sample Unit Plan 2.1, a "Travel Day to Hawaii," for examples.) Many teachers begin by creating and photocopying a blank form with several headings (see Figure 2.1). This form can be filled in at the beginning of each week or each unit. This is a typical outline, but it neglects some important areas of lesson planning, as we shall see later.

Lesson plans are constructed within the general framework of a unit and should reflect the goals of that unit. You need to be alert, in constructing daily plans, to how activities can move your students toward an understanding of the unit's general goals—how daily activities can make those goals more meaningful. This requires a careful match between student readiness and interest and the activities you plan.

Subject Area ＿＿＿＿＿＿＿＿＿＿＿＿＿ Date ＿＿＿＿＿＿＿＿＿＿＿＿＿
Objectives:

Procedures:

Materials:

Evaluation:

Figure 2.1 Lesson plan form

The first consideration in making a lesson plan is the objective or purpose. Is there a special concept that you hope students will acquire? The next step is motivation. What can you do to capture students' attention? This may involve relating the experiences of students to your objectives. Student interest and involvement in the lesson may be triggered by an artifact, a learning game, or a planned classroom experience.

Beginnings are important. They help to shape the motivation of students. Teachers should try to effect a smooth transition from what students already know to the new material. In general, sequence your instruction from the simple to the complex. Sometimes a brief review by a student of what was done in yesterday's social studies lesson is helpful. Try to create an organizational framework for ideas or information so that students know where things are going. It is often valuable simply to state the purpose of the lesson. Some teachers turn lessons into guessing games for their students, who must figure out where they're going and why. This generally does not help the learning process, especially for slower students.

In writing out procedures, teachers often do not use enough detail. What does "read and discuss the textbook" mean? Read aloud? Read silently? Read one paragraph silently and then discuss? Will students discuss questions in small groups? You can see that "read and discuss the textbook" is open to a wide variety of interpretations.

During the lesson, be attentive to the responses of the students. Is there a sense of accomplishment among them? Finally, think about closure, or ending the lesson. Will you depend on the bell to close the lesson? That can leave students dangling in mid-thought. A better way is to draw attention to the end of the lesson, to help students organize their learning, and to reinforce what they have learned. Have a student summarize the lesson for the class, or do so yourself.

A good lesson, then, usually consists of the following areas:

Objective to be achieved
Concept or major idea(s) to be taught
Teaching strategies to be used
Motivation for the lesson
Materials and resources needed for the lesson
Closure for the lesson, including independent work and follow-up
Evaluation to learn whether objective(s) are achieved

The typical outline in Figure 2.1 that lists objectives, procedures, materials, and evaluation therefore neglects motivation, concepts to be taught, closure for the lesson, independent work, and follow-up. Lack of attention to these areas sometimes results in dull lessons when just a little more planning could turn the lesson into an exciting and useful learning experience for the students.

2.8 SMALL GROUP WORK: LOCATING INTERESTING LESSON PLANS

It would be exhausting to develop all your lesson plans by yourself in the area of the social studies. Look at teachers' guides and resource units for ideas for lesson plans. Find three lesson plans you like. Explain why they appeal to you.

ORGANIZING AND SCHEDULING

Time for teaching is a valuable resource. Many elementary students attend school for more than five hours a day, and the trend in the reform movement is to increase the number of minutes that elementary students spend in school. But when you subtract lunch time and recesses, most teachers probably have only about four hours a day actually to teach.

How much time should be spent on teaching the social studies? Many school districts give recommendations. The minimum usually is fifteen minutes a day for the first grade with an increasing time allotment each year. But the fourth grade, around thirty-five minutes a day is usually recommended, and by the sixth grade, social studies usually occupies a full period of approximately forty to forty-five minutes.

These time allocations, however, presume that subjects are not integrated. Typically, first-grade language arts (reading, writing, listening, speaking, spelling, handwriting) are allotted *two to three hours* each day. This means that if you integrate different areas, such as language arts (reading stories about the culture you are studying, writing a thank-you note to a community worker who spoke to your class), you can greatly increase the number of minutes devoted to social studies instruction. Integrating science and social studies is also worthwhile; studying the geography of a given area lends itself easily to the study of that area's plants, animals, climate, and the like. Integrating social studies with music, art, dance, and drama is natural, especially when you are studying a particular culture.

When is social studies typically taught during the school day? In many schools the basic subjects, reading and math, are taught in the morning "prime-time" hours. Social studies is generally relegated to the afternoon in such programs. By integrating subject matters, however, you can bring social studies content into the morning hours when students are fresher and better able to learn.

You may not have complete control over scheduling block time and subject areas. In most schools, physical education, music, art, and other such subjects are taught by specialists whose schedules will dictate part of your own scheduling. In addition, students are often grouped for reading and/or math and may go to different rooms for these subjects. Again, you may have to follow prescribed time allocations for such classes.

Most teachers, however, can make decisions on how to use the time available. You will probably want to set up a "normal" daily and weekly schedule. You may decide that you would rather teach social studies on Monday, Wednesday, and Friday for a longer block of time than every day for a shorter period. Time allocations may change depending on the activities. A field trip or a local guest may dictate changes in the normal schedule. However, most classrooms eventually move into routine scheduled times for different subject areas or learning periods. Teachers differ on how to schedule and organize their class time. As long as time is used wisely, these differences are probably not important.

SUMMARY

Planning is important for effective teaching. Teachers usually block out a year's social studies curriculum by determining what units will be taught during the year. The unit approach with a theme and sequential lessons provides better learning experiences for students. Ideally, lesson plans should be detailed enough to make teaching of the social studies effective and interesting. Teachers also have to plan so that citizenship and multicultural education as well as other goals and skills are treated as a day-long concern (see especially Chapters 6 through 8).

SUGGESTED READINGS

Allen, Jack, ed. *Education in the 80's: Social Studies.* Washington, D.C.: National Education Association, 1981. An overview of the social studies.

Beyer, Barry K., and Gilstrap, Robert. *Writing in Elementary School Social Studies.* Boulder, Colo.: Social Science Education Consortium, 1982. How to use writing as a resource in the teaching of social studies.

Brophy, Jere E.; Rohrkemper, Mary; Rashid, Habim; and Goldberger, Michael. "Relationships between Teachers' Presentation of Classroom Tasks and Student Engagement in Those Tasks." *Journal of Educational Psychology* 75 (August, 1983): 544–552.

Davis, James E., and Haley, Frances, eds. *Planning a Social Studies Program: Activities, Guidelines, and Resources.* Boulder, Colo.: ERIC Clearing House for Social Studies/Social Science Education, Social Science Education Consortium, 1977. Old, but still good.

Dick, Walter, and Carey, Lou. *The Systematic Design of Instruction*, 2d ed. Glenview, Ill.: Scott, Foresman, 1985. Organizing learning and instruction effectively.

Eisner, Elliot W. *The Educational Imagination*. New York: Macmillan, 1985. Sees much of teaching as an artistic enterprise.

Fredericks, Anthony D.; Meinbach, Anita Meyer; and Rothlein, Liz. *Thematic Units*. New York: HarperCollins, 1993.

INSTRUCTIONAL STRATEGIES

This chapter illustrates the use of various instructional strategies with social studies topics. The more methods or teaching strategies you have, the better you will be able to accommodate your students' diverse learning styles. The following areas are highlighted in the chapter:

1/ General Consideration of Methods
2/ Direct Teaching
3/ Inquiry Modes and Critical Thinking
4/ Cooperative Learning
5/ Role Playing
6/ Simulations

GENERAL CONSIDERATION OF METHODS

What methods or instructional strategies should be used to teach elementary social studies? Planning instruction is like planning a trip; you need to consider several elements (see Tables 3.1 and 3.2).

To teach effectively, you should have a wide repertoire of teaching methods. Using a variety of strategies will help you meet the varying needs of students, who have different styles of thinking and learning. Of interest is Howard Gardner's

TABLE 3.1   ELEMENTS IN PLANNING

Planning a Trip	*Planning for Choice of Method*
What is my goal(s)?	What is my goal(s)?
What transportation will be used? Various forms?	What method will be used? Various forms?
How much time is available?	How much time is available?
What will I do?	What activities will be used?
What shall I pack? How much?	What materials or resources are needed?
What information do I need?	What background do the students need?
What if there are delays?	What adjustments may need to be made?

TABLE 3.2   ELEMENTS IN PLANNING FOR METHODS

Student Characteristics	+	*Content Characteristics*	+
Reading abilities		Significance	
Other basic skills		Available materials/resources	
Cooperative abilities		Survey versus in-depth coverage	
Attention span			
Motivation needed			

Environmental Characteristics	+	*Instructional Possibilities*	=
Schedule		Exposure: story, film, text, guest	
Space/room arrangement		Skills to be taught: library, cooperative learning	
Size of class		Creative: role play, research	

Possible Instructional Sequence
Introduction–overview
Motivation
Development
Student reproduction of knowledge
Culmination, summary, conclusions

theory of multiple intelligences.[1] Gardner identifies seven basic intelligences. (See Chapter 4.)

> Verbal Linguistic (language)
> Logical/Mathematical
> Visual/Spatial
> Body/Kinesthetic
> Musical/Rhythmic
> Interpersonal (understanding of other individuals)
> Intrapersonal (understanding of ourselves)

Gardner believes that individuals possess all seven of these intelligences but we differ in the relative strengths of each of these. However, the schools tend to focus primarily on the first two intelligences. This means that teachers need to provide experiences that use and extend all of the seven intelligences of children.

3.1   *ON YOUR OWN: FINDING YOUR STYLE*

What learning style are you most comfortable with? Does your style of learning have any relationship to the methods you are most confident with in your teaching? Have you consciously adopted one or more methods in your own teaching experience? Jot down the strengths and weaknesses of your "style."

To meet the wide diversity in student background and learning styles, it is wise to use a wide range of teaching methods. For example, with a fifth-grade class studying the history of the U.S. West, you could begin with an exercise on planning a trip to the pre–Civil War West. Have the students, organized in small groups, decide how much they should spend on various supplies and what articles they should put in the covered wagon. (There are computer programs such as *The Oregon Trail* that work on a similar theme, but if you do not have a computer in your classroom, the small group exercise can work very well.)

Have the students analyze their findings. In a whole-class discussion, they can gain insights from other groups' experiences about what is important for making the trip, and the class can rank the priority items for moving west. (Discussion and list-making favor verbal students.)

Introduce literature and songs about the pioneers to enhance the students' understanding of the settlement of the West. Have students learn or listen to songs like "Oh, Susannah" or "Sweet Betsy from Pike"; talk about the *Little House* books

---

[1]Howard Gardner. *The Unschooled Mind: How Children Think and How Schools Should Teach* (New York: Basic Books, 1991).

or television shows. Teach square or country dancing. To use another strategy, give a short lecture on abstract concepts such as freedom and lawlessness on the frontier. Have students read the appropriate textbook pages and do workbook assignments. Involve the nonverbal students in a range of projects to make or do: putting together a short play on the West, making maps of wagon-train routes, and so on. More verbal students might write "pretend" diaries, songs, or poetry on the West. Finally, have students evaluate their own efforts to see how these projects could serve as stepping-stones for future learning.

The variety of activities in this unit on the West provides channels for a wide range of learners and their abilities. Students start with a concrete experience (planning a trip to the West) and move into concept development (lawlessness, freedom, etc.). Furthermore, the students find applications for the materials and concepts as they develop their own projects. In the process of evaluating their projects, the students engage in analysis and also move into the affective domain by sharing their projects with other members of the class. You will meet many needs in this series of lessons.

In addition to the learning needs of students, certain environmental factors may also influence your choice of teaching methods. Large class size might make some methods inappropriate. The physical environment of the school or the social climate of a given class may not be conducive to certain methods. Simulations, for example, may be noisy. If the walls are thin and a simulation would bother other classes, using this activity would not be a considerate choice. In addition, each class has its own personality. Often you hear experienced teachers say, "No group reports this year. My kids just don't mesh well enough."

Therefore, many factors need to be considered when you think about teaching methods. Each method represents one possible route to more successful learning for your students, and different methods may be more appropriate for different topics and skills.

All teaching methods, however, have some common elements. Each one involves teacher direction of student thinking processes. All require preparation, concern with motivation, setting up of the learning experience, and the creation of some evaluative technique to assess whether students have gained in knowledge, skills, values, or social participation—the four goals of social studies.

DIRECT TEACHING

Much attention has been focused in recent years on an instructional method known as *direct teaching*, or *direct instruction*. The main purpose of direct teaching is to present knowledge and skills that will enable *all* students to *master* the material being taught.

The most popular direct-teaching model, also known as Clinical Teaching, Target Teaching, or Instructional Theory into Practice (ITIP), was developed by

Madeline Hunter. What response do you have to these various titles? Do they suggest that Hunter is interested in having teachers sharpen and target their teaching skills so that students can gain higher levels of achievement? Direct-teaching advocates argue that this approach—which includes structured content, the carefully explained introduction of new material, considerable student practice, and frequent recall and comprehension questions—can improve achievement, especially for lower socioeconomic status students.

The Hunter model has been successful in part because it begins from a realistic assessment of what goes on in many classrooms, including social studies classrooms. It recognizes that the textbook is still the major vehicle for social studies instruction. Unfortunately, teachers often simply assign sections of text and worksheets without much explanation of the material covered. The Hunter model, which is a specific form of direct teaching or lecturing, can be used to help teachers convey content more effectively. A second reason for the popularity of the Hunter model is that it was developed at a time when some educators were questioning the value of the looser, less direct, or less structured teaching strategies, such as role playing, simulations, and value exercises, which relate more closely to the affective domain.

Districts and individuals have added to and modified the Hunter mastery teaching model. For example, Hunter did not include closure in her steps and many districts have incorporated this activity. Therefore, do not be surprised if you find certain district guidelines using direct teaching models that include more or fewer steps indicated, as follows.

Five-Step Lesson Plan (an interpretation of the Hunter Model) [2]

1. Anticipatory Set
   a. Focus students
   b. State objectives
   c. Establish purpose
   d. Establish transfer (if possible)
2. Instruction
   a. Provide information
      Explain concept
      State definitions*
      Identify critical attributes*
      Provide examples*
      Model
   b. Check for understanding
      Pose key questions

---

[2]The starred items are particularly critical when you are teaching an abstract concept (e.g., democracy). They may not be relevant or appropriate when teaching a practice-oriented concept (e.g., state capitals). Thanks to Bill Crandall for the development of the table.

Ask students to explain concept, definitions, attributes in their own words*
Have students discriminate between examples and nonexamples*
Encourage students to generate their own examples*
Use active participation devices
  3. Guided Practice
    a. Initiate practice activities that are under direct teacher supervision
    b. Elicit overt response that demonstrates behavior
    c. Provide close monitoring
    d. Continue to check for understanding
    e. Provide specific knowledge of results
  4. Closure
    a. Make final assessment to determine whether students have met objective
    b. Have each student perform behavior on his or her own
  5. Independent Practice
    a. Have students continue to practice on their own
    b. Provide knowledge of results

Here are the steps in a direct-teaching model:

1. *Anticipatory Set*: Get the students focused on the lesson. Use material relevant to the objective and related to students' past experiences or interests. Use when introducing new learning, after an interruption, or at a point of change to a new subject.
2. *Objective*: Tell the students what they are going to learn.
3. *Purpose*: Tell the students the benefit of the learning. Explain why you are teaching the lesson. (Objective and purpose are sometimes combined.)
4. *Input*: Analyze the knowledge and skills that need to be learned. Present the material.
5. *Modeling*: Tell the students what to look for. Provide a perfect model. Demonstrate what the end product of the learning will look like.
6. *Check for understanding*: Monitor the learning. Adjust your instruction to accommodate where the students are.
7. *Guided practice*: Actively involve all students. Monitor their activity. (Understanding and practice are sometimes combined.)
8. *Closure*: Tie the learning together. Recapitulate. Summarize.
9. *Independent practice*: Assign classroom work and homework, to be done independently.

What are the key elements of direct teaching? *Pacing* and *learning for mastery* are important. Students spend a high percentage of their time on tasks that they will successfully complete. In contrast, regular instruction too frequently skips many of the elements of direct teaching and leaves students frustrated, either because they are not sure *what* they are supposed to have learned, or because they don't know *why* they are learning it.

The direct-teaching model may remind you of what a public speaking instructor would say: Tell them what you're going to say, say it, and then tell them what you've said. That is, in fact, a large part of direct instruction. In addition, however, the emphasis on "set" is an attempt to relate actual student experiences to the objectives— to bring students into a more active participation in learning. Direct teaching attempts to stimulate student interest and involvement in the lesson by explaining to students the importance of what they are learning and by presenting the content clearly. Furthermore, the lesson is planned in detail, so the teacher avoids meandering along trivial or personal paths. Finally, direct teaching gives students an opportunity to practice what they have heard and then to reinforce it with further assignments.

When is direct teaching appropriate in the social studies? Certainly, teachers need to explain ideas and concepts to students whenever instruction begins on a new unit of work, a new concept, or a new project. Direct-teaching methods can help. Here is how direct teaching using a textbook might work:

A teacher, Mr. Smithy, wants to explain the concept of *organization*—a group that has at least two members who have common interests and rules. His teaching objective is for students to distinguish organizations from nonorganizations. To *set* the lesson, Mr. Smithy points out that many members of the class belong to organizations: José is a Cub Scout and Maria is a Brownie. What other students, he asks, belong to these or other organizations? Mr. Smithy explains that religious or after-school sports groups are also organizations.

Then Mr. Smithy tells the students that they are going to learn about organizations, which form important parts of our modern society, because it is useful for the students to be able to identify them. In other words, he explains the *objective* and *purpose*. In the *input* stage, he may give examples of organizations. The city council is an organization; it has more than two members, rules, and common interests. The local personal computer club is also an organization. Members have common interests, pay dues, and come to meetings to find out more about how to use their computers. The Parent-Teacher Association (PTA) is an organization; stamp clubs and after-school soccer teams are organizations.

Mr. Smithy then gives examples of *non*organizations. The local shoe repair store employs only one person. It is not an organization. A group of individual shoppers in a shopping center is not an organization, even though it includes more than two people, because the shoppers do not meet regularly or follow common rules.

Mr. Smithy explains to his students the main characteristics of an organization. He continues to provide examples of organizations and nonorganizations. He summarizes the main distinctions again. Then Mr. Smithy has the class read the pages in their textbooks about organizations.

After the class finishes reading, Mr. Smithy *checks their comprehension* by asking questions about what is and what is not an organization. Then he gives a worksheet to the class and has students check on a list the words that represent organizations and those that do not. The list may include *people at a movie theater, the Sierra Club,* or *people walking in the park.* Mr. Smithy supervises this activity, providing *guided practice.*

After allowing time for this exercise, Mr. Smithy and the class go over the correct answers on the list. In *closure,* the students summarize again the main characteristics of an organization.

Finally, for homework, Mr. Smithy has students ask their parents what organizations they belong to (unions, churches, clubs, etc.). Students then create, independently, lists of organizations to which their parents belong. This provides *independent practice.* Mr. Smithy may check these lists to be certain that students have an accurate understanding at this point of what an organization really is.

In the above example, Mr. Smithy assumed that all students could read a textbook, which is not necessarily true of all class members. By identifying the key ideas before giving students the reading assignment, however, he ensured that even students who were not good readers would find the assignment easier. In effect, he had built in "readiness" for the reading experience. He used the textbook to reinforce his own teaching and to help students understand a concept.

Simply creating all the elements of a good direct-teaching lesson is not sufficient. You must *communicate* those elements to your students. Breakdowns can occur in direct teaching as well as in any other teaching method. Because much of the instruction in this method depends on your speaking to your class, your vocal delivery is important. If you use poor diction, mannerisms, or digressions, or show a lack of clarity, these may interfere with your delivering the information effectively to your students. The level of abstraction may be too great for a particular group, and students may simply "tune out." Students may also ignore what you are saying if the lesson goes on too long. Their attention may be diverted by physical distractions in the room or by other students. Concrete examples will always help maintain student interest, as will having students use their other senses by employing visual aids or requesting a written response. Too often lecturing is a passive activity for students, who remember little of what they have heard. If you follow the Hunter model carefully, however, step by step, you won't fall into the trap of overusing the lecture.

In some districts and states, administrators have gone overboard with direct teaching and expect all teachers to use it almost all the time. Madeline Hunter did not encourage this rigid dependence on her model. Used exclusively, direct teaching can stifle creativity in teachers and prevent them from exploring different teaching strategies in different situations. Direct teaching obviously has many good points. Whenever you explain or lecture to a class, you would do well to check the steps of the direct-teaching model. Introducing lessons with clear goals and making ideas logical and cogent are helpful principles in conveying knowledge and skills. As with any teaching strategy, however, direct teaching should not be employed day after day in the social studies program. Daily repetition of the same process is dull for both student and teacher unless you are an exceptionally enthusiastic advocate of this method. Direct instruction may be particularly effective for teaching facts and skills to low-ability classes, but the teaching of higher-level thinking skills may best be done by other methods.

3.2   *ON YOUR OWN: EXPLORING THE PROS AND CONS*

Would you like to teach in a school or district in which direct teaching is emphasized? List the advantages and disadvantages of this situation. You may want to read criticisms of the direct-teaching model, which note that only limited research has been conducted to support the claim for improved learning.

INQUIRY MODES AND CRITICAL THINKING

What do the words *inquiry, problem solving, inductive thinking, critical thinking, discovery learning*, and *thinking skills* have in common? They all refer to the processes that everyday citizens as well as scientists and scholars use to discover knowledge, make decisions, and solve problems. The schools have always claimed to do more than just teach the three R's. One goal of education has been to foster the thinking skills that are desperately needed outside the classroom by all members of society. Many critics believe, however, that thinking is a process rarely encouraged or manifested in most classrooms.

How many times have you wished you could have done something different after things have gone awry? "If only I could do things over again" is frequently heard as we discuss our personal problems with others. This human capacity to learn from experience is our greatest potential resource for building a better personal future. Instruction in the processes of critical thinking is even more vital for the future of our lives as citizens. Teaching decision-making skills is essential in the curriculum of the social studies. In making decisions, ranging from minor ones like what book to choose from the library for recreational reading to major ones such as evaluating what is the best way for the nation to have good health care services, children as well as adults must determine the alternatives and then choose wisely among them. Decisions made without careful consideration of the alternatives and the consequences of each can be costly in terms of the quality of our lives.

When thinking skills are not taught, many students (and inevitably, many adults) lack confidence in their own abilities as thinkers. For most, critical thinking is a *learned*, not an *innate*, skill. Those without it feel unsure of themselves and believe that they cannot generate good ideas. This lack of confidence is true even of those students who receive high grades in all subjects on their report cards.

In the 1960s, a reform movement began, in recognition of the need to teach thinking skills. More than fifty new social studies projects were created at that time, and many of them had some emphasis on teaching thinking, most commonly called inquiry. Although educators in the 1970s showed greater concern with values and relevance of materials to students, an interest in teaching thinking skills has manifested itself again in the 1980s and 1990s for many reasons. Our society in general is more concerned about being able to compete in a worldwide market. Only if its youth are educated to think, this argument goes, can the United States survive as a leading industrialized nation with a high standard of living. In addition, citizenship goals have always emphasized the need for teaching all children to think.

Although in practice, thought processes differ from one person to the next, the following steps outlined by John Dewey are a good starting point for "thinking about thinking."[3]

1. Define the problem.
2. Suggest alternative solutions to the problem; formulate hypotheses for testing.
3. Gather data to support or negate hypotheses.
4. Select supportive hypotheses or reject unsupported ones.

This sequence translates into the following steps for teaching thinking skills.

   1. Introduction—problem, question, or dilemma posed
      Example of activities:
         What are our images about Mexico?
            Small groups brainstorm; chairpersons report back to the class.
            Teacher presents items on Mexico gathered from media.
   2. Development of a hypothesis (tentative answer)
      Example of activities:
         Teacher leads a discussion of ideas generated from brainstorming and teacher/class select the best one; hypothesis could be that our images of Mexico are not accurate or it could be the more specific hypothesis that Mexico is facing serious financial (or political or social) problems.
   3. Gathering data
      Example of activities:
         Teacher presents data in charts.
         Students extract data from the textbook.
         Students collect data (group or individual research).
         Students classify and interpret data.

---

[3]John Dewey, *How We Think* (Boston: D. C. Heath, 1933), 72.

4. Hypothesis accepted or rejected
Example of activities:
Class/teacher evaluates data and methods of research.
Class/teacher states a conclusion.
Students suggest further questions for investigation.

We use these processes of problem solving in our everyday lives. Assume that you go to your car in the morning and it does not start. Definitely a problem! You listen and it seems to be making a funny noise as you try to start it. You form a hypothesis: The battery is dead. Then you get help from a friend or neighbor who charges the battery. It works! Your hypothesis (the cause of the problem was a dead battery) has been supported.

Students also face decision making or problem solving on many different levels in their own lives. They may make plans for a birthday party and have to decide whom to invite or what activities to plan. They need to decide how to use their leisure time. Should they watch television, read a book, or play soccer? They may need to resolve problems in getting along with classmates or siblings. They may need to figure out a way to earn money. Students may also have grave concerns about how they should behave in school or outside the classroom.

Problem-solving skills, then, have universal value. Anything that the schools can do to sharpen students' thinking skills now will have a big payoff in the future. Certainly, both individuals and our society face many problems that can be solved only through informed and logical thinking by citizens. But developmental stages are important, and there are limits to what children can do in thinking and problem solving. Many students at younger ages, for example, cannot think abstractly. In addition, children who are impulsive and not motivated toward intellectual tasks may not show much interest in thinking activities in school. In teaching students to think, you need to consider the formal process as well as the specific needs of your students.

Defining the Problem

To resolve any problem, we must first be able to recognize it and define it. This is the first thinking ability that you should encourage in your students. A good way to approach this first step at the elementary level is through *inductive reasoning*. In inductive thinking, an individual perceives a particular pattern of relationships based on a finite number of items or events. It is a way of generalizing from experience or data.

To encourage inductive thinking to help students recognize that culture influences art, you might bring in pictures or show filmstrips on the art and architecture of a particular society such as that of the Mayans or the ancient Greeks. After they have seen a series of art "products" from that culture, have the children try to state something about that culture's beliefs. How are women and men depicted?

Does most of the art represent gods and goddesses? What does that suggest about the importance of religion? By beginning with the concrete objects and encouraging students to generalize from them, you will help students grasp the concept that culture influences art. In contrast, simply asking your students how cultural beliefs affect a society's art will present a far more difficult problem for them.

Many forms of problem solving begin with inductive reasoning. Teachers often try to trigger student thinking by presenting a discrepancy between what students *think* they know and some new data. Ask your students what images they have about a given nation. Contrast this with actual data. Or raise a controversial question such as what a community should do about housing the homeless or controlling pollution. Contrast the students' solutions with what is actually being done.

Generating Ideas

The second step in thinking is to generate ideas or hypotheses (tentative answers) to help explain why a problem is occurring. Try to draw forth as many ideas as possible without making any judgments. Even silly ideas should be accepted to encourage all students to participate.

You might ask individual students to jot down as many different ways as they can think of to improve the common bathtub or, for more of a social studies flavor, their local transportation system. We recommend that each student work by himself or herself for a minute or two before moving into small groups to share ideas. Always have students do some individual thinking first. Students should not get into the habit of believing that they can think only when they are part of a group. A good strategy is to have students think alone, then form pairs or small groups and share ideas.

In the group, each student will usually find out that the others have different ideas. Some might think that public transportation should be increased; others might think that workers need to arrive at their places of employment at different times to avoid commuter congestion. It is good for students to learn that not everybody perceives the world and solves problems in the same way. In some exercises, especially at the beginning, you may not want to focus on determining the *best* ideas. In fact, students should be encouraged to brainstorm and generate ideas without making judgments about which ones are best. Students who are accustomed to questions with only one right answer (what is the capital of Chile?) may find the notion of many right answers both confusing and exciting.

Class activities can help students learn to select good ideas, decisions, or solutions. In the following example, students take the role of an explorer and try to determine solutions to particular problems. The exercise encourages cooperation rather than competition. Notice also that the exercise tries to break down the steps of thinking. It does not simply pose the problem, but first provides background information. Unfortunately, teachers often pose problems too broadly. In this exercise, the student is led step by step through the process to see what ideas will work best in the particular situation.

SAMPLE LESSON PLAN 3.1

Deciding Which Ideas Are Best

In 1542 the Spanish had a claim, or right, to the land in California. This was a land in which 300,000 Native Americans lived. But in the 1700s the Russians were moving down from Alaska. They wanted the rich otter fur trade. The British were also coming closer to "Spanish" land.

Around 1700 the Spanish had settlements in Baja, California (now part of Mexico). To protect their claim, the Spanish government decided to send soldiers and missionaries to California to teach the Indians and to create a permanent Spanish settlement.

The military leader of the group sent to California was Captain Gaspar de Portola, the governor of Baja, California. The religious leader was Father Junipero Serra, a Spanish priest and missionary.

Captain Portola had to decide how to move his group to San Diego, 640 kilometers (400 miles) north of Baja, California. He had two choices: to go by water or by land.

1. Put yourself in Captain Portola's place. List the most important consideration he should think of in making his journey._____

_____

Ships at that time were small, about thirty meters (100 feet) long. A crew might number twenty. The winds might blow the small ship off course. The captain had poor maps. The crew and passengers might get ill from not eating the proper amount of fruits and vegetables, especially if they were at sea for a long time.

By land there was possible danger from the natives. The group had to bring enough food since they could not depend on living off the land. They had to find water. The trip was also slow since most people walked only a few miles (kilometers) each day. There were not enough mules and horses available to carry everyone and all the group's supplies.

2. Captain Portola had to consider an additional problem. In 1769, the year the trip was to start, Father Serra was fifty-five years old. He was short and walked with a limp. How do you think Father Serra should travel? Why?_____

_____

3. Captain Portola also wanted to bring some cattle and horses with

him to California. The animals would be useful in the new settlement. What would be the best way for them to travel?_____

_____

4. Now, with these considerations, what choice do you think Captain Portola should make on how to travel to California? Why?_____

_____

Captain Portola decided to "hedge his bets." He would use three ships and two land groups, one land group going ahead of the other land group.

5. Was this the best plan? Why?_____

_____

6. Captain Portola had to decide whether he, the leader, should go by land or by the sea route. Portola was a skilled army leader. Which way would his talents be best used?_____

_____

Captain Portola and, surprisingly, Father Serra went by land. Limping and riding, Father Serra, with great determination, made it to San Diego. There the land group met the group that had gone by sea. One of the three ships was lost at sea, and many from the voyage were sick and died. The land party also had lost men from illness. But even with these hardships, Captain Portola was successful in establishing the first permanent European settlement in California. Had he used the best ideas in his decision making? What would you have done differently?

3.3 SMALL GROUP WORK: TAKE THE STUDENT ROLE

Pretend you are a student. Work out the exercise on Captain Portola. Then share your responses with a small group or with the class. Do you think the above exercise helps students to think? What if a student decides that Portola should have done something other than what he actually did? Should the student's idea be accepted? How would you respond?

Students need a lot of practice in generating ideas and then in deciding which ones are best. Usually, if a student's explanation of events or situations considers all the relevant facts, it is an idea worthy of consideration and should not be rejected. Ask your students to make sense of or to generate ideas out of puzzling things, such as why Stonehenge in England was built or why Indians called Mound Builders built their large structures in certain parts of the United States. Most students will enjoy thinking about and looking at data about the Loch Ness Monster or, in the United States, Big Foot and drawing conclusions about the possible existence of these "monsters." Or children's own experiences can be used to generate ideas. What can be done about the big kids in other classes who bully younger children? Or what do we do when all children want to paint at the easel at the same time? Students can also be given more formal social studies exercises, such as trying to account for the growth of large cities in their state. All these examples can serve as springboards for thinking and for generating ideas (i.e., hypotheses) to be tested.

Gathering Data

After identifying the problem and suggesting promising ideas to explain or solve it, the third important step in problem solving is gathering data to support or reject the hypothesis. It is important for students to acquire data from a variety of sources. Finding information often involves skills best taught directly, as with the direct-teaching model. Thus, in teaching the more creative thinking skills, you may find yourself using direct-teaching methods.

Information Skills

1. Finding information in a book
   Using a table of contents
   Using an index
   Using a glossary
   Using an appendix
2. Finding information in a library/media center
   Using a card catalog
   Using the Dewey Decimal System
   Using encyclopedias
   Using an atlas
   Using an almanac
   Using other reference books
   Using a telephone directory
   Using on-line computer services

In many cases, before students can find information and data to support their hypotheses, they must be able to use the library and books appropriately. Usually, your school librarian will be helpful in explaining how to use the library and how to collect information, including using computer data bases. Worksheets (on how to find encyclopedia information about the Mongols, the Suez Canal, or the growth of railroads, for example) can be helpful.

Here are other examples of activities that encourage information skills. Photocopy for each student the one-page Quick Reference Index of *The World Almanac and Book of Facts.* Then ask students to give the *category* in which you would look to learn about major earthquakes, the population of Canada's provinces, where nuclear reactors are located in the United States, and so on. Similarly, prepare an abbreviated copy of the telephone numbers of government offices. (In real life, people often need to telephone government agencies about such things as how to fill out an income tax form or how to secure a dog license.) Then explain how to find government office telephone numbers in the pages of a telephone directory. Finally, ask students to find and write down the telephone number for offices such as Animal Control, Birth Records, or Boating or Building Permits.

Students may also assemble their own data from interviews and questionnaires, but they must be taught to ask questions in an objective manner and to communicate clearly what is being asked. Most students will need your assistance in designing an interview sheet or questionnaire to gather data, for example, on how local residents view traffic problems in their neighborhood. Poorly designed interview forms and questionnaires may yield misleading information that is of little value in proving or disproving a hypothesis. Such questionnaires also may reflect unfavorably on the school and the teacher.

Specific Inquiry Skills: Observation and Listening

Observation is a systematic approach requiring careful examination of behavior and phenomena. Teachers constantly direct children to see which object is larger, the differences between two geometric shapes, and how deciduous trees lose their leaves as weather turns cooler in the autumn. Science for young children has a heavy emphasis on the skill of observation. However, observation of behavior of people is more associated with the social sciences. Observation may sound deceptively easy, but it is hard to "tell it like it is." Students must be aware of the distinctions among an action they observe, the *inferences* or meaning they attach to the action, and the value judgment they place on the action. An inference carries one beyond the observable and into the realm of speculation. However, this speculation should not be just guesswork. The problem of looking at (and listening to) people and then making some inferences about their behavior is quite complex and filled with pitfalls. It is difficult to observe objectively people we know well. Objectivity may not be easy in reporting behavior and then making inferences about it when the activity involves family and friends. Frequently, both children and adults are unwilling to be harsh or make negative comments about friends and family; however, not everyone has the same degree of charity or kindness in judging behavior. Some are more severe in their judgment of a situation, whereas others are more lenient.

Thus, it is important to have many opportunities not only to observe a given person or group but also to get some agreement among the observers on the action being observed. An observation by just one person may be very perceptive but again it could be very misleading. Thus, ideally two or more observers are necessary.

Even having more than one observer does not completely solve the problem.

Children as well as adults respond differently even while looking at the same behavior. You may "see" hostile behavior if you are ready to believe a person is hostile. In a certain sense, you have a set or perspective that acts to focus your observation. Human behavior can also be studied from many points of view. From similar observations, two individuals will stress or see different actions, or make different inferences. Some observers report a great deal of detail while others see only gross actions. The site where the observation takes place is also important. The observer may be influenced by the crowd or the general atmosphere.

Yet observation can be a source of data in problem solving. What are the most likely examples that elementary school teachers may use? Usually they are school problems. How are children acting on the playground and are they friendly or unfriendly? Are children recycling by putting their glass bottles, paper, or cans in the right containers? Ecology offers many possibilities for observation. How much food is wasted in the school? What do the trash cans show after lunch? Students can observe the waste paper basket within their own classroom. Are paper and other supplies being wasted? Do students reuse their paper lunch bags by putting them into their backpacks? In all these examples, students might observe which of their practices are contributing to caring for their environment and which are not. In structuring observations, teachers can assist students to look for actions, not people, that contribute to creating or solving a problem.

With technology becoming increasingly available to schools, students know that not all direct observation has to be limited to the look-see-record variety. Videotapes and recordings can also be used as ways of collecting data on behavior. Recording behavior makes it available to be restudied and rechecked as needed. However, all students know from watching television that when the camera pans a group of people who know they are being observed, the people often will behave differently from the way they would act if they had not known they were being observed or recorded.

Teachers must help students define peer pressure if they are observing how groups may try to influence individuals. Students generally must be directed to look at specific aspects of behavior and move away from global assessments about individuals—she is a wonderful, friendly person or she is a lonely nerd; he never wastes food and is protective of the environment or he is a complete slob and never recycles.

Teachers can help students *before* they go out to observe by having them role-play what is to be observed and use guide sheets to record their observations. Checklists or rating forms are often very useful. After students agree on what they have observed, they can discuss the inferences and judgments they can make on the basis of the data. Should the class work with the rest of the school to reduce waste and recycle more? Taking action reminds students of the value of thinking and makes the action more likely to be successful.

Observation skills are also used constantly in viewing media, in role playing, and on field trips. Having students become critical about television viewing is especially important as television is one of the most pervasive sources of information of many students. Constantly check what reaction students have to a film or picture you have shown or what they may have seen at home; they may differ on what they remember seeing/hearing, the inferences they make, and their judgment or evaluation of the material. By continually making students aware of the skills they need to use in observation, you can help many of them become more careful observers. Observation skills should not be a hit-or-miss activity; students need to be given instruction and help to use the observations skills as they interact with people.

Listening skills are similar to observation skills and are also critical in learning. A great deal of the school experience involves listening. Listening is stressed in the whole-language approach. As children learn to listen, they can learn from others and expand their world. As in reading, the goal in listening is to grasp the main ideas. Students need to remember the most important things they hear.

Students must be encouraged to listen for the main theme—the major idea or thought that runs through the material. After students identify the main ideas and understand what has been said, the second stage in listening is to evaluate the content and ideas. Children often do not recognize that others may have a different frame of reference. When listening to a different frame of reference, students must identify the feel of the situation and see the problem the way the speaker sees it. This skill is called "sensitivity" or "empathy." Before students hear a tape or record, assign to some of them roles such as those of labor leaders, Native American tribal leaders, or Asian immigrants. Ask students to listen and react to the song or poem the way the individual in their assumed role would react. Compare their reactions to those of the rest of the class; in this way, many students become more aware of how their own frame of reference (also true in observation) allows them to hear certain messages and ignore others. In addition, students realize that different people speak in different ways.

Teachers have also used the rumor exercise in their class to illustrate how easily messages can be distorted. The original message is given to one child or group and each person repeats this to the next person. The last member reports orally. Typically, the story, having passed through many versions, is likely to be very different from the original. This activity can be followed by a discussion of the difficulty people have in transmitting messages accurately, and of the effects of poor listening habits and the insertion of bias.

What can teachers do to encourage students' listening skills throughout the whole school day? Sometimes it is necessary to take time out for teaching these skills, as in debriefing in cooperative learning groups to encourage students to be courteous listeners and not talk all the time. Check the amount of listening required in your class; young children have short attention spans. Try to vary the amount of listening with the opportunity for them to interact with others. Help students see the importance of listening by having them record the amount of listening they do both during the school day and outside school. Initially, tell your students what to listen for or to focus on; later they can learn to listen without your assistance.

Accepting or Rejecting a Hypothesis

After students gather data, they need to classify and organize the information. Finding relationships and classifying facts under main headings requires skill. Students must be able to see, for example, that data on immigrants might belong in several categories, such as the problems immigrants face and the successes they have had. In addition, students will often have to analyze and interpret their information to decide what it really means. Only then are they in a position to accept or reject their hypothesis, the final step in the thinking process. Do the data support the hypothesis?

We have shown here that you will probably have to use a variety of methods to teach problem solving or thinking. Sometimes students will work in small groups; other times, they will work alone. In some cases, your role will be indirect as you try to encourage students to generate as many promising ideas as possible. In these cases, your role is not to judge but to encourage an atmosphere in the class where ideas are welcome and not subjected to ridicule by other students. On the other hand, for specific skills, such as how to find information in an atlas, direct teaching may work best. But it is not enough just to drill students in these skills. Worksheets or other teaching tools should be as entertaining as possible so that students will want to use the skills after they do the required assignments. Teaching skills that students will not use in the future is not beneficial for either the students or the school.

In teaching thinking skills, then, present a variety of open-ended problems or questions that students can use to practice their thinking skills. Make sure the students become interested in the problems, and don't pursue a problem if most children seem bored by it. Also, don't foster dependency in students by giving them too much help. Be positive about their ideas, and remember that many children have not had much experience in thinking and will not become creative thinkers in merely three weeks. Remind students that making mistakes is part of the learning process and they should not be discouraged if their first ideas do not work out. Finally, make the encouragement of critical thinking a goal in everything you do and every lesson you teach, throughout the year.

3.4   ON YOUR OWN: JUST THE FACTS!

How much thinking do you believe goes on in a typical social studies classroom? Does it occur during the whole day? If you believe that little thinking takes place in most classrooms, list three reasons that you believe lead many teachers to concentrate on having students recall facts instead of emphasizing thinking.

COOPERATIVE LEARNING

Cooperative learning is a form of small group instruction that is getting increasing attention in education. In cooperative learning, students work together in small groups to achieve a common goal. There are many reasons for this technique's growing popularity, but the primary one is that research, usually filled with conflicting findings, consistently shows that cooperative learning can result in higher achievement among participants and can also help them develop social skills through participation in small groups. Such group skills include listening to others, offering ideas, asking questions, and compromising to resolve conflicts. In addition, students often come to like their classmates and the subject area even more after engaging in cooperative learning. They may feel more successful and have increased self-esteem. These are powerful reasons to use cooperative learning. Although not necessarily the only way to teach, cooperative learning is one more strategy you can use to deliver content and to teach skills.

Cooperative learning has many definitions. Some educators include peer teaching and cross-age tutoring as examples of cooperative learning. But these forms of tutoring lack an important element of cooperative learning: individual accountability. In cooperative learning, each member of the group is to learn the subject matter or to complete the task and is evaluated on his or her performance. This accountability seldom occurs in tutoring, as the tutor is normally not tested in the subject area that she or he is teaching. Tutoring also implies an unequal status relationship in which the tutor knows the material while the person being tutored is presumed to be less able academically.

In contrast, cooperative learning presumes that all students will make some but different contributions to the group's task. In other words, they are *all* members of the group and each is dependent on the other group members (i.e., one member of the group does not have all the answers).

Some definitions stress the size of the group. *Cooperative learning* consists of three or more students who are united in a common purpose to complete a task and to include every group member. Elizabeth Cohen suggests that the group size be limited to no more than five members.

In summary, cooperative learning is a method in which a group is given a task to do that should include the efforts of all the students in the group. Students directly interact with each other. They do not just sit silently next to each other working on their own assignments. In addition, cooperative learning includes the element of individual accountability. There should be no "free ride" in which any student does not contribute to the group's efforts. Instead, each student is held accountable for learning the subject matter or contributing to the task. Accountability is often determined by tests or teacher evaluation of group work and presentations (see Table 3.3). To encourage the group effort, some teachers assign a group grade on a test as well as the presentation (if given) so that the more able members of the group take some responsibility for teaching the material or skills to all members of the group.

TABLE 3.3   TEACHER EVALUATION OF COOPERATIVE LEARNING

Group	Work		Presentation	
Names	Used Time Well	Encouraged Others	Quality of Information	Effectiveness In Delivery
1.				
2.				
3.				

Why do experts recommend cooperative learning? In a classroom, the average student during a discussion has only one chance out of twenty-five (or whatever the class size may be) of having the opportunity to speak at a given moment. But if she or he is in a small group of four, the probability of speaking goes up to one in four. This means that there is more interaction among students, an important factor in learning both content and social skills.

Adults spend a great deal of time in small groups. Most of us interact with our families and friends. In community affairs, organizations, and clubs, a task is frequently assigned to a small committee. For teachers, it is almost impossible to avoid being put on a committee to work on some project to help improve the school.

In order to function in our society, everyone needs the skills to participate in small groups. Usually the activity is pleasant; most of us enjoy the socialization and companionship. But this is not always true. Have you ever been in a three-person group in which the other two members "ganged up" on you and tried to impose their views? In real life, three-member groups are often unstable regardless of the setting—three persons sharing an apartment or three people on an outing. Or have you been in a small group that was unpleasant because one person knew all the right answers and would not listen to others? Just putting individuals or students into a small group is not a guarantee that the work on the task will proceed well or that the contributions of all members will be valued.

With these cautions, the *first task* for a teacher using cooperative learning is to identify the lessons that are appropriate for cooperative learning. Ideally, there should be more than one answer or more than one way to solve the problem. If just factual answers from a textbook are asked, students will look to the brightest member of the group for all the answers and the rest of the group will just copy them. The task must be challenging and rewarding, requiring a variety of skills such as reading and writing.

The teacher's *second task* is to make some organizational decisions. These include five areas: group size, team formation, use of roles, room arrangement, and materials. Size, as noted previously, is a very important characteristic of cooperative learning. In the past, some group work has divided the class into three more or less equal groups, typically with seven to ten members. This is far too large for effective small group work. In general, younger children profit most from smaller groups. In fact, two children is the proper group size for many primary children. Groups of three, four, or five are appropriate for more mature children. Group members must be able to see the nonverbal clues that other group members give as well as hear what everyone is saying. If the group is too large, members cannot monitor what is happening. Five should probably be the largest size for a group.

In assigning groups, especially early in the year, you need to look carefully at the academic achievement and the personalities of the class members. Almost all experts recommend heterogeneous grouping—mix students by ability, gender, ethnic groups, and so on. One way to do this is to make a list of students by academic achievement, from the highest to the lowest. If there are to be groups of three, put into each group a high-ability member, a middle achiever, and a low achiever. Ensure that the gender and ethnic distribution are mixed. That means there should be a fairly equal distribution of girls and boys and of minority students. If you know that two students don't get along, do not, at least initially, place them together. However, later in the year, after their small group skills improve, you might *want* to assign them together. Avoid placing best friends on the same team. They will tend to talk and interact only with each other and ignore other members of the group. As a final suggestion, many teachers color code the groups. The names of all members of the blue team or group are under blue. These color-coded materials are posted so that all students can easily see what team they belong to.

Even with your best judgment in assigning groups, some groups may have difficulty working together. There may be personality clashes, ranging from minor bickering to insults that end in tears. What causes some of these conflicts in the small group? Often it is the recognized stable hierarchies of "smart" and "slow" students. Most students in most classes within a short time categorize every member of the class as smart, average, or dumb, usually based on a verbal ability (such as reading). These attitudes about ability can carry over into students' small groups. Groups frequently take less advantage of the contributions and skills of students who are labeled dumb, despite your plea that everyone participate and that all work together.

Thus, students may quarrel about who is to do what and who should make decisions. In effect, they play power games, just as adults do. Higher-status students want to have leadership roles, and lower-status students resist being in a group that does not seem to appreciate their talents. In many cases, "slower" students withdraw by physically moving away from the group or by disrupting it.

To avoid these problems, some teachers assign roles to each member of the group. This is the third organizational decision. One student is the chairperson, another is the secretary, a third is responsible for getting the supplies to the group, and a fourth is charged with seeing that the group stays on task. Some teachers prepare cards with the title of the role—"chairperson" or "secretary"—to empha-size that each member of the group is to perform a certain role.

Here are some roles that students can play in small groups:

Chairperson or Facilitator
   Organizes the group's work
   Makes sure the group understands its job
   Takes the group's questions to the teacher *after* trying to get answers
      from the group
Recorder or Secretary
   Writes down the group's answers on the group's answer sheet
Checker
   Checks that everyone can explain and agrees with the group's answer
Encourager (eventually all members should be this)
   Keeps people feeling good about working together
   Shows interest and excitement about the group's work

Some teachers include other roles such as reporter, but often it is easier for the secretary to read his or her own writing than to give it to another student to try to decipher. Of course, these roles should be rotated throughout the group so that each student has a chance to assume each of the roles. You need to monitor what is going on. Occasionally, students do not take their assigned roles and thus allow leadership, for example, to pass on to another student who has not been assigned that role.

Roles may have to be taught and evaluated. You should explain clearly what is expected in each role. Sometimes a teacher may want to use the role of a stu-dent observer who checks carefully what is happening in the group. Another way is for the group, at the end of the work session, to process how they have worked together. One way to do this is for the teacher to ask whether everyone in the group participated and to ask the group to consider this question; another way is by using a group self-evaluation form (Table 3.4). Students should be given an op-portunity to process how the group is working. This does not have to be done every day but is often a neglected element in cooperative learning.

The teacher's fourth organizational decision concerns the room arrangement

TABLE 3.4   GROUP SELF-EVALUATION

	Usually	*Sometimes*	*Never*
1. Every group member participated.			
2. Our group used its time wisely.			
3. Every group member did his or her job.			
4. Group members encouraged each other.			

for the groups. Ideally, the groups should be in a circle, preferably without tables or other obstructions. The group members should be close enough to each another to communicate and removed enough from the rest of the class that they do not get distracted by the noise and activities of the other groups. In addition, the teacher needs to be able to circulate among the groups without encountering physical obstacles.

You should consider what materials are needed for the group to complete its task. Will the members have to share one set of materials per group or will there be a textbook for everyone? Do students need a place to write or will oral discussion be the focus of the group's activity? Your decisions can influence the amount of interaction that the students have in their group.

These are the general steps for implementing cooperative learning. Usually it is wise at the beginning of the year to set up group learning experiences so that students can get to know one another better. At this point, the lessons do not have to include academic social studies content. Have the students in groups make collages, illustrating things they like to do, or have them share information about themselves with other members of the group. A favorite task is to develop a team name or sign to identify the group such as "The Experts" or "All-Stars of Room 2." Small groups might make poems on topics such as birthdays or a holiday. To do this, have individual students first jot down ideas or short phrases on the topic. These ideas can be incorporated into the group poem, which one member of the group might then read to the class. You might also want to post a copy of the poem, signed by all members of the group. The purpose of these activities is to teach students to use the ideas of *everyone* in the group and to take pride in *the group's final product*. In effect, this is team building in which each member develops a respect for everyone in the group.

As students get to know each other in the group, you may want to move into different formats of cooperative learning. One is group investigation, which requires each student to find material and decide how to communicate his or her learning to the remainder of the class. Perhaps you have decided that for the whole class to cover all the material in the textbook on Native Americans would take too much time. Instead, you decide to divide the students into cooperative groups, having each group study in depth a single nation or tribe. You can assign the nation or tribe, or let the group, with your approval, select the one they want to study. After being directed to the appropriate sources of information (with the help of your school librarian), the groups share with the rest of the class what they have discovered.

A more complex form of cooperative learning is Jigsaw (Table 3.5). Here students teach each other factual content. Each child is assigned to both a learning team (the original home team) and a study group. Typically, content or a textbook chapter is divided into sections. On the elementary level, this probably should not be more than four pages. On the topic of the American Revolution, content could be divided into the following sections: The American Army, The American Navy,

TABLE 3.5   JIGSAW

Steps
1. Design a lesson with a clear objective for the task. The task should be communicated both orally and in writing.
2. Choose the group size and composition (mixed groups are better).
3. Assign roles, materials, and room arrangement.
4. Have students do individual reading of information.
5. Have each expert group study the information and decide how best to teach.
6. Send experts back to home teams to teach their information.
7. Assess learning.
8. Process how well the groups did (expert and home teams).

Foreign Aid, Loyalists, and Prisoners. Often the teacher prepares a list of questions to be answered on each section.

In every home team, each team member is assigned a number. Then all of the "1's" get together. All of the "1's" study the same materials, such as the content on The American Navy. All of the "2's" study the content on Foreign Aid. Each group becomes an expert in the content it has been given and thinks of ways to teach its content. Then these experts return to their home team to teach the information related to their topics to the other home team members. Within the group members take turns teaching the information they have become experts in. Thus, each member teaches his or her assigned content to the rest of the group and learns from the others the content they were assigned to teach. Finally, after studying the content in their own home group, all students in the class are tested on content from all of the chapter sections. Typically, each student receives two grades from the test: an individual score as well as a team score. Realizing that their grades are partially dependent on the achievement of the home team, students are encouraged to do their best in group work.

The teacher acts as a timekeeper; sometimes this can be a problem in the expert group, in which material may not be covered. Students often request more time. Each phase of Jigsaw need not be done on the same day.

In Jigsaw as well as other forms of cooperative learning, grading can be a problem. Sometimes the "smart" students overparticipate, and the less able students contribute little (or find their contributions undervalued by the group). Often students see as unfair the teacher's insistence that all members of the group be given the same grade. If you explicitly require that all students in some way participate in the group's efforts, the "able" students will be more likely to make sure everyone is included so their grades will not be lowered. Some teachers use the whole group's score on tests to determine whether there is improvement and give extra points to the groups that improve.

Teachers also have to decide how long a given group stays together. Some teachers like to change the groups after a number of weeks so that students will learn to work with a variety of different personalities. Others keep the same groups for months, especially if the focus is on teaching social participation skills, such as having members encourage each other. These skills take time and practice, and often they can be applied more effectively if the group members already know each other.

In addition to pointing out possible pitfalls of cooperative learning, we also want to emphasize that this can be a very productive method. The class atmosphere may improve as students get to know one another better and learn to work together. Everyone enjoys the class more. Furthermore, the academic achievement level of the class may increase.

Cooperative learning does require special attention and planning by the teacher. Make your assignments and instructions clear so that the group does not take too much time trying to determine what has to be done. In addition, you must monitor carefully what is going on. Is one group constantly bickering? Is one student always ordering the other members of the group around? If these problems persist, even after processing, you may have to show students how to make improvements in the group. Role playing at "being bossy" or demonstrating other problems can also provide a rewarding opportunity for students to become aware of how to improve their small group skills.

3.5   *SMALL GROUP WORK: TRYING OUT SMALL GROUP TASKS*

The best way to learn how to use small group or operative learning is to do it yourself. Experience firsthand what it is like to be a member of a small group. Try the following formats and see how you like the experience. First, brainstorm in a group for a few minutes on the advantages and disadvantages of small group work. The rule here is that no one is allowed to discourage any ideas. Then write down a few ideas on how you think small group work could be used in teaching social studies. Now convene a second group and try to move toward consensus by choosing the three best contributions. How were the experiences different?

ROLE PLAYING

What is role playing and how does it work? *Role playing* is a method of problem solving that enables participants to explore alternative solutions to a given problem. It is an *unrehearsed* dramatic presentation, usually more appropriate for children age nine or older. Role playing is especially useful for dealing with controversial issues.

The impetus for role playing can be provided by reading the class a story or a law case or by having students view an open-ended film or filmstrip or photograph showing conflict. Classroom problems such as lack of sharing or breaking school or class rules can also be used for role playing. When you use problems in your own class such as dealing with the class bully, however, do not use actual names, and disguise the incident on which the group is focusing.

The basic steps in role playing are the following:

1. Present the open-ended problem. Set the stage by asking, "Have you ever . . . ?" or "How did you feel when you were . . . ?" Then say, "Today we're going to hear a story about Kyle (or any name other than that of a member of your class) who got into a similar jam. Think about how you would feel if you were in such a situation." Next, read the story up to the conflict point. Encourage students to identify the problem and talk about how the people in the story feel.
2. Select the participants or role players. Ask for volunteers to play the various roles. The rest of the class serve as observers.
3. Begin the role play. Enact how the story might end. Have students pretend to be characters with the feelings and ideas of the people in the specific situation.
4. Discuss the solution, especially in terms of its realism. Ask the observers if there are alternative ways of solving the problem.
5. Explore the alternative possibilities in further role playing.
6. Discuss the several role-playing experiences and, if possible, summarize what has been learned.

Role playing can be a safe way of exploring alternative behavior. It allows us to express feelings or opinions without risking disapproval. Many of us, when we are driving on the freeway or sitting at our desks at the end of the day, have said to ourselves, "If only I had said this or that, the situation would have been better." Students need to know that sometimes alternative ways of acting lead to better solutions. Role playing offers a safe opportunity to explore.

Role playing also can help prepare students to cope with conflict resolution and problem solving. Role playing is used, for instance, to help students "say no to drugs." Proponents of this approach in substance-abuse education believe that it is not enough just to tell a student to say no to drugs. It is better to act out situations, such as a party at which one student offers alcohol to another student. Showing different ways in which a student can refuse alcohol while still remaining "friends" with the offerer may be important to students. In addition, this approach can suggest to the "straight" student that it is possible to find activities other than alcohol use to share with the user—a step to help the substance user.

Using role playing in substance-abuse education also illustrates another value of role playing. Role playing can deal directly with issues on which students might be reluctant to give their opinions in other formats, such as what to do if you see two children fighting or if you meet a friend after you have heard that this friend has told lies about you. By providing a situation in which students are and yet are not themselves, you give them a chance to bring out feelings and opinions they might otherwise not be willing to express.

Most students enjoy participating in and watching role playing. It provides an opportunity for more active involvement than many other classroom learning experiences, and it is more personalized. Acting out the dilemma of a pioneer child who must decide if he will report to his Native American friend that the tribe's camp will be raided the next day involves the students in what has happened in the past. Many teachers say they are using role playing to play out historical events (e.g., the Constitutional Convention of 1787) much as they actually occurred. Technically, when students act in a prescribed fashion and merely duplicate the historical event, they are doing *dramatic play* and not role playing. Mock trials, often used with older children who are already familiar with the procedures used in courts, are also an example of using drama. For example, students can reenact the Salem witch trials, Socrates' trial, or other important trials in history. To be successful, students need a good background in the time period as well as knowledge of court procedure. *Reader's Theatre* is another dramatic presentation in which the lines of the students, as in a play, are already fixed and not given as alternatives. This is not to deny the value of reading a play or script, especially if students themselves have made the script. It merely points out the differences in dramatic play and role playing. The focus of role playing is the concept of *alternatives*, or other ways the story or historical event might have ended (see Figure 3.1).

You may encounter students who are reluctant to volunteer to role-play, espe-

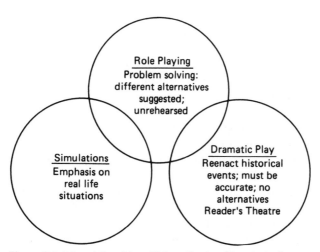

Figure 3.1 Interrelationships of interactive teaching strategies

cially at first. Others are often born hams who want to play roles every time. Do not let these "actors" take over the stage completely. Start with less controversial or emotional issues so that students become more at ease in role playing. Continue to encourage the shy students to volunteer, and as students get used to the format of role playing, they will become more eager to play a role. However, be careful not to cast students in the roles they occupy in the minds of their classmates. Do not put the class clown in a role in which he or she plays the class clown. Instead, put each student in someone else's shoes. The class bully should play the role of the weaker student who wants to have a turn in a game. Continually emphasize the role that the student is playing and avoid calling the student by his or her real name. Refer to the police officer or the landlady rather than to the specific student.

Sometimes students have a difficult time maintaining their roles. They start to giggle and often are distracted by the response of their audience. Members of the audience, too, must play their role appropriately. You may want to comment on this before or after the exercise. Usually, with time and practice, students are better able to maintain their roles.

Initially, you may find that many students want to play the enactment as it "should" be. In other words, they will play a role in a kind and loving manner and do all the right things. You need to ask if this is how it really happens. Some teachers are bothered if students enact negative, although realistic, behavior. They think that the class may model the wrong pattern. This is especially true, for example, if a student role involves pretending to take drugs or acting according to some other behavior that the community strongly opposes. But this should not be a major concern if you have an appropriate discussion and debriefing on what was going on. You can ask students who acted in negative roles how they felt. Often they will say that they were uncomfortable about how they acted. Thus the debriefing stage is one of the most important parts of role playing. By sharing feelings and answering questions at the end of the enactment, students may see further alternative ways to act.

Teachers sometimes believe that they must force a generalization from the role-playing experience. They want the group to come to a conclusion—for example, "If you are not hostile in a situation, there is more chance that you can solve a problem." But sometimes students are not yet ready to reach that conclusion. In those cases, it is best to drop the matter. Perhaps in a later experience, the group will come to that or a similar conclusion.

Role playing in the social studies offers the possibility of moving into the affective domain. It can help teach children to empathize with others by showing them how it feels to be in someone else's place. It can tap the emotional responses of students to certain situations while still moving toward a rational solution to a problem. This is one of the values of role playing. Often role playing can be a springboard for further study on a given topic. For this reason, it can be a successful method for the teacher of the social studies.

3.6 *SMALL GROUP WORK: DEVELOP A ROLE PLAY*

Try role playing in your class. You might use the scenario of a principal walking into a class when everything is confused and out of order. Assign roles of the principal, student teacher or teacher, and a few students in the class.

SIMULATIONS

Simulations are learning activities that present an artificial problem or event. The situation described tries to duplicate reality but removes the possibility of injury or risk. Pilots, for example, learn to fly by using a simulator, while both the military and business worlds may use simulations to learn how to win a campaign or where to locate a new factory. In many cases, a computer records the responses of the trainees or participants in the simulation.

Like role playing, a simulation allows the trainee or the player to try out a role and make decisions in a safe environment. But unlike role playing, which focuses on problem solving, simulations have a gamelike quality in which there are players, roles, and an end goal, such as winning. Because of this, many students think that simulations are fun, and they are motivated to do their best. Often they are put in a conflict or crisis situation, such as a political situation in the Middle East or South Africa, and are asked to play high-ranking political and military leaders or other important roles. Usually, they compete with others. One simulation, "Seal Hunt," tries to encourage cooperative behavior, but most simulations are based on competition.

In education, simulations were used initially without a computer. Students played simulations such as "Star Power," which set up an unequal division of power and resources, and were supposed to learn what it was like to be a member of certain power groups. In another social studies simulation, "Farming," set in western Kansas in three different years, students acting in teams of two made economic decisions on what to invest in—hogs, wheat, livestock, and so on. The simulation tried to duplicate the reality of farming in the 1880s, and at the end of the simulation, many of the couples (students) found that they had lost their money. Part of the purpose of this simulation was to bring to life the problems that farmers were facing after the Civil War. One of the advantages of well-designed simulations is that they can make abstract concepts such as oversupply or power more meaningful for students. In addition, simulations provide almost immediate feedback to the students on how they are doing, which is a key to motivation.

We are now seeing more computer-based social studies simulations. In most of them, the individual student interacts with the computer program, playing the role of the king-priest of an ancient city making economic decisions, for instance, or trying to win a political campaign in the United States. Other examples are the well-known "Oregon Trail" or the "New Oregon Trail," where players travel on the Oregon Trail making decisions faced by the original pioneers. There are many variations of this as children pretend to travel on the "Santa Fe Trail" or go to the gold mines of California ("Golden Spike"). In a few games, such as "Geography Search," students act in teams to try to locate valuable resources. In these cases, there is often competition between different teams in the same classroom.

Neither computer nor noncomputer simulations in the social studies are usually designed commercially for the primary-grade levels; they are for middle grades and beyond. However, primary teachers may design their own simulations, setting up, for instance, a post office, hospital, or other community institution.

Along with many promises, there are also pitfalls in using simulations in the classroom:

1. In some cases, especially at the middle school level, students may have to learn complex rules in order to play. They may be unable or unwilling to listen to a long explanation, and you may find it best to have students learn by doing, even if some encounter frustration.
2. Some students are motivated in simulations only when they have important roles to play. They find it unfair that they have to play poor people or members of a group who are discriminated against. You may find that students are reluctant to accept these roles, although the roles are necessary to the simulation.
3. Simulations can have management problems. They are often noisy. Occasionally, students get so involved in playing the simulation that they actually become hostile and even start fights. You must constantly scan the classroom to monitor what is going on.
4. Teachers sometimes believe that simulations misinform students by oversimplifying. If a student plays the role of a United Nations delegate, for example, the student may then believe that he or she knows all about the United Nations. Some teachers also worry that simulations encourage unethical or immoral behavior, as when students choose to drop bombs and start wars or to take resources from poorer players.

As you can see, some of these concerns are similar to those associated with role playing. As with that approach, discussion and debriefing are essential to clarify what actions players choose to take and what effects those actions have on other players. Thus in "Seal Hunt," students must realize that their decision not to share resources may have forced other students to starve. In the "Mercantilism" simulation, which is set in colonial America, students, eager to make money, find they are often engaging in both slavery and smuggling. It is important in debriefing to clarify what the students are actually doing and to explore the consequences of such behavior.

The strong advantage of a simulation is that students are often highly enthusiastic and motivated. There is a minority of students, however, who would rather read the textbook and answer the questions at the end of the chapter; not all students are the same. You must therefore determine whether a simulation has achieved the desired objectives. Do the students now know more about understanding different cultural groups? Do they feel more empathy for disadvantaged people or developing nations? Like any other method, a simulation is worthwhile only if it conveys knowledge, skills, or changed values.

3.7   *ON YOUR OWN: RESEARCH BY DOING*

Acquire a simulation. Your curriculum library or computer library may have some to choose from. Good sources of what is available are *Interact*, P.O. Box 997, Lakeside, CA 92040 or Social Studies School Services, 10200 Jefferson Boulevard, Culver City, CA 90232-0802. Secure the teacher's manual. Review the simulation, step by step, to see how it works. Do you see possible difficulties? What does it seem to teach? Secure reviews, if possible, from teachers or from computer journals on how the simulation is rated.

Other methods do exist for teaching the social studies. Some teachers individualize instruction and set up learning centers. Others may use supervised study as their main activity for teaching. Sometimes questioning is listed as a distinct method, although questioning is part of almost all methods. In particular, the Taba approach, which uses teacher questions to move students to concepts and generalizations, is often recommended. (See Chapter 4.) Different methods are more appropriate for certain students and for achieving certain objectives; no method will work all the time for all teachers and all students. Since you are the decision maker, you must decide what combination of methods is best suited to achieving your objectives.

SUMMARY

Each teaching method has certain advantages. The direct-teaching learning model can be useful to impart certain information and concepts. Inquiry methods are extremely important in teaching students how to think. Cooperative learning or other small group activities can teach knowledge *and* social skills. Role playing and simulations are more interactive methods that can touch the affective domain. Questioning skills are an integral part of all methods. The choice of methods depends partly on what you are trying to achieve. In general, by using more variety in your teaching methods, you will be more successful in adapting to the diverse learning styles of your students.

SUGGESTED READINGS

Chance, Paul. *Thinking in the Classroom*. New York: Teachers College Press, 1986. Excellent overview of several types of current thinking programs.

Cohen, Elizabeth G. *Designing Groupwork*, 2d ed. New York: Teachers College Press, 1994. Good pointers.

Horn, Robert E., and Cleaves, Anne, eds. *The Guide to Simulations/Games for Education and Training*, 4th ed. Beverly Hills, Calif.: Sage, 1980. Older, but good list of simulations and games.

Hunter, Madeline. *Mastery Teaching*. El Segundo, Calif.: TIP Publications, 1982. Advocate of direct teaching.

Johnson, David W., and Johnson, Roger T. *Learning Together and Alone*, 4th ed. Englewood Cliffs, N.J.: Prentice-Hall, 1994. Excellent on cooperative learning techniques.

Orlich, Donald C.; Remaley, Anne L.; Facemeyer, Kevin C.; Logan, Jerry; and Cao, Qin. "Seeking the Link Between Student Achievement and Staff Development." *Journal of Staff Development* 14, no. 3 (1993): 2–8. A critical report on the effectiveness of the Hunter model.

Shaftel, Fannie R., and Shaftel, George. *Role Playing in the Curriculum*, 2d ed. Englewood Cliffs, N.J.: Prentice-Hall, 1982. Best text available on role playing.

Slavin, Robert E. *Cooperative Learning—Theory, Research, and Practice*, 2d ed. Needham Heights, Mass.: Allyn & Bacon, 1995. Reviews research, theory, and applications of cooperative learning.

Stahl, Robert J., and Van Sickle, Ronald L., eds. *Cooperative Learning in the Social Studies Classroom*. Bulletin 87. Washington, D.C.: National Council for the Social Studies, 1992. Good examples.

Taba, Hilda. *Teacher's Handbook for Elementary Social Studies*. Palo Alto, Calif.: Addison-Wesley, 1967. Excellent on thinking strategies.

Chapter 4

SOCIAL STUDIES in the PRIMARY GRADES

Curriculum considerations for primary-grade social studies are divided into the following sections in this chapter:

1/ Primary-Grade Social Studies Curriculum
2/ Guidelines for Integrating Social Studies in the Primary-Grade Curriculum
3/ Classroom Environment and Scheduling

Although the goals, standards, and strategies outlined in the previous chapters provide general guidelines for social studies curriculum and instruction at all levels, you will want to focus specifically on the particular needs and competencies of the younger child when you consider social studies issues to be presented in the primary grades. Children's statements such as, "The moon was at my house last night, not yours," and "My bike is going faster than that airplane!" reveal the many ways in which young children commonly invent explanations for the complexity of our world. Children from ages five to eight are just beginning to accumulate the information and experience that we take for granted in the intermediate-age child. They are becoming aware of their individuality. They are exploring interaction and cooperation with others. They are grasping for explanations of their vast, challenging physical environment.

An effective social studies curriculum for the early years is rooted in an awareness of the cognitive, psychological, and social tasks specific to the five- to eight-year-old child. All the academic knowledge about child growth and development and personal wisdom you have gained through experience with young children will help you as you organize initial plans for social studies instruction.

As a brief reminder, however, of the crucial nature of guidance from these sources, let us restate three precepts before looking at specific elements of the social studies curriculum for early grades. First, the content of the social studies program as well as the ways the social environment of the classroom and school are structured can have significant impact on the child's social vision. Second, young children are capable of, indeed require, discussion of moral and controversial issues as prompts to taking different perspectives and learning about people and situations that have multiple roles and meanings. Third, young children need learning strategies that activate their various kinds of intelligence—linguistic, musical, logical-mathematical, spatial, bodily-kinesthetic, personal, and social—and evaluation strategies that build on individual strengths as well as work toward developing all the intelligences.[1] Using these general principles as compass points can help us chart rich and well-founded social studies curricula for young children.

PRIMARY-GRADE SOCIAL STUDIES CURRICULUM

To explore the elements of a social studies curriculum for young children, we will examine new national standards recommended as essential content. Further, we compare two versions of topical guides around which primary-grade social studies are organized. Then we review the various kinds of skills and competencies young

---

[1]Howard Gardner, *Frames of Mind: The Theory of Multiple Intelligences*. New York: Basic Books, 1983.

children are expected to develop, and discuss guidelines for integrating social studies with other curricular areas. Finally we consider various materials for implementing the curriculum, and we outline the specifics of organizing the classroom environment and scheduling social studies activities.

Content Design Alternatives

As we saw in Chapter 1, content for primary grades generally elaborates on the developmental needs of children. One approach to content organization that attempts to meet developmental needs is known as the *expanding horizons* model. According to this model, the curriculum extends gradually from the individual to wider social circles. This approach, popular since the 1930s, attempts to build on the child's growing awareness of the world beyond the self.[2] Frequently, the study of social and economic roles—such as parent, authority, citizen, worker, consumer, producer—is part of this sequence, thereby adding dimensions from social sciences to the basically geographic content design. However, among the national standards recently developed by professionals from the disciplines of history, geography (geography standards are discussed in Chapter 5), civics, and government, in only the history standards is the expanding horizons model used.

Recognizing that most students in primary grades are exposed to history as part of an integrated study rather than as a separate subject, the National Center for History in Schools (the History Center) endorsed eight standards.[3] Note that the history focus is added to the traditional expanding horizon model.

1. Family life now and in the recent past; family life in various places long ago
2. History of their own local community and how communities in North America varied long ago
3. The people, events, problems, and ideas that were significant in creating the history of their state
4. How democratic values came to be, and how they have been exemplified by people, events and symbols
5. The causes and nature of various movements of large groups of people into and within the United States, now and long ago
6. Folklore and other cultural contributions from various U.S. regions and how they help to form a national heritage

---

[2]Lavone Hanna, Gladys Potter, and Robert Reynolds, *Dynamic Elementary Social Studies*, 3d ed. (New York: Holt, Rinehart and Winston, 1973).

[3]National Center for History in Schools, *National Standards for History: Expanding Children's World in Time and Space* (Los Angeles: National Center for History in Schools, 1994.)

7. Selected attributes and historical developments of societies in such places as Africa, the Americas, Asia, and Europe
8. Major discoveries in science and technology, some of their social and economic effects, and the major scientists and inventors responsible for them

The intent of these standards is that history content in the primary grades be alive and centered on people, not events or dates. There is a dual focus in this list. One is on history of the children's own families and of people, ordinary and extraordinary, who have lived in the children's own community, state, nation, and the world. It is suggested that stories, myths, legends, and biographies be used to study these histories. The second focus is on diversity of backgrounds of people highlighted in the study for each of the expanded horizon topics.

Primary-grade standards for civics are expressed in the form of organizing questions.[4]

1. What is government and what should it do?
2. What are the basic values and principles of American democracy?
3. How does the government established by the Constitution embody the purposes, values, and principles of American democracy?
4. What is the relationship of the United States to other nations and to world affairs?
5. What are the roles of the citizen in the American political system?

To many primary-grade teachers the standards in civics will seem too advanced for young children. The intent of these guiding questions, however, is that primary-grade instruction include a beginning exposure, rather than expect an expert mastery-level understanding, of the concepts and procedures on which civic life in the United States is based. (Chapters 5 and 6 discuss citizenship education in greater detail.)

The following are two versions of how one state outlined primary-grade social studies content. Both are from California. Both predate the publication of national standards. They are, however, convenient as examples of the changes taking place in content recommended for primary-grade social studies. Compare the 1981 and 1987 outlines. The 1981 guide represents a more traditional expanding horizons model. The 1987 guide incorporates more attention to history, geography, and diversity in the traditional topics as well as new methods (use of literature).

---

[4]Center for Civics Education, *National Standards for Civics and Government.* Calabasas, Calif.: Center for Civics Education, 1994.)

SAMPLE TOPICAL GUIDES 4.1

Example A: 1981 California History—Social Science Framework[5]

Kindergarten—Myself and Others in My World

Finding my way in my world
The uniqueness of me: My similarities and differences
My needs and the needs of others: How people grow and change
Self-awareness and the employment of my five senses
My parents—their jobs and jobs that I can do
Special occasions in my life
Cooperation and conflict between friends and classmates in work and
    play
Songs, stories, games, and dances my friends and I like
Rules and why we need them
Learning to listen and listening to learn

Grade One—People at Home and at School

Relationship of home to school
Getting from home to school safely
Time and my life
Roles people play in my family and at my school
Families—my own and others in the community and the world
Meeting needs at home and at school
Cooperation, conflict, and communication at home and school

Grade Two—People as Members of Groups

Getting around in my neighborhood
Groups to which I belong
American ethnic groups; their roles and contributions
People and the groups they form or join
Roles within groups (e.g., leaders, followers, innovators)
How groups use resources

continued

[5]Many states follow similar grade-level topics. This one comes from California State Framework for History—Social Sciences (Sacramento: State Department of Instruction, 1981).

SAMPLE TOPICAL GUIDES 4.1 (CONT.)

Rules, responsibilities, and group norms
Communication, problem solving, and decision making in groups
Cooperation and conflict within or between groups
How art, music, and dance influence and enrich group life
People who have contributed to the groups to which I belong

Grade Three—People as Members of Communities

My community — where is it?
What is a community?
Our community — its past, present, and future
How community groups rely upon and influence one another
The diverse cultures and people who make up and contribute to our
  community
How our community is governed
Cooperation, conflict, and communication within our community
Appreciating and preserving the beauty of our community and improv-
  ing the quality of life in it
Comparing our community to other communities in the United States
  and in the world

Example B: 1987 California History—Social Science Framework[6]

Kindergarten—Learning and Working Now and Long Ago

Learning to work together
Working together: Exploring, creating, communicating
Reaching out to times past

Grade One—A Child's Place in Time and Space

Developing social skills and responsibility
Expanding children's geographic and economic worlds
Developing awareness of cultural diversity, now and long ago

---

[6]*California State Framework for History— Social Sciences* (Sacramento: State Department of Instruction, 1987).

Grade Two—People Who Make a Difference

People who supply our needs
Our parents, grandparents, and ancestors from long ago
People from many cultures, now and long ago

Grade Three—Understanding Continuity and Change

Our local history: Discovering our past and our traditions
Our nation's history: Meeting people, ordinary and extraordinary, through
  biography, story, folk tale, and legend.

Comparison of these two content outlines reveals that the most recent outline places greater emphasis on history. Within the historical perspective, concepts from various social sciences and the humanities are interwoven—group norms and rules from sociology and political science, ritual and ceremony from anthropology, form and function of legend and myth from folklore, study of human characteristics from literature. This interlacing forms a set of topics grounded in the social sciences but organized according to this version of what is appropriate for the child's stage of development.

An additional perspective currently coming into greater practice in the selection of social studies content for young children also arises from the developmentalist point of view. Arguing that children bring to school an intuitive knowledge of how their world works, proponents of this approach emphasize the importance of exploring values as the essential foundation for any content design. Myth, legend, and tale as social studies content sources, rather than insistence on engagement with reality, are materials used to capitalize on the interests of young children. Recognizing the significance of fantasy and story line in the thinking of young children, the examples we provide them need to be seen as "sense-making tools"[7] for building a more conscious understanding of their social lives. Using fantasy sources to discuss good and evil, kindness and cruelty, selflessness and greed can provide safe avenues for the young child to ponder human behavior and values. This approach resonates well with many experienced teachers of young children and some social critics calling for a curriculum that teaches values. It is possible to make any topic more satisfying to young children by emphasizing its storytelling potential.

---

[7]Kieran Egan, "Individual Development in Literacy," *Literacy, Society and Schooling: A Reader*, ed. Suzanne de Castell, Allan Luke, and Kieran Egan (Cambridge: Cambridge University Press, 1986), 250.

4.1 SMALL GROUP WORK: USING FANTASY AND STORY LINE AS CONTENT SOURCES

> Everyone knows the tale "The Little Red Hen." How can this story be used for a social studies lesson? What human qualities do the characters represent? Is the hen justified in doing what she did at the end? How could everyone be satisfied in this story? Can you think of a contemporary or home version of this story? Explore the global possibilities, using versions of this story and comparing different kinds of bread—tortillas, chapatis, pita, fry-bread. Discuss with your colleagues your ideas about using this kind of content for social studies.

Still, some educators find fault with content designs that do not specifically incorporate social issues with which young children are most concerned. Many young children fear they might be shot at on their way to school. Others must live in conditions of conflict within their families and with caregivers. Truly, violence, hopelessness, environmental degradation, and health-related concerns figure prominently in the minds and lives of many young children. Many teachers, feeling that they are not trained as counselors nor equipped to improve the child's home life, are afraid to confront these issues. They feel that school needs to be a safe place where the child can be exposed to knowledge that provides hope, which can come from finding out about other worlds. As a result of such feelings, these teachers tend to choose social studies topics they believe will not be upsetting or offensive to young children. Yet experience suggests that trying to conduct social studies instruction primarily from a textbook or a state-mandated guide that eschews unpleasantness and conflict will not go far toward connecting what is studied in school to the real lives of children.

There is renewed recognition that in any content design, the starting point should be topics that are elaborated with a specific understanding of the lives of the students in a specific class. Whether these concerns come directly from their lives or indirectly through the media, young children need social studies content that helps them grow in their abilities not only to survive and cope but also to seek ways of improving their lives and their communities. And fantasy sources or fiction may permit the necessary distancing from children's real situations to initiate exploration of these concerns. Let us return to the topical guides from California to see this point.

As an example, the 1981 California content list suggests that teachers guide children to explore family roles that reflect families of children in the class. Many children have caregivers who may be single, or older relatives, or not biologically related, or in same-sex relationships. Whatever the home constellation of caregivers may be, young children need to feel that they and their situation are respected as they are. Further, they need to see that even though what they may have or do at home is different, all children have learning tasks in their home lives. The same grade level from the 1987 California list offers another way to explore the child's role by looking at it from a historical perspective. Awareness of immigrant or pioneer children's responsibilities in an earlier time provides present-day children with important samples to draw from in seeing themselves and their situations as part of a social process that others have passed through successfully. Thus, the first rule of content selection is that it must lead from or be related to the group of individuals in a given class. Every class is different. Sometimes a class is different from one day to the next! Topics and units taught last year will need to be rethought and redesigned if they are to be used as content for this year's class.

Two recent children's trade books illustrate ways to explore the same first-grade topic of family roles and/or a child's place in time and space using the structure of story line and genre of fantasy, but focusing on the plight of being homeless. Maurice Sendak's *We're All in the Dumps with Jack and Guy*[8] employs the distancing device of obscure English nursery rhymes to explore the humanity and family feelings among the homeless. Salt Lake City adolescents living in homeless shelters chose a similar device to explore the point of view of being homeless in their recent book, *The Homeless, Hibernating Bear*,[9] by making the protagonist a bear lost in the city. The lost bear encounters problems similar to those encountered by homeless children. The anthropomorphism, endowing an animal with human thoughts and actions, allows young children having no direct contact with homelessness a distance that protects while sensitizing. Through either of these fantasy vehicles and the problem-solving discussions these can provoke, children become more informed and empathetic as they move to the next step of deciding what they can do to help homeless people in their school and community.

In concluding this brief survey of social studies content for the primary grades, we should underscore four points. One is that learning activities about social studies topics can be organized in formal teacher-planned sessions as well as flow informally from an event that catches student interest. A second is that social studies content can come from nontraditional sources. Social studies content may, but does not need to, come from a textbook. Content may, but does not have to, come from a bookbound source. Third, choosing topics requires that the teacher perceive how familiar with the topic children are, and what potential the topic has to assist children to grow in problem-solving ability. Finally, some topics are more important than others to children. This does not mean selecting topics according to results of a student opinion poll. Rather, it means that teachers are responsible for helping children connect to their lives a foreign or apparently insignificant topic. Important topics are those that offer children the concept of belonging to a diverse world, the context to understand who and where they are, the tools to resolve issues, and a sense of caring that prompts striving for better conditions for all people. Topics that meet these criteria can be defended as part of the social studies program.

---

[8](New York: HarperCollins Children's Books, 1993.)
[9]*Kids Livin' Life.* (Placerville, Calif.: Gold Leaf Press, 1993).

The Context of Skills and Competencies

In addition to the topical grade-level outlines, curriculum guides usually list skills and competencies children should acquire while studying the suggested topics. A recent restatement of these by a national task force of social studies professionals captures the major categories that are typically addressed.

> Skills and competencies in social studies should equip children with the knowledge and understanding of the past necessary for coping with the present and planning for the future, enable them to understand and participate effectively in their world, and explain their relationship to other people and social, economic, and political institutions . . . provide students with the skills for productive problem solving and decision making as well as for assessing issues and making thoughtful value judgments. Above all, the social studies help students to integrate these skills into a framework for responsible citizen participation, whether in their play group, the school, the community, or the world.[10]

Some of these skill areas are also developed in other subjects. Lists of reading competencies include research and study skills. Math lists include problem solving, critical thinking, telling time, and locational skills involving work with grids. Children are gaining study skills when they gather information for a report by observing how groups solve conflicts at recess or by interviewing a parent on the tools that the parent uses in his or her work. They are growing in decision-making skills when they compare several solutions to the issue of how to distribute the playground equipment during recess. They are growing in problem solving when they test their predictions about which is the most productive way to get classroom jobs done. Although an integrated curriculum can incorporate most of the skills and competencies related to social studies, below we survey competencies and skills that are seen as more specifically related to the social studies to make sure we know what they are.

Citizenship, the Fundamental Social Studies Skill.   Some of the skill areas pertinent to the social studies should be taught throughout the day. Citizenship is such an area. Younger children need special guidance in citizenship skills. They are dealing with the idea of authority in their lives. Their parents, teachers, the traffic patrol guard, the school yard aide, and older children give them orders and rules to follow. Unless you highlight the need for rules and order, children may believe that authority is magical or capricious, not to be questioned, and resident with whoever has the most power and size.

---

[10]National Council for the Social Studies Task Force on Early Childhood Elementary Social Studies, "Social Studies for Early Childhood and Elementary School Children Preparing for the 21st Century," *Social Education* 53, no. 1 (January 1989): 14–23.

Discuss why we have specific rules. Once the reasons for the rules are clarified, you should play the devil's advocate to help the children learn to question authority using a principle or reason. For example, if the children agree that the traffic patrol guard lets them cross after he or she has checked that traffic is stopped, ask them what they should do if they are told to cross while the patrol guard is laughing and joking with someone and has not checked the traffic, or if a friend crosses against the wishes of the guard, or if the guard keeps the children waiting when there is no visible reason.

Posing dilemmas such as what to do if a baby-sitter exceeds his or her authority is a natural prelude to role-playing alternative solutions (see Chapter 3 for a basic explanation of role playing). Teachers find that young children are more easily involved in trying out ideas when they can act through simple stick puppets. The puppet serves to move direct focus of the audience from the performing child, which seems to ease the child's anxiety about self-expression.

Making up rules and practicing the use of authority open a child's understanding of justice and fairness. When children have real experience in rule making, they should be led to discuss how rule making and enforcement happen in the adult world. You can promote these exploratory conversations by bringing a newspaper to class and talking about what the president, or another public figure with power, is doing and what that person's role is in rule making.

To extend the exploration of concepts of authority and power beyond the immediate experience of the students, you should discover what they know about figures in authority. In this diagnostic phase of theme development, teachers need to interview the students: Who is the president? How does a person get to be president? What does the president do? Why is the president important to us? Can a president make a rule by himself or herself? Is the president's power limited? Or, relate the idea of authority to the class: Who should decide what we do in this class? Why do teachers get to organize what we do? Why do teachers follow rules? How are these rules made? Should rules ever be changed? Should teachers ever be changed?

Student answers can help us know where to start our current events discussions. Typically teachers will need to "go with the flow"—that is, we need to extend our students' information by bringing in pictures and stories based on what they give us as starting points. The information students offer should be taken at face value and with seriousness. Laughing or finding fault with what a student offers will guarantee that the student will be less genuine the next time you ask what he or she thinks or knows.

Our ultimate goals are to help students see that those who have power in our system are real people. They retain their authority by following established rules and are subject to losing it if they do not adhere to these rules. Discussions in the classroom about situations that involve civic values such the consent of the governed and rights that have responsibilities will help students understand the bits and pieces they gather from television. We are helping them build a background for interpreting events, a vital citizenship skill. Citizenship skills can be enhanced within the classroom as well. Chapter 6 details a middle-grade approach that sets up a class government, treating the classroom as a microsociety. Primary-grade children can also profit from assuming classroom responsibilities, devising classroom rules and procedures, and solving problems. Allowing students to organize classroom procedures and rotate classroom responsibilities gives them practical experience in citizenship skills.

Thinking Skills That Form Habits of Mind.   The degree of sophistication in children's thinking has long been the subject of research and debate. Developmentalist theory suggests that children move through stages in their thinking abilities. Critiques of developmental perspectives suggest that young children are capable of complex and philosophical thought. Bringing this thought to a level of consciousness is second nature to some teachers. Others find they need models and suggestions to offer instruction in the processes of thinking. Among the several strategies devised to help children develop skill in organizing ideas is the simple scheme developed by Hilda Taba.[11] Three basic steps in this by now classic strategy are these:

1. Teacher enumerates and lists students' responses to an opening question
2. Students group the responses
3. Students label or categorize their groupings

In this strategy teachers promote large or small group discussion through questions that follow these steps. For example, to explore the concept of rules, a teacher might ask, "What comes to your mind when you hear the word *rules*?" Recording student responses as they are given, the teacher tries to elicit a variety of responses, accepting all without regard to whether they are accurate. Working from the original responses, the next question according to the strategy would be "Can we group any of these?" "What is the reason you put _____ and _____ together?" Finally, "What title can we give to this list?" This line of questioning can also be used for guiding students in the formation of generalizations.

Recall teachers in your experience who prompted you to think. What kinds of questions did they use? Weren't they always asking how we knew something to be true? To explain how we arrived at a conclusion? To give a reason(s) for a decision? This probing attitude should become second nature to teachers when dealing with individuals or group discussions. If you learn specific approaches for prompting student thought, these techniques can help you internalize this mode of verbal interaction with students. Teaching thinking skills must be a permanent instructional activity.

---

[11]Hilda Taba, *Teaching Strategies and Cognitive Functioning in Elementary School Children*, Cooperative Research Project no. 2404 (Washington, D.C.: U.S. Office of Education, 1966.)

Map and Globe Skills from Immediate Surroundings.   Map- and globe-reading skills are among those specific to the social studies. Younger children need concrete experiences in spatial awareness before they are presented with maps. They need to practice, as is done on "Sesame Street," the locational prepositions, for example, *under, around,* and *beside.* Songs and games such as "Simon Says" or "Mother, May I?" can help them learn *down, up, over, under, through, around, behind, between, left* and *right.* Students must grasp these concepts firmly before they can learn about cardinal directions. Learning north, south, east, and west is best pursued outside at varying times of the day with the sun as a guide by which students can orient themselves to local landmarks. Once the students have learned that they can use the sun to find directions, and that their interpretation of the sun's position will vary according to whether the time is morning or afternoon, they are ready to transfer the skill anywhere. When they learn, for example, that the swings are to their east as they stand outside their classroom door, they are ready to name the direction of other landmarks from that point. After a series of varied, real experiences with finding direction, students are ready to transfer the idea of cardinal direction to the pictures they make of their classroom, school, route from home to school, and neighborhood.

Pictures and models that translate real physical space to a representation of it present conceptual challenges to any age. Young children can best begin this process by manipulating blocks and toys on a sand table or a floor area to replicate the classroom, the playground, a room, or a city street or block. Movable objects permit students to be experimental and free from worrying about ruining a painting or drawing with a mistake.

After miniatures of concrete settings are arranged, the further abstraction of representing them on paper begins to make sense. Before replicating the concrete, teachers may organize activities calling for pictorial representations or clay models without requiring that they be to scale or oriented to the proper direction. Software that permits manipulation of objects on a street grid or fictive landscape can be useful as reinforcement but not as a substitute for activities that engage children with physical, not "virtual," reality.

A globe is a model of our planet. Kindergarteners need exposure to this concept. After they learn their location on the model, they can begin learning names and shapes of continents as well as locations for places in the news they discuss. Outline globes that portray relief, landforms, and bodies of water with no printing are best.

Accumulating an index card file of place names as these are introduced and the places are located on the globe provides an excellent set of material for "changes of pace" and "filler" games during all-class sharing or activity change times. The cards can help students build verbal cues to incidental sight vocabulary and geographical locational skills. If these cards are numbered to coincide with numbers fixed on the globe, the globe can become one of the activity station choices for individuals or small groups during work periods.

Time and Chronology Skills Related to Student Lives and Histories.   Time and chronology are, in part, social studies skill areas. Most programs usually introduce "telling time" using a clock and, sometimes, a calendar. Telling time in periods longer than a day needs to be part of the primary-grade daily routine. A year-long timeline or journal of class events can help students with this skill. One of the classroom jobs can be to record student-selected significant events from yesterday on the class timeline or in the class journal. This practice helps students build a sense of continuity and recall. Another way to stretch children's sense of chronology is for them to create a personal timeline for which they research and portray their own individual timelines on developmental tasks such as learning to walk, talk, eat alone, dress, and ride a tricycle. Students record the information on note cards that they illustrate; these cards can then be sorted and sequenced.

Studies have found that many young children are unaware of or fear change. Teachers need to involve children in activities that call attention to change as a natural part of living that they experience as they grow. Here are key questions that you can use to focus students on changes: Is something different? What is changing? What is causing the change? What do you think might happen because of the change?[12]

Observing change in their own height and weight by keeping individual charts helps children see change in themselves. Collecting weather and season data on temperature, rainfall, snowfall, the length of days and nights, the changes in the moon, and the changes in vegetation and animal habits helps children see the cyclical nature of some changes.

Change in the human life cycle also needs to be illustrated. Contact with older people as classroom helpers or storytellers as well as books about growing, changing, and dying assist children to become more comfortable with the idea that, even with change, there is a continuity of life provided through our families and that change, including the loss that comes with it, is necessary for growth.

GUIDELINES FOR INTEGRATING SOCIAL STUDIES IN THE PRIMARY-GRADE CURRICULUM

Developmental psychologists tell us that materials used with young children should prompt them to interact, create, and manipulate. We are also told that children respond best to stories that are related to integrated themes. When we look at the kinds of topics suggested for the primary grades in social studies content designs, we sense two dilemmas. One is the apparent distance between the learning-mode prescriptions and the nature of social studies topics. The second is the difference in orientation between the separate subject tradition of curriculum designs

[12]C. Sunal, "The Child and the Concept of Change," *Social Education* 45, no. 6 (October 1981): 438–441.

and the more child-centered approach to organizing early school programs. How can we help children learn about families in other parts of the world, or about how groups use resources? How can we manage to teach the crucial basics of literacy and still include all the other subjects? In the first apparent dilemma, we have topics that may be distant from the children or represent abstract ideas that are difficult to present in a concrete manner. In the second, we become overwhelmed by the expectation that long lists of topics be covered in the ever more crowded school day.

Integrated Thematic Instruction
Connects Students to Curriculum

The scheme for organizing curriculum known as integrated thematic instruction is recognized increasingly as a way to build on the child's mode of perceiving the world while providing a rationale for reducing the segmented-day approach to curriculum organization. Organizing activities around a theme or problem allows development of basic skills as they flow from and make sense in relation to the chosen theme. Organizing programs around integrated themes represents a departure from the practice of listing skills and then organizing activities that develop them following a logically derived sequence from simpler to more difficult. Further, integrated theme instruction does not necessarily observe the chronological approach to organizing topics, nor does every theme lend itself to including all the traditional ways of social science knowing.

Several general questions are important when you are planning for integrated thematic instruction:

- Is the theme one that will interest and extend the knowledge of students?
- Are there facets of the theme that can incorporate various ways of thinking and knowing derived from various kinds of information?
- Can adequate resources be located to provide students with adequate input that represents more than one point of view?
- Does development of the theme incorporate working with a variety of skills and modes of expression?

One planning device for this approach to organizing instruction is a brainstorming technique known as the idea or theme web. Typically, a theme web is developed by a grade-level teaching team. The chosen theme may come from the social studies topical guide—community, cooperation, family, heroes, changes, farms, celebrations. In a first meeting, using free association, members of the team jot down ideas and subtopics of the theme on a large, shared sheet of paper or chalkboard. The second phase of this process is to group ideas and subtopics into clusters. From this first sort, new ways of naming or grouping emerge as the group discusses what each cluster means. Working groups need to appoint a scribe who will record their ideas on a chart or chalkboard all the group can see. This listing will capture the resources and activities mentioned as the discussion evolves. Eventually the group settles on a set of subthemes or questions radiating from the larger theme. The third phase of this meeting is to review the general questions/criteria and decide whether to proceed with planning based on the theme or to revise or to abandon it.

In preparation for a second meeting, team members work individually to put together resources that can be used to "teach" the theme. This search takes teachers beyond the text, gathering sources from children's fiction and nonfiction books, reference books, maps, films, and videos. The list could also include manipulables, costumes, pictures, artifacts, resource people, computer software, newspaper files, and local field trip possibilities. Sorting through resources in a team meeting naturally brings to mind the kinds of activities that would be appropriate to help students to learn from these sources. Involvement of school media center personnel and municipal librarians will be essential.[13]

4.2 *SMALL GROUP WORK: BRAINSTORMING THEME DEVELOPMENT AND SUBJECT INTEGRATION*

With a partner, brainstorm primary-level ideas about the theme of water. Use the idea-clustering web based on questions children might ask about the theme "Water, a Basic Resource," beginning your discussion with the questions on the left side of Figure 4.1. Follow these steps: (1) Add more questions as you survey those already listed. (2) Discuss what kinds of ways of knowing or what subject matter sources are implicit in each and whether you need more variety. (3) Evaluate the possibilities of actually gathering the resources required to let students investigate this theme. (4) List the kinds of skills and modes of expression this theme would elicit from students, assessing whether it presents enough variety.

Now, develop the second set of ideas that comes from the questions about the second theme web, "Looking for Our Roots." Do you find the same subject connections? Would the theme promote different ways of knowing? Of expressing? You need to discuss the questions this exercise raises as you explore integrated thematic instruction with your classmates.

Doing the small group activity (4.2) probably gave you a sense of the freedom you can have in planning the integrated approach. There is not one best or

---

[13]Integrated theme instruction is part of the integrated language or whole-language curriculum perspective. See Christine C. Pappas, Barbara Z. Kiefer, and Linda S. Levstick, *An Integrated Language Perspective in the Elementary School: Theory into Action*, 5th ed. (White Plains, N.Y.: Longman, 1995) for an extensive elaboration of this approach.

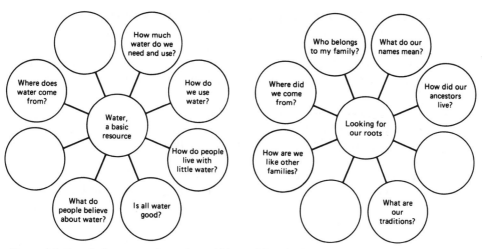

Figure 4.1 Sample themes, and questions children might ask about them

only answer to what is included as part of the theme. With this freedom comes the responsibility for choosing a worthwhile theme. Some themes that have been frequently used with young children deserve to be reconsidered. Think of the topics or themes you recall from your own primary-grade days. Would they meet the criteria for integrative themes you have just been considering? Would these same themes relate to the real concerns many children have today? Integrated theme planning can also relieve teachers worried about covering a long list of topics. Broad topics, rich with content possibilities, will engage students in various kinds of skill development and occupy them profitably for longer stretches of time, relieving your concern for covering specific, lengthy topical lists. Did this exercise bring up questions about skill exposure and practice? Teachers need to be sure to build in adequate time for teaching and reinforcing beginning decoding and numeracy skills. Striking a balance between thematic exploration that permits integration of social studies and science while providing impetus for development of literacy and math skills is crucial to the thematic approach to instruction.

Using "Passive Media" in Primary-Grade Instruction

Choosing a topic that follows traditional grade curriculum or flows from an integrative theme approach does not resolve the issue of opening vistas beyond students' immediate experience of that topic. Most social studies topics require the unlocking of information conveyed by print or voice or video. There are some guidelines that teachers can follow when using "passive medium" materials with young children so that profitable interaction occurs between the children and the material.

Instructional Checklist for Using Books and Media in Primary Grades

Keep input session short—ten to twenty minutes.

Elicit predictions—"What do you think will happen?"—or questions—"What does this (picture or title) make you wonder?"—to set direction and focus.

Use explicit objectives—"Let's read to find. . . ."

Explain new and/or important vocabulary.

Break up exposition by asking children to answer questions, demonstrate, predict.

Provide visuals to accompany print information.

Conclude with discussion, chart making, predicting, summarizing.

Follow with a related activity that prompts the child's expression about the topic read or viewed.

These are general instructional steps in reading or viewing for comprehension. Teacher's editions of social studies texts usually contain such guidelines. Using them when you work from library or trade books and visual media will also increase student focus and engagement.

Children who are learning English as a Second Language (ESL) can benefit from all these suggestions. In addition, they will require repeated interactive exposure to visuals plus individual and small group tutoring and discussion with other students and adult aides that permit them to hear and imitate vocabulary as well as to use gestures, movement, and art to show and extend their comprehension. It is good to keep in mind that learning another language takes time. Typically, social usage precedes academic-related expression by several years.

Having surveyed the general guidelines for primary social studies instruction, let us examine the various sources—textbooks, unit materials, trade books, holidays—of the social studies curriculum for young children.

Role of Textbooks and Reading Materials

Textbooks should not be the principal element of primary social studies programs. Textbooks from social studies series can be used as a resource. Distributing the books and finding the page steals precious minutes from instructional and attending time. Teachers have developed several ways to manage using the text as a resource. For example, they do not distribute individual copies of the texts. Instead, they use one textbook as a storybook and read or storytell essential passages to the children, who are seated in close proximity so that they can see the illustrations as the teacher shows the copy.

Newer textbooks come enriched with "big-book" illustrations that facilitate teacher-led group "reading" and "re-creating" with chart story writing. Beyond the more traditional reinforcement of content through group production of a chart story, researchers in English as a Second Language (ESL)[14] suggest that teachers can help children comprehend content embedded in print and visual texts by creating additional visualizations. This can be done by developing categories, constructing timelines, developing flowcharts or cycle outlines, clustering ideas using webbing from a main topic, or building charts to be filled with data as part of group instruction. A listening-post center through which children rotate can be used to bridge aural and visual decoding. Typically, for this activity teachers record the text passage, including management directions and questions or comments they want children to reflect on as they follow along in their books.

Helping ESL children, and all children, acquire language and understand the ideas expressed by the words requires teachers to assemble a rich diversity of reading materials around the themes being studied. One way is to present sources that range in difficulty from picture books to items for independent reading, and offer a variety in genre—from fiction to poetry, letters, reference materials, and other nonfiction sources. Teachers can also include all kinds of visual aids such as photographs, filmstrips, and audiotaped and videotaped materials. Teacher presentation, individual study, reading teams, and learning centers can be organized as ways for children to gain information.

Using Trade Books for Theme Development

The extensive use of trade books for primary children can be a natural strength for social studies topics. Children love to listen to stories. They empathize with stories more easily than with video or film. Stories are an easy and malleable way to deliver social studies content. Stories are more accessible and personalized than most text and video treatments. Levstik[15] argues that children's historical fiction, because of its narrative, or storytelling, format, makes historical understanding much more accessible to children than do social studies textbooks or other media treatments.

Selecting trade books or storybooks that illustrate social studies topics for young children is a continual updating process. Recent analyses of popular children's trade books have pointed out the care teachers must exercise when choosing library books to read to children. For example, Patrick Shannon found that popular children's books rarely, if ever, portray characters who work together for collective goals.[16]

Less stereotyping is found in newer books. Wilma Dougherty and Rosalind Engle reported that Caldecott and Honor Books, published in the 1980s for young

[14]Margaret Early, "Enabling First and Second Language Learners in the Classroom: Language Arts in English-as-Second Language," *ESL* 67 (October 1990): 567–575.

[15]Linda S. Levstik, "Mediating Content through Literary Texts," *Language Arts* 67, no. 8 (December 1990: 848–853.

[16]Patrick Shannon, "Hidden within the Pages: A Study of Social Perspective in Young Children's Favorite Books," *The Reading Teacher* 39 (March 1986): 656–663.

children, have markedly reduced the portrayal of men and women in traditional gender roles.[17] However, age stereotyping is still portrayed in many trade books for children. Sister Regina Alfonso alerted teachers to stereotypes of age they should look for in children's books: the elderly are senile, they must be grandparents, they are all alike, they depend on their children.[18] Sunal listed books that offer sensitive views of different kinds of change that confront children.[19] The Association for Childhood Education International and the Children's Book Council Joint Committee have published bibliographies focusing on "positive values in a threatening world." Here is a composite list selected from these two sources on the topic of change.

Books to Read to Children on Dealing Positively with Change[20]

Aliki. *The Two of Them.* Greenwillow, 1979. Child shares grandfather's last days.

Bunting, Eve. *The Man Who Could Call Down Owls.* Macmillan, 1984. Powerful fantasy about good and evil.

Cazet, Denys. *Christmas Moon.* Bradbury, 1984. To handle grief, animal character remembers loving ways of grandfather.

Cook, Ann; Gitell, Marilyn; and Mack, Harb. *What Was It Like When Your Grandparents Were Your Age?* Pantheon, 1986. The United States in photographs between 1920 and 1930.

Cohen, Miriam. *Jim's Dog Muffins.* Greenwillow, 1983. Child learns to accept loss of pet dog.

Delton, Judy. *The New Girl at School.* E.P. Dutton, 1979. Sensitive, realistic treatment of making friends at new school.

da Paola, Tomie. *Now One Foot, Now the Other.* Putnam, 1981. Grandfather's stroke frightens child.

McGovern, Ann. *If You Lived in Colonial Times.* Four Winds, 1964. Describes daily life—clothes, food, school.

Power, Barbara. *I Wish Laura's Mommy Was My Mommy.* Lippincott, 1979. Child adapts to mother working.

---

[17]Wilma Holden Dougherty and Rosalind E. Engel, "An '80's Look for Sex Equality in Caldecott Winners and Honor Books," *The Reading Teacher* 40 (January 1987): 394–398.

[18]Sister Regina Alfonso, "Modules for Teaching about Young People's Literature: Model 2: How Do the Elderly Fare in Children's Books?" *Journal of Reading* 30, no. 3 (December 1986): 201–205.

[19]C. Sunal, "The Child and the Concept of Change," *Social Education* 45, no. 6 (October 1981): 438–441. C. S. Sunal and B. A. Hatcher, "A Changing World: Books Can Help Children Adapt," *Day Care and Early Education* 13 (Winter 1985): 16–19.

[20]Association for Childhood Education International and Children's Book Council, "Positive Values in a Threatening World," *Childhood Education* 62 (January–February 1986): 195–198.

Singer, Marilyn. *Archer Armadillo's Secret Room*. Macmillan, 1985. Grandfather and grandson unite to oppose family move.

As social attitudes change, children's literature attempts to portray these changes. Teachers need to be alert to these shifts. One easy technique to use in evaluating a book that presents social issues is to check the publication date. This is not to suggest that all older books should be ignored. That would force us to abandon some excellent literature. However, when reading pre-1970s books, call the students' attention to any change that has occurred. Ask them to think of ways in which something is different now. Looking at literature from the perspective of period helps children to develop their powers of critical thinking while internalizing historical context.

Several sources will help you select antibiased children's literature. Publications of the Council for Interracial Books for Children are invaluable guides. That group's *Human Values in Children's Books*, published in 1976, is continuously updated in the council's periodical *Interracial Books for Children Bulletin*.[21] Recent issues of this periodical have focused on topics such as teaching preschoolers about work, Martin Luther King, counteracting bias in early childhood education, homophobia and education, children of interracial families, children's books, and economic issues. General reference books in children's sections of libraries can assist an initial hunt for books related to a topic. Especially useful are *A to Zoo Subject Access to Children's Books*[22] and *Children's Books in Print*. In addition, *Social Education* publishes an annual listing of notable books in children's literature.

Unit Planning for Active Learning

Textbooks and curriculum guides may present excellent content. To bring that content to life for most young children, you will need to collect and present material that your students can enjoy for its intrinsic merit while you use it to take students into expressive activities. Units of instruction that include manipulation of materials help students internalize ideas. They involve children in a multidisciplinary exploration of a topic. Variety in modes of intake as well as recapitulation and creative expression keep children's interest high and provide for accommodating individual differences in students. In planning a unit, check to see that activities include listening, viewing, painting, writing, classifying, touring, community action, and dramatic expression.

A unit outline on the hospital is presented here without listing the objectives. The story line is presented by the teacher using a curriculum guide supplemented with trade books and photographs. Note the kinds of materials that would be needed to carry out this unit.

---

[21]*Interracial Books for Children Bulletin*. Published eight times a year by the Council for Interracial Books for Children, 1841 Broadway, New York, NY 10023.
[22]Carolyn Ward and John A. Lima, New Providence, N.J.: R.R. Bowker, 1993.

SAMPLE UNIT PLAN 4.1

Active Learning: The Hospital—Second Grade

Story Line	Activities	Skills
Feeling sick	Poem Sick faces on wet pastel	Describing words Painting
How do we know when we are sick?	Drama in pairs: mother/child, doctor/child; nurse visits	Problem-solving discussion using descriptive words and medical instruments: thermometer, light, stethoscope, etc.
	Medicine precautions	Labeling; poetry writing
Accidents	Collage figures of accidents	Painting
	List preventable, nonpreventable accidents	Discussion; classifying; list cause-effect
	Design working body	Cutouts fastened with brads
Serious illness	Design ambulance Admission Hospital layout Dialogue nurse/patient	Cut-paste model Fill-in form; writing Draw floor plan Role playing
Hospital life	Ward pictures List hygiene rules Patient's diary Diets	Labeling Discussion Sequence drawings Classification
Hospital workers	Collage figures Job descriptions	Painting Classification
People going home	How people get better, worse	Discussion
	Healthy faces Rules	Compare sick-well Creative writing

In this unit the materials were chosen to foster artistic and written expression and to provide a positive, open-ended forum for discussion of fears about acquired immune deficiency syndrome (AIDS) appearing in young children. The teacher used storybooks, pictures, some medical instruments, and a visiting nurse in addition to the curriculum guide. Materials resulting from this unit would be voluminous. They would include word cards and lists of pertinent vocabulary, chart stories, a collage of figures representing kinds of accidents and kinds of hospital workers, model ambulances, drawings of hospital interiors, paintings of healthy and sick faces, poems about feeling well, and stories about the hospital. Each visual product of the unit topic can be used to help children discuss what they are learning, thereby organizing their thoughts.

4.3 *SMALL GROUP WORK: BRAINSTORMING AN ACTIVE LEARNING UNIT OUTLINE*

Here is another possible story line for a first-grade unit on transportation. Without gathering specific materials, develop a hypothetical activity sequence on this topic. You need not elaborate the skills that relate to these activities. Your goal is to provide activity variety that assists children in understanding the story line, or subtopics. Compare your list with that of a colleague.

Story Line	**Activities**
My favorite way of travel	
Wheels that move things	
Wings that move things	
Moving big and little things	
People who work in transportation	

Holidays as Social Studies Curriculum

Holiday units are often a major component of social studies for young children. Decorating classrooms using holiday themes is a tradition in many primary classrooms. Children learn to associate symbols such as cupids, shamrocks, turkeys, and pumpkins with certain months of the year. Too often, however, children receive little or no explanation for the meaning of these symbols. They may be read a poem or story about the folklore of the holiday followed by an art project replicating the holiday's symbols. They may not gain any substantive information about the symbols they are reproducing. They do not know that the shamrock represents the Christian trinity of the Father, Son, and Holy Ghost or that the rabbit and the egg have been associated since pre-Christian times in Europe with the coming of spring and fertility. Extending our holiday and symbolic repertoire beyond the Eurocentric tradition into other cultural traditions must become part of our agenda. We must learn that the meanings of the animal symbols of the Chinese zodiac may vary from one Asian culture to another as do the celebrations of the New Year based on it. We need to respect religious positions, such as the Muslim aversion to portraying illustrations other than geometric abstractions in ornamentation because of the Koranic requirement of avoiding images, or the Seventh-Day Adventist aversion to having their children participate in school holiday celebrations that are not sacred times according to their reading of the Bible.

Using holiday materials that explain these symbols and their lore is part of cultural literacy that children deserve to have. Where do we begin educating ourselves about the significance of familiar symbols and the meanings of holidays not part of our own cultural experience? The religious composition of a class is the place to start. If the group has Christian, Jewish, Muslim, Hindu or Sikh, Santeria, or Buddhist students, a note to parents at the beginning of the year inquiring about special religious dates they wish their children to observe can begin to personalize the holiday calendar for your class. Ask these questions of parents: Are there special religious days for which your child needs to miss school or have special considerations at school? Would you or a member of your faith like to share a story or symbol of a holiday with the class? Does your child celebrate a birthday?

Next you need to consult a basic reference book such as an encyclopedia to inform yourself about the religion and sacred days parents mention. Some parents are reticent about requesting special attention or consideration regarding their religious practices. If they are not Christian, they often feel that American schools will not include learning about their beliefs in a school program. Devout Muslims may assume teachers know that their children are to eat little or nothing during the days of Ramadan and may be tired at school during this month as they eat a large meal with a family gathering late in the evening.

Some holidays are particularly American and, as such, deserve special note. Days appropriate for young children to commemorate are Columbus Day, Veterans Day, Thanksgiving, Martin Luther King Day, and Presidents Washington and Lincoln Days. Most of these days are best commemorated with a brief story followed by a creative activity.

Young children can understand the significance of Martin Luther King with few materials beyond a photograph and a recording. Barbara Green of Olinder School, San Jose, California, began by asking her class of second and third graders how they would feel if some of them could not come to this class because of the color of their skins, because of their religion, or because of how much money their parents have. After the children responded, Mrs. Green introduced a photograph of King. She told them his name and the story of his fight to end racial discrimination by allowing blacks to have the same access as whites to public places and jobs. Following recess, Mrs. Green played a recording of King's "I Have a Dream" speech, and the children discussed King's dream. Mrs. Green asked if they had dreams of their own that they would like to see happen to make this a better country for everyone.

The floodgates opened! Children expressed dreams about eradicating poverty, unemployment, violence, and war that were far beyond Mrs. Green's expectations. This discussion led to a writing assignment in which the children expressed their dreams of social justice (see Figure 4.2). The results were read and discussed with another classroom group. This four-part experience gave these second and third

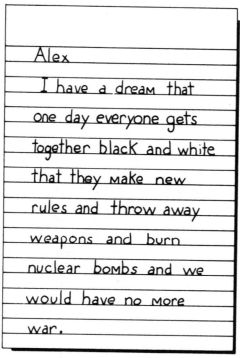

Alex

I have a dream that
one day everyone gets
together black and white
that they make new
rules and throw away
weapons and burn
nuclear bombs and we
would have no more
war.

Figure 4.2 The content of this writing sample may be surprising; it reveals that young children, in their own way, do think about our most crucial issues.

graders a personalized, age-appropriate understanding of why King is honored with a national holiday.

Celebrating Columbus Day and Thanksgiving is a tradition in nearly every primary grade. With our growing sense of revisionist history, most elementary teachers have come to rethink the approach they take in presenting the historical background of these days by taking into consideration American Indian points of view. Knowing, for example, the fuller story of Squanto makes him the complex, star-crossed hero of the folkloric feast. Squanto was a translator for the Pilgrims as a result of a long series of misfortunes with Europeans. Squanto's European contact included being captured, enslaved, taken to Spain to work, escaping to England, earning his freedom, and coming back to his land in order to be with his own tribe only to discover they had all been killed in battles or died of diseases introduced by the Europeans. In his legendary role as peacemaker between two groups that did not understand each other, Squanto was probably doing what he thought necessary for his own survival. Squanto was the last Patuxet.[23] Although his people

---

[23]When possible, the name of the American nations should be used. Recognizing the proper tribal names helps young children internalize that not all American Indians were alike.

did not survive, commemorating his story is important as a tribute to those who are peacemakers.

Multiple points of view and critical thinking about the meaning of Columbus Day that evolved from the 1992 quincentennial of the European discovery of America have led us to see that the ways we traditionally related this event to young children and the children's literature we used to assist us are full of one-sided perspectives that may gloss over or contain errors of historical fact and its interpretations.[24] Older versions of the Columbus story ignore the fact that the Americas were settled long before the "discoverers" arrived, that native groups had their own religions and cultures and social organizations, and that European contact was a genocidal experience for some native groups. Young children can understand the arrival of Columbus as a problematic situation about territory that was resolved in favor of those who had the deadliest weapons. Before you recount the Columbus story, you can lead young students to ponder the influence of European explorers by hypothesizing what America would be like today had the Europeans not come seeking resources and trading opportunities here. These guesses should be recorded and evaluated as to how they might be positive or negative. Or, in sharing an old version of Columbus, ask students to think how each part of the story would be told if a native of the island had written it.

By presenting national holidays such as Columbus Day and Thanksgiving in ways that promote valuing the complexity of historical events instead of passing along myth and stereotype, we are integrating critical thinking about historical events into school holiday commemorations.

CLASSROOM ENVIRONMENT AND SCHEDULING IN PRIMARY GRADES

Implementing the social studies in the primary classroom involves more than simply presenting the subject matter. Ideally, the goals of social studies teaching will be furthered by the manner in which teachers arrange their classrooms and schedule social studies experiences.

Classroom Environments That Support Social Studies

To organize your classroom space for optimal learning, take into account the variety of activities and positive social groupings young children need. Children need spaces to call their own. Designate a "cubby" or locker-type space for each child where he or she can keep snacks, lunches, clothes, and personal supplies. This removes the necessity of assigning a permanent table space or desk for each child,

---

[24]See William Bigelow, "Once upon a Genocide: Christopher Columbus in Children's Literature," *Language Arts* 69 (February 1992): 112–120.

and allows you to arrange tables to serve a variety of purposes in spaces children can rotate through during the day.

Teacher-led large group activities usually occur in an area near a chalkboard that has floor-sitting space for the children and a chair for the teacher. Teacher-led, small group activities often have a special corner with chalkboard, pocket charts, teacher chair, and semicircular arrangement of children's tables and chairs. Seat-work groupings are usually in the middle of the room. Other activity sites include an easel or art area, a listening-post center, a dramatic play area with clothing and props, a writing-reading center with books displayed (perhaps a typewriter or computer is available), and a construction area with art and model-building supplies. Folders for accumulating children's work and boxes for keeping workbooks and text materials are arranged within the children's reach near the areas where the materials will be used (see Figure 4.3).

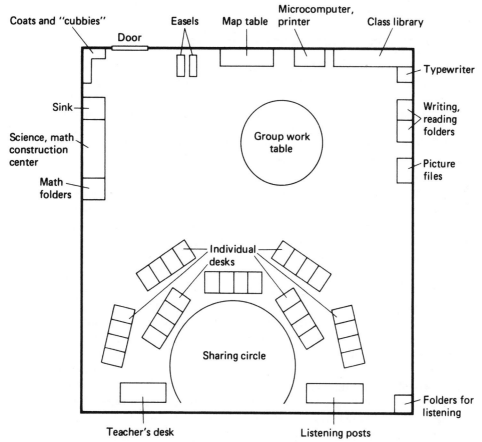

Figure 4.3 Classroom arrangement shows structured choices for children. Children keep their work portfolios near the appropriate activity centers.

Social studies teaching in the primary grades involves only three permanent materials: a globe, a picture of Earth taken from space, and a map of the world. Textbooks and workbooks may also be part of the materials. Most of the teaching aids in vibrant social studies programs are those the teacher has located and selected. As unit topics and seasons change, different materials are needed. Build files that assist you in bringing new stimulation to your classrooms that can be introduced throughout the school year.

Materials related to social studies topics can be placed in any of the activity areas—the globe and maps and the daily class journal can be in the reading-writing area, textbooks and related tapes can be in the listening area, community helper or other theme props can supply the dramatic play area—and can be renewed as topics change. Classroom-display areas such as bulletin boards can be used to build collages and murals of social studies topics as children produce them. Teachers who provide a background for murals and collages or work displays find that children can be put in charge of arranging the rest of the displays.

Scheduling Predicts Instructional Approach

In the way they schedule the school day, teachers express their values about what is important for a young child to learn and how that learning takes place. Some teachers follow a more traditional early childhood schedule by breaking the day into work periods. Each period is separated by a snack, recess, physical education, or another large group activity. Children rotate from one activity center to the next during different work periods. While the teacher works with a small group on something such as reading, other groups of children might be engaged in seat work or might be at the listening center or in the easel area.

Each day begins with planning that suggests what each child must accomplish that day and what options each child has in choosing activities. Children manage their own movement by placing their names in pocket charts for option centers at the beginning of each work period. Then, as a child finishes, he or she makes a place for the next child in line.

Another pattern designates periods for each subject throughout the day and week. Social studies may be scheduled three days a week, from after lunch until the afternoon recess. There are benefits and disadvantages to this pattern. Designating a specific time for social studies guarantees that each child will receive some exposure to the subject. For younger children especially, however, that kind of exposure may seem unrelated to other areas of the curriculum and other times of the day. Also, it may limit strategies of instruction to large group intake of reading or visual information and limit responses to completing worksheets. Young children need to be engaged actively. For learning to be significant for them, their listening or viewing needs to be followed by opportunities to build, dramatize, or do some other expressive activity.

Ideally, from our point of view, social studies for young children should be seen as part of an integrated day in which a social studies or science theme provides the informational focus for activities in reading, writing, drama, and art. Basic programs in reading and math skills would continue to be part of the child's daily experience. But language arts, music, art, and physical education would be organized around the current topic under study in the social studies or science. Film and videos would continue to be shown. They would be part of an ongoing study. That is, they would be preceded and followed by intake and expressive activities and would not be merely an afternoon filler or reinforcement of a reading assignment.

Informal Teaching and Social Studies Curriculum

When children are asked to participate in sharing, they often introduce topics that may influence your scheduling and instructional plans. Through the informal method of capitalizing on children's interest, teachers construct social studies-related experiences. For example, if a child tells the class that his pet was hit by a car, you might turn the discussion to the general theme of what we do when we lose someone we love. The following day, you could bring in Judith Viorst's *The Tenth Good Thing about Barney*, a story about a boy's grief when his cat dies, to read to the class and discuss. Sensitive teachers attempt to respond to these teachable moments.

Developing an extended instructional sequence based on such a teachable moment requires much planning and scheduling flexibility. Certainly, organizing instruction based on children's interests is an honored early childhood ideal.

There are several issues to consider in deciding whether the teachable moment merits further class time and attention. First is the issue of attention span. Sometimes when children ask questions, they want only a "yes" or "no" answer, not an elaborated response. We must develop a sixth sense for determining which questions and issues children can sustain with a more detailed exploration. Even when we believe the topic is within the children's attention span, our judgment about which topics really will add to the growth and development of the group is essential.

A second factor in determining how far to pursue a child-initiated topic is the issue of dignity or trust. Children may reveal confidences or home situations of abuse within families. Teachers, by law in many states, must follow up such confidences and suspicions by reporting them to the school or legally authorized personnel charged with defending children's safety and health. However, to elaborate a mini-unit on child abuse based on concerns about an individual child or a group of children would most probably abuse that child's or that group's dignity within the classroom. This could also damage the children's trust in the teacher.

On the other side of the argument is the need to provide children with proactive models rather than perhaps leaving them helpless by ignoring a topic or denying the appropriateness of a topic for young children. Issues concerning unfairness should not be ignored. Exploring ways to seek justice through discussion and role playing that probes different sides of an issue offers valuable, enduring experience and insight to children. Seeking justice through group action such as requesting to speak to the principal or writing letters to the editorial section of the newspaper or to an organization or politician are indelibly instructive to all children.

Adding to the daily schedule social studies–related explorations that spring from children's interests is a laudable practice. The same is true of holiday-related social studies schedules. Both types of scheduling are enriching. Neither, however, can replace deliberately planned social studies programs. Reliance on holidays and student-initiated issues for social studies content most surely will short-circuit exposure to the comprehensive understandings and thorough skill development guaranteed by more formal social studies instruction. There is no substitute for a teacher-planned curriculum that systematically engages young children in learning more about who and where they are.

SUMMARY

The content and processes associated with the social studies are as essential to the young child's growth and development as any curricular area. National standards support the importance of including historical, geographical, and civics strands in content for the primary level. Curriculum outlines at the state and local levels as well as in published textbook series will incorporate these emerging expectations. Effective instruction in the social studies for children in the primary grades is experiential and integrative. Concepts are presented in ways that involve children in exploring who and where they are and in thinking critically about what they explore to construct and reconstruct their understanding. Materials and strategies expose children to a variety of people and cultures and problem-solving possibilities. Informal teaching that capitalizes on children's concerns is an enrichment of the basic social studies program that intentionally involves children in exploring facets of their world.

SUGGESTED READINGS

Bigelow, William. "Once upon a Genocide: Christopher Columbus in Children's Literature." Language Arts 69 (February 1992): 112–120. Critically reviews Columbus biographies from perspective of natives.

Boutee, G. S.; La Point, Sally; and Davis, Barbara. "Racial Issues in Education: Real or Imagined?" *Young Children* 49 (November 1993): 19–23. Presents African-American adult perspectives of young children's "playful" ethnic and racial interactions with suggestions for addressing them positively.

Derman-Sparks, Louise, and the A.B.C. Task Force. *Anti-Bias Curriculum Tools for Empowering Young Children*. Washington, D.C.: National Association for the Education of Young Children, 1989. Broad view of curriculum inspires this essential early childhood publication.

Egan, Kieran. *Teaching as Storytelling: An Alternative to Teaching and Curriculum in the Elementary School*. London, Ontario: Althouse Press, 1986. New interpretation of how and what children of different ages learn about their social world.

Feldkamp-Price, Betsy, and Smith, David Lee. "Teaching about Indians? Use the Real Stuff!" *Teaching K–8* 25 (October 1994): 57–59. Lists sources and activities to confront misconceptions about Indians.

Gardner, Howard. *Frames of Mind: The Theory of Multiple Intelligences*. New York: Basic Books, 1983. Groundbreaking discussion of the multiple kinds of intelligence.

Lamme, Linda Leonard. "Stories from Our Past: Making History Come Alive for Children." *Social Education* (March 1994): 159–164. Uses familiar, quality children's trade books to demonstrate how to lead young children to discover links between the books and their own lives.

Matthews, Gareth B. *The Philosophy of Childhood*. Cambridge, Mass.: Harvard University Press, 1994. Critique of Piaget and Kohlberg suggests developmental hurdles not precise and sees more similarities than differences between adult and child thought processes.

Paley, Vivian Gussin. *Kwanzaa and Me*. Cambridge, Mass.: Harvard University Press, 1995. Long-time kindergarten teacher-writer of University of Chicago Laboratory Schools illustrates use of storytelling method as way of letting children reveal their concerns that permits teacher to supply creative alternatives to problems as she recounts encounters with racial and social problems that informed her reflective teaching.

Pappas, Christine C.; Kiefer, Barbara Z.; and Levstik, Linda S. *An Integrated Language Perspective in the Elementary School: Theory into Action*, 2d ed. White Plains, N.Y.: Longman, 1995. Well-grounded curriculum/methods text for realistically implementing whole language approach.

Parker, Walter C. *Renewal in the Social Studies*. Washington, D.C.: Association for Supervision and Curriculum Development, 1991. Outlines newer directions in curriculum development and need for it.

Seefeldt, C. *Social Studies for the Preschool Primary Child*. Columbus, Ohio: Merrill, 1989. Methods text focusing on early social studies instruction from developmentalist, whole-child perspective.

SOCIAL STUDIES in the FOURTH THROUGH EIGHTH GRADES

In this chapter we discuss the teaching of social studies from grades four through eight with special emphasis on strategies and materials that move beyond the basal textbook:

1/ Children in the Middle Grades

2/ The Social Studies Curriculum: Content

3/ Current Events/Current Affairs

4/ Teaching Controversial Issues

CHILDREN IN THE MIDDLE GRADES

Teachers who have experience with both the primary and middle grades are very clear about the developmental differences between these age groups: "I love teaching fourth graders. They can think and they enjoy discussion." "My first graders are so loving! They still confuse me with their mothers." "Kindergarteners are so active. They need to change activities every twenty minutes."

Cognitively, middle-grade children are ready to incorporate a wide span of spatial and temporal relationships in their thinking. Just as middle graders are extending their personal range of familiar space by roaming farther from home on their bikes and skateboards, they are ready to learn about unfamiliar places in social studies. The contrasting ways of rural and urban or desert and rain forest life interest them. Middle graders are able to see themselves in the context of time. Their curiosity about prehistory and earlier human times grows. They are eager to conjecture about the future.

Psychologically, middle-grade children are focused on personal competency. They like recognition for what they can do, whether as an outstanding speller or a whiz at drawing or a standout in recess team sports. Middle graders like quick-paced and varied activities. Class or small group games such as baseball and Twenty Questions or trivia contests are appealing as content-review strategies. Projects that involve them in producing concrete products such as graphs, models, and murals gratify their need for variety and evidence of their competence.

Socially, middle-grade children are entering the age of reciprocity in friendship and human relations. They comprehend the social consequences of their actions. When they are in a group, they are eager to seek fairness. They relish opportunities to make rules, to enforce them, and to establish consequences for breaking them.

All these children are growing and developing, but there are individual differences in their rates of growth. The areas sketched above are, nevertheless, some of the typical changes in the ways that middle-grade children see and interact with the world, and they should influence how you orient your social studies program. As you examine content, strategies, and materials for middle-grade social studies, keep these general characteristics in mind.

Remember two other points when you begin teaching social studies to fourth through eighth graders. The first is that developmental levels may vary dramatically within each grade and, as with any teaching, you need to be aware of these variations and adapt your presentation of content and methods to the readiness of your students. The second point is that at some time in this grade range, probably at the sixth- or seventh-grade level, students will enter a middle school or junior high school where, typically, schedules will be divided into specific periods for each subject. Students may even begin changing classrooms for different subjects, as they do in high school.

The advantage of this environment is that the teacher will often be a specialist in his or her field and therefore will have more background and interest in the subject matter. The disadvantage, however, is that subject matters tend to be even more compartmentalized, with less and less integration between them. To avoid these difficulties, more middle schools are scheduling one teacher for an extended period—a core class for two or three periods. The intent is that "kids in the middle" will get both basic academic and exploratory subjects in a setting with a wide range of extra or co-curriculum and guidance services. But even in middle schools, some teachers tend to split the core period into separate subject content times.

Almost all experts recommend some degree of integration, particularly the integration of language arts into the social studies. We strongly encourage you to include language-arts content and methods in your social studies teaching, no matter what the organizational structure of your classroom time, since the two areas both complement and reinforce each other. See Chapter 8 for specific tips on using language arts in teaching social studies.

THE SOCIAL STUDIES CURRICULUM: CONTENT

What is currently taught in a typical fourth- through eighth-grade social studies program?

Grade 4: State history, geographic regions
Grade 5: U.S. history
Grade 6: World cultures, history, and geography
Grade 7: World cultures, history, and geography
Grade 8: U.S. history

As you can see from the topics, history and to a lesser extent geography have been emphasized at these grade levels. Concern about effectively covering the range of topics in U.S. history—from Columbus to the latest president, or ancient civilizations to the most recent war—in one year has made social studies curriculum designers of the California Framework and other areas try to divide up the content and not repeat it. Thus, in California the framework in the teaching of U.S. history gives the fifth grade the Colonial-Revolution period, the eighth grade the nineteenth century, and the eleventh grade the twentieth century. How widespread this idea will be in teaching both U.S. history and world history is uncertain. Should we continue the traditional one-year broad survey chronological approach? A division of content would allow more depth and detail than is presently possible with the typical broad coverage of hundreds of years of content in one academic year.

History and geography have traditionally been emphasized at these grade levels, although there has been an attempt in the past twenty years to include more of the social sciences—political science, sociology, economics, and anthropology. Similar to using themes for integration of several subject areas (science, art, etc.), often an *interdisciplinary* social science approach is very worthwhile. In this approach, several of the social sciences and history are used to explain a topic. To consider nearly any problem—unemployment, poverty, crime, health care, changes in the family, violence in our society and in the world—requires using data and research methods from several of the social sciences and history. No one academic discipline such as economics can give the full picture. Areas of the humanities such as film and novels further personify and visualize social studies topics. This curriculum approach works especially well in a theme- or issues-centered approach in which students examine topics such as world peace or population trends.

This broadening of the social studies framework reflects a similar broadening in research in history. Historical research now emphasizes analysis over narration, a thematic or topical approach over a strictly chronological one, and more statistics, oral history, sociological models, and psychoanalytic theories. This new history focuses on everyday family life—patterns of recreation, for instance—rather than just on the lives of political, military, and social leaders and their institutions. We are seeing an increasing amount of research about women, minority groups, and community groups in history. Similar trends have occurred in other disciplines of the social sciences as well. All this is reflected in what students are taught about social studies.

History

You are aware from the media that the kind of history that features people's story of the past is a controversial issue for the schools. Parents, religious leaders, and members of political organizations and of ethnic groups speak at school board meetings regarding their concerns about their group portrayal or their lack of coverage in the textbooks and other materials that are being considered for adoption or are already in the classrooms. Whose history is to be presented? How much attention should the various groups receive? Should multiple perspectives be presented, such as showing how immigrant women or white male managers saw the growth of the industrial revolution in the United States? If more attention is given to various individuals and groups, will all students be exposed to the core values and cultural heritage of the American society as well as the global society?

There are no easy answers to these questions. Part of your response depends on your values. In general, more conservative educators usually advocate teaching all children a core of historical knowledge to maintain the mainstream culture and the democratic values that tie together all Americans and give us our shared heritage and national identity. This group is concerned that there is now too much emphasis on diversity and not as much on teaching about mainstream American history. However, more liberal educators tend to believe that the histories of too many groups have been left out of American textbooks and the children from these groups do not see themselves or their groups in the textbooks they study. Thus, they claim that not enough attention has been given to the various individuals and groups that make up the diverse American society and more multiple historical perspectives from people of color and women are needed. In a similar manner, the debate continues over whether the world history/world culture course has too much of a European-centered focus. Should non-European history/cultures be given more attention?

Another issue is curriculum integration in social studies. Some argue that history should be taught mainly as a separate subject in the social studies program. The proponents in favor of the separate subject approach believe that the teaching of history has been so diluted during the past twenty years by concentration on other social sciences that students no longer learn history as history. They cite research about students' gaps of knowledge, such as when the Civil War took place. Currently some curriculum experts value greater integration in all subject areas, while other advocates and scholars recommend teaching academic disciplines primarily as separate subjects, believing students will learn more with this approach. These advocates, if they do recognize other subject areas and the humanities, generally want their subject are to be the primary focus or the "queen" of the area, with the other social sciences and the humanities in a more subsidiary role.

A controversy about the teaching of history immediately arose with the publication of three books in 1994 presenting history standards:

> *National Standards for United States History: Exploring the American Experience (5-12)*
> *National Standards for World History: Exploring Paths to the Present (5-12)*
> *National Standards for History: Expanding Children's World in Time and Space (K-4)*

What history to teach and how to teach it were examined carefully by the National Center for History in the Schools (History Center), which produced the National History Standards Project (see Chapter 1). Representatives from the History Center proposed an integration of historical thinking (skills) and historical understanding (what students should know).

The five types of historical thinking for all grade levels are as follows:

1. Chronological Thinking
2. Historical Comprehension
3. Historical Analysis and Interpretation
4. Historical Research Capabilities
5. Historical Issues—Analysis and Decision-making

The content standards in history for Grades K–4 consisted of four topics with eight standards (see Chapter 4). The American history content was divided into ten eras with four eras devoted to the twentieth century; two to four standards for each era were established, for a total of thirty-one standards. Each standard stated what students should learn for the particular period; there are about 200 pages of examples of student achievement to reach these standards. For example, the report indicated that students are to know the causes of the American Revolution, the ideas and interests involved in forging the revolutionary movement, and the reasons for the American victory. Examples of student achievement for grades 5–6 include the following: reconstruct the chronology of the war; identify and compare leadership roles of two major leaders such as George Washington, Benjamin Franklin, Thomas Jefferson, John Adams, Samuel Adams, John Hancock, and Richard Henry Lee; and draw evidence from novels on how the war affected the lives of people (*Jump Ship to Freedom, My Brother Sam Is Dead, Johnny Tremain,* and *War Comes to Willy Freeman*). For grades 7–8, examples include assessing leadership of both American and British military leaders, analyzing the varied responses of Native American nations to the American Revolution using the Iroquois and Cherokees as case studies, and examining the Revolutionary War from the African-American perspective.

The World History Standards (5–12) are divided into eight eras with thirty-nine historical understandings standards. Era 1 is Beginnings of Human Society; the series ends with Era 8, The 20th Century. This is followed by about 250 pages giving examples of student achievement of the standards.

Even before the publication of the *National Standards for United States History* in November 1994, conservatives and other individuals and groups protested against the report, stating that it was a "politically correct" document concentrating on "multiple perspectives." Lynne Cheney, former head of the National Endowment for the Humanities, in a *Wall Street Journal* editorial October 20, 1994, criticized the document as a too "gloomy" picture of America, one that is too critical of all things white and too uncritical of all things, brown, black and other.[1] As evidence, she reported the number of times historical subjects were cited in the *National Standards.* According to her count, Sen. Joseph McCarthy and/or McCarthyism is mentioned nineteen times, the Ku Klux Klan seventeen times, the Seneca Fall women's rights convention nine times, and Harriet Tubman six times whereas important male heroes such as Paul Revere, Daniel Webster, Robert E. Lee, Alexander Graham Bell, Thomas Edison, Albert Einstein, Jonas Salk, and the Wright brothers were not mentioned at all. She and other critics felt that not enough attention was being given to the positive aspects of U.S. history in its long struggle for liberty, equality, justice and dignity and too much emphasis was placed on the country's failures.

---

[1]Lynne V. Cheney, "The End of History," *Wall Street Journal*, October 20, 1994.

The media and its commentators picked up on this controversial topic. Headlines in the leading newspapers and magazines had such titles as: "Conflict over a New History Curriculum," "The Hijacking of American History," "Instead of Western Civ, It's Multiciv," "History According to Whom: Let the Debate Continue," "History Rewrites Itself," and "History without Heroes?" In general, the critics condemned the standards for being manifestations of left-wing "political correctness" and extravagant multiculturalism. The criticism also focused heavily on the American history document (5–12) and then the world history standards. The comments were almost exclusively devoted to the examples given of student achievement (the bulk of the document) and not on the standards. Hardly anyone commented on the five historical thinking standards that were to be used from grades K through 12 except to say that they demanded more critical thinking of students than what had typically been required in most history courses.

It is difficult to predict the impact the history standards will have, especially with the political controversy surrounding them. Apart from the debate on political correctness, one concern has been the sheer number of content standards for U.S. history and the length of each of the three documents. Teachers believe there is not enough time for most students in most schools to meet these ambitious standards. One social studies expert stated that an average fifth-grade teacher would have to teach nothing but history all day long for three years to meet the fifth-grade standards. In addition, some believe that the performance standards have emphasized what students should "know" at the expense of what they should "do," a direction that might lead teachers to require students simply to memorize a lot of facts.

The history standards do reflect more multiple points of view than most teachers now use, and this is a concern of the conservatives who feel that too much of traditional American history and Western civilization is being left out. On the other hand, the history standards may not be extensive and complete enough to satisfy those who want even more attention to diversity. These new standards thus clearly illustrate the debate in our society on what children should learn about American and world history. The teaching of these subjects is inherently controversial. As teachers attempt to interest students in how the knowledge of the past informs their present, we would hope that the content selected will illuminate the ideals that attract and connect us while honoring the diverse experiences of individuals and groups seeking to enjoy the promises of these ideals.

5.1 SMALL GROUP WORK: VIEWPOINTS ON U.S. HISTORY

The History Center staff recommended devoting three full years to the teaching of U.S. history, somewhere from grades five through twelve. Only about one-third of the states now have this requirement. In your group, list the reasons you think the three years is either a good or poor idea.

In teaching history, we can never be certain that every elementary student has a mature sense of historical concepts that are not easily understood, such as time and change. Therefore, your teaching of these abstract concepts should include as much specific, concrete material as possible. Specific help in teaching chronological skills is included in Chapter 9. There are several other practical possibilities that can lead you beyond reliance on a textbook, however. Texts are important; they provide basic information and are an important resource. But part of the problem in teaching history is that students cannot see how the material relates to their daily lives and their relationships with the larger world. You can help them broaden their perspective by using the following techniques.

Oral History.   Students enjoy exploring the past through creating oral histories, a method that historians are using increasingly, especially with groups like immigrants who tend not to leave traditional written records. Historians obtain oral data not only from famous or powerful people but also from members of a given community (an Indian pueblo), from a given period or national background, or from people who observed or participated in a specific activity (a strike or a protest march). These kinds of firsthand accounts fascinate children.

To use oral history in your classroom, first determine a topic that is relatively narrow—what life was like in an elementary school twenty, thirty, or fifty years earlier, for example. Don't expect students to question people about their whole lives; instead, define the topic clearly, focusing on a short span of time. Together with your students, create a short list of questions and have these printed out. Students might ask, for instance, what subjects were taught, how large the classes were, if students in a single classroom were all the same age or different ages, how long the day lasted, what games were played, and how the teacher enforced discipline. The questions should be clear, and each child should have his or her own printed copy.

Practicing interviews in the classroom often helps. Have your students role-play. At first students tend to ask only the questions on their list, ignoring any possibilities of interchange that might arise during the interview. You can encourage them in the role playing to move beyond the interview questions while still being certain that they gather the required material.

You need to determine whether students will tape the interview or take notes. In either case, role playing in the classroom will help them develop their skills. Taping requires good equipment that should be tested before use. If they will take notes, students must know that they cannot expect to take down every word; you will need to work with them on listening skills. A form with the questions and spaces provided for answers is very helpful to many students. They can take notes directly on the form, or if they tape the interview, they can transfer the information onto the form later.

Children can interview anyone who fits the category for the information required—parents, grandparents, community members, even the school principal.

When the data are gathered, you can use the information not only to help your students understand history—what went on in elementary schools in past years—but also to help your students understand the work of *historians*. How do historians weigh the information provided in oral histories? Did the respondent, for example, stretch the truth? Did he or she *really* walk three miles to school every winter through three feet of snow? Does he or she remember only the pleasant things? By compiling all oral histories that the class has gathered and comparing them, your students should be able to determine those areas on which most respondents agree. If there is a local historical society, its members may be able to confirm or disagree with some parts of the material you have collected. Finally, your class will have a valuable picture of what life was like in earlier years—of *history*—and they will have acquired it through active participation in the process of historical research.

Family History.   The same kind of active participation can be achieved through creating family histories. Many teachers use units on immigration, urban life, or other concepts that actually depend on students' family histories for part of their content. Data from student family histories in effect are used to support or disprove generalizations.

Encourage students to make their own histories. When and where were they born? Have they seen their birth certificates? What do other family members remember about them as they were growing up? What do they remember about themselves? Are there photographs to analyze? What about written reports? Report cards? Certificates? Have these historical documents been saved along with "artifacts" like baby shoes? Students can make grade-by-grade timelines and the whole class can correlate them with historical events for each year.

Usually, your job in creating family histories is to structure the necessary data. Do you want to record birth dates and addresses of parents and other family members? The various jobs held by all family members, including grandparents? Use prepared worksheets showing the information to be gathered, such as family trees with blanks to be filled in. Determine what data you need and then structure a way to report the data. This helps students complete their tasks and makes analysis of the data simpler.

Looking at Objects of Historical Significance.   In addition to learning from oral histories and family histories, students can gain insights from seeing historical objects. This is particularly important in understanding the community's roots. Cemeteries can be remarkably useful classrooms. If one is near your school, walk through it with your students. Provide guidelines about the information they should gather; a worksheet can be useful also. Look at the headstones and monuments of the graves. Ask students to list the name, gender, age, and occupation, if it is given, of the person buried in each grave you look at. Have one student write down interesting inscriptions from headstones. Students may be surprised to note, when the data are collated, that many more infants and children died in the past than do so today. This observation may lead to a discussion of mortality rates and the reasons for their change. Did husbands generally survive their wives or did wives outlive their husbands? Did occupation, if it is provided, seem to affect the age of death? How and why?

In addition, a walk through an older section of your community or a trip to view historical buildings can be valuable if it is well planned. You might also want to visit your local historical society or museums where artifacts represent what the community was like years ago. Often it is best to visit such museums at the end of a unit so that students will have learned something about the tools or other objects they will see.

Students can also be encouraged to bring to the class artifacts that their families may have. Families may have written records, such as a relative's discharge from the army, or a penmanship book written by a student many years ago. Warn students to be careful, however. If the artifacts are valuable, replacing or repairing them is almost impossible if they are lost or damaged.

Children's Literature and Magazines.   A fourth strategy to bring history or any of the social sciences to life is the use of children's literature or trade books. Literature can bring past events into the lives of students. Literature is usually more people centered than text material and can give fresh insight into the ways of life in our culture—past and present—as well as cultures of other places and times.

Biographies and novels are especially powerful. Stories can combine historical incidents with emotion and conflict. Kieran Egan suggested that, for students up to the age of seven, stories with clear conflicts between good and evil and fear or security are best.[2] Students from eight to thirteen are in the romantic stage and prefer to read about people who struggle courageously with real problems. Children want to know how Sojourner Truth felt in the face of great odds, for instance, and will often be interested in books depicting human suffering. Today, more emphasis is placed on reading books that have content themes instead of isolated books unrelated to each other.

Where can social studies teachers find good books? Each year the journal *Social Education* publishes a list of notable children's trade books in the social studies field. These books are selected because they (1) are written for readers from kindergarten through the eighth grade, (2) emphasize human relations, (3) represent a diversity of groups and are sensitive to a broad range of cultural experiences, (4) present an original theme or a fresh slant on a traditional topic, (5) are easily readable and of high literary quality, and (6) have a pleasing format and, when appropriate, illustrations that enrich the text. The number of good books is increasing. Who would not be excited by a book such as *The Inheritance* by

---

[2]Kieran Egan, "What Children Know Best," *Social Education* 43, no. 2 (February 1979): 130–139..

Claudia Von Canon (Houghton Mifflin), set in Spain at the time of the Inquisition? The hero comes home to claim his father's estate; his father, suspected of helping the Jews, committed suicide rather than submit to the Inquisition. The hero has to decide whether to stay in his hometown under suspicion of the Inquisition or flee for safety.

Biography and autobiography on the lives of people such as anthropologist Margaret Mead; Thomas Gallaudet, a pioneer in education of the deaf; Native American Pocahontas; and others are always popular, as are folktales and legends of various cultural groups. In addition, books on controversies such as acid rain or the nuclear arms can provide students with different viewpoints.

Consult your librarian to see what is available in your school library that is related to the social studies. Indicate your preferences for future orders. Some teachers will read aloud to the class a portion from a interesting book to entice students to read further. Take care not to kill student enthusiasm by assigning only dull reading reports.

There are also history magazines for young people. The most popular is *Cobblestone*, which focuses on U.S. history with articles on entertainers like Annie Oakley and the Wild West; explorers like Robert E. Peary, who went to the North Pole; Joseph, chief of the Nez Perce, and so on.

Cobblestone is found in many public libraries and the back issues may be of interest to teachers. The same publisher (7 School Street, Peterborough, NH 03458) also has a children's magazine, *Calliope*, which features world history; *Faces,* for world cultures/multicultural studies; and *Odyssey*, which has articles on space and astronomy.

These four strategies—collecting oral histories, exploring family histories, looking at historical objects and places, and reading historical literature—will help children get a sense of the past and make history come alive for them. Other techniques include role playing or dramatic play. Have children research various occupations in a New England town at a particular time, and then set up shops (general store, blacksmith forge, print shop, church, jail, bakery, inn/tavern, furniture/cabinet shop, barber/doctor shop, and the like). Include in your debriefing discussion an analysis of how accurately the children played their roles. Try a *history day*, increasingly popular in some states, in which children portray life in Colonial or earlier times. These techniques require active participation from students and move well beyond traditional textbook teaching.

Geography

Responding to the criticisms that most Americans are almost illiterate in geography, the National Council for Geographic Education (Geography Council) sketched out a broad, ambitious set of eighteen national standards setting out what students should know and be able to do in geography from kindergarten through the twelfth grade. Their document, *Geography for Life: National Geography Stan-*

dards 1994, emphasizes the value and importance the council places on geography for all citizens throughout their lives. These eighteen standards specify the essential knowledge, skills, and perspectives that students should have to be informed, effective, and responsible citizens.

Building on previous work of the National Council for Geographic Education and the 1984 guidelines of the Association of American Geographers, the National Council for Geographic Education essentially retained the following five basic themes for geography education from kindergarten through twelfth grade, although the names and emphases changed in some cases.

1. Location—position on the Earth's surface
2. Place—the physical, human, and observed characteristics that distinguish one place from another
3. Human-Environment Interaction—how people have modified or adapted to natural settings
4. Movement—movement of people, ideas, and materials
5. Regions—areas that display unity

Realizing that their standards were difficult to remember, the Geography Center organized them into the following six clusters:

The Geographically Informed Person Knows and Understands . . .

The World in Spatial Terms
(Standards 1–3)

1. How to use maps and other geographic representations, tools, and technologies to acquire, process, and report information from a spatial perspective.
2. How to use mental maps to organize information about people, places, and environments in a spatial context.
3. How to analyze the spatial organization of people, places, and environments on Earth's surface.

Places and Regions
(Standards 4–6)

4. The physical and human characteristics of places.
5. That people create regions to interpret Earth's complexity.
6. How culture and experience influence people's perception of places and regions.

Physical Systems
(Standards 7–8)

7. The physical processes that shape the patterns of Earth's surface.
8. The characteristics and spatial distribution of ecosystems on Earth's surface.

Human Systems (Standards 9–13)	9. The characteristics, distribution, and migration of human populations on Earth's surface.
	10. The characteristics, distribution, and complexity of Earth's cultural mosaics.
	11. The patterns and networks of economic interdependence on Earth's surface.
	12. The processes, patterns, and functions of human settlement.
	13. How the forces of cooperation and conflict among people shape human control of Earth's surface.
Environment and Society (Standards 14–16)	14. How human actions modify the physical environment.
	15. How physical systems affect human systems.
	16. The changes that occur in meaning, use, distribution, and importance of resources.
The Uses of Geography (Standards 17–18)	17. How to apply geography to interpret the past.
	18. How to apply geography to interpret the present and plan for the future.

There is some overlap of the five themes (1984) and the six clusters (1994); the clusters, developed more recently, place more emphasis on skills, especially problem solving, and perspectives. This change was probably an attempt to steer teachers away from the focus on facts, such as where cities and nations are located, and map skills. Physical systems now also receive more attention. For example, eighth-grade students are responsible for describing the ocean circulation system and its role in climate systems and to draw pictures of ecosystems in various parts of the world.

As with the history standards, the impact of the geography standards is uncertain, although the geography standards are likely to be less controversial. Remembering all eighteen standards, even if they are organized under six essential elements, is a chore. Some teachers liked the older five themes because they were easier to recall and moved from the simple to the complex. Another basic problem is that many teachers had no geography courses in college. Funds for retraining teachers will be necessary if teachers are to have a geographic perspective. An additional problem is that geography has lost ground as a separate subject in both the middle and high school curriculum. The subject generally receives scant time and attention in the total school curriculum. Where does it belong? The Geography Council stresses the importance of integrating geography across the curriculum at the elementary level. But giving geography enough attention at all grade levels, even in an integrated approach, will be a problem. Time is always at a premium in the classroom. If geography is to receive more time during the school day, what will be removed or deemphasized? Also, the success of some of the standards may require new instructional equipment, including the latest technology to generate computer maps and to enable students to become familiar with satellite imagery.

On the positive side, the Geographic Alliance Network that has been established in many states has been reaching out to teachers. The network is funded in part by the National Geographic Society, which has supplied materials and sponsored teacher workshops for wider inclusion of geography in the curriculum. These steps may help to implement the geography standards.

To see how geography standards could be used, let us look at South Africa.

1. The World in Spatial Terms (the 1984 term was *Location*)
   What is in the news about South Africa?
   Where is the capital of the country? Is it the most populous city?
2. Place
   What is the climate like in South Africa?
   What are the physical features of the country?
   What is the cultural background of the people?
   How is South Africa different from or similar to your community?
3. Human Systems (the 1984 term was *Human/Environment Interactions*)
   Where do most people live in South Africa?
   How have the people of South Africa changed their environment?
4. Environment and Society (the 1984 term was *Movement*)
   What are the major exports; imports?
   Where are the major roads; airports?
   Does South Africa have major ports?
5. Regions
   Is South Africa similar to its neighbors in its government, culture, and religion?

Using some of the new guidelines of the Geographic Council, we could add the following:

6. Mental Maps (Seeing the World in Spatial Terms)
   What images or mental maps do you have of South Africa?
7. Applying Geography to Interpret Present and Future
   Do you think that it is likely that South Africa will change its political system?
   Do you think South Africa will have more or fewer conflicts with its neighbors?

Chapter 9 provides more detail on teaching the interpretation and making of maps. But note that a critical concern about how geography is taught is that too often *only* map skills are stressed rather than all the major concepts of geography as outlined by the National Council for Geographic Education. Students may learn the topography of their state or nation but pay little attention to how that topography has been modified or how people have adapted to the natural settings. In studying Brazil, for instance, students often learn that Brazil has a large forest area and that its major cities are located on the coast but not that Brasilia, its capital, was carved from a high plateau once thought uninhabitable, or that the migration of the Japanese into Brazil has changed the character of the nation.

A second criticism of how geography is taught is that thinking skills are underemphasized and low-level memorization is overemphasized. The Geography Council strongly emphasized geography skills to try to correct this weakness. It is not enough for students to know where the Nile River is; they should also know the consequences of its being where it is and its connections to other parts of the world. Rather than having students simply locate cities on a map, have them find common elements about the locations. They may be surprised to note that some 90 percent of all major cities are located near waterways. For those that are not, like Madrid or Phoenix, ask them to hypothesize *why* not. Do politics and technology influence the location of cities? Are newer cities more or less likely to be located near waterways? Why? Also, rather than having students learn only about the climate of their own region, have them compare it to other climates. How does climate influence the way we live? The way we dress?

There is no best way to teach *either* geography *or* history. As with history, however, you need to make geographical concepts concrete by designing learning experiences for your class that use their environment and fall within their range of readiness. Take your students on a walk around the school, and then have them make a map of the route as they recall it. Walk the same route again, this time making maps as you go. How closely do their remembered maps resemble their actual maps? What problems do mapmakers face when confronting new territory? (Three-dimensional maps, with boxes or blocks representing buildings, can be fun to make, but may take more time than the concept requires.)

Make students aware of how the place they are studying relates to the place where they live; let them locate on the map the places they are studying. Use the textbook maps to point out the major cities of your state for your fourth grade class, or the major sites of revolutionary battles for your fifth-grade class. Calculate how many hours it would take to get from your community to Philadelphia, where the Constitution was written, by horseback or carriage and by plane; measure it off. If you live four days by horseback, talk about it on Monday, and on Thursday remind your students that they would just now be arriving at their destination.

In addition, try to tap as many actual student experiences as possible. Ask your students where they have lived or traveled, and have them talk about those places. Ask where the students in the class were born and plot these locations on a map. Or investigate and map the local shopping center or main street, classifying the types of stores and shops found there. Students can also map the interior of a supermarket, indicating aisles, major food categories, and other sections. In addition, students can find items from the supermarket that come from other parts of the world and plot information about imports on a map. Talk about your travel experiences as well.

Using controversial issues also helps to bring life to major geographical concepts. Some ecology or environmental issues lend themselves naturally to a consideration of major concepts of geography. Should a given piece of land in the community be developed? How should it be developed? Should it be made into a shopping center or housing for low-income groups? Such discussions can lead to a better understanding of the advantages and disadvantages of using a land site for different purposes as well as showing how people can modify their environment. All these techniques, and especially using the local community as a concrete illustration, can help to improve geography education by moving beyond the textbook.

5.2 *ON YOUR OWN: YOUR POSITION ON GEOGRAPHY*

What do you remember about your own exposure to geography in elementary school? Jot down some things you remember about how geography was taught. How comfortable do you feel about teaching geography? Have you had a college-level course in geography?

Economics

Knowing about the economic world is important for every student. All students will eventually need to have skills and knowledge to be able to earn a living. In addition, economic or financial considerations invade almost every decision we make—large or small. Students face the problem of whether they can afford to buy a certain piece of sports equipment or a bicycle. Governments as well as families face the problem of what to do with limited financial resources. Scarcity and limited resources are always a problem and are the main focus of economics. Therefore, economic education is necessary if one is to be an informed citizen.

An important source of resources for teaching economics is the National Council on Economic Education, 432 Park Avenue South, New York, NY 10016. This organization will send you information on where your local or state centers on economic education are located. You can secure sample units and background information from these centers to help you plan the teaching of economics in the classroom.

The National Council is seeking funds to create national curriculum standards for economics. Its projected completion date is 1997. Economics, in comparison with history, geography, civics, and government, was not listed by Congress in 1989 as one of the areas to be tested for at the fourth, eighth, and twelfth grades, but was added in 1994. Because economics was designated late as a critical area for student testing, and because its standards are still being developed, teachers of social studies will probably not be aware for several years how to change the way they incorporate economics into their teaching.

Economics, like history and geography, often contains difficult concepts. Gross national product, scarcity, income distribution, depressions, comparative advantage, opportunity cost, and so on can be hard for students to understand. In addition, economics (a policy science) addresses ideological issues, and some groups become very upset if the schools appear to be advocating anything but our present economic system. Free materials, including videos from business, labor, or other groups, should be viewed with a critical eye when you present them to students. But the controversial nature of economics can be a plus by adding interest and relevance. How much money should be allocated for defense or welfare or research on AIDS? Students often have opinions on these issues.

As with concepts in history and geography, abstract economic concepts can be made concrete more easily if you use the community and other resources in addition to the basic textbook. Students can see which jobs are performed in their own community and make comparisons with jobs of other historical periods. Field trips and resource people will help students understand local businesses. Students can participate in simulations like *Mini-Society* (Addison-Wesley) to begin learning how economic concepts work in our society.

Some teachers follow up field trips and visits from resource people by having students make and sell some product of their own, such as school T-shirts, cookies, or holiday gifts. In this way, students can actually act out the various roles involved in producing and selling a product or service.

Two areas related to economics are consumer education and career education. These areas are the more "practical" or personal side of the teaching of economics. Often these areas are integrated into other curriculum areas. For example, should the unit on how to write checks to be part of a math unit or a social studies unit? Your district may have guidelines about teaching them; if not, you will want to decide how much to include in your own curriculum. For both, but particularly for consumer education, you will need to determine whether a specific unit should be included each year or whether the topic should be integrated into other units. Many experts feel that unless they are taught as separate units, these topics will get scant attention.

Consumer education lends itself well to correlation with other subject matter like math and language arts. Students can make price comparisons of similar products at the supermarket. They can become more aware of the intent of advertising through analysis of commercials on television and ads in newspapers and magazines. Consumer education can be linked with the study of nutrition and ways we can improve our food buying and eating habits. Consumer education helps students develop skills to live more intelligently in the real world.

In a similar manner, the rationale for career education is that all adults need to be self-supporting, and this need usually involves employment. Some argue that girls and minority groups need specific career education to help them raise their sights and prepare to enter more responsible jobs and nontraditional careers. The recent rapid changes in the job structure, however, suggest that *everyone* has to be prepared to make work and career changes, and therefore a flexible attitude toward change as well as skills is necessary in the adult work market.

Career awareness and exploration can take many different formats. For the primary grades, parents who have various careers can bring what they wear to work and what they use as tools or equipment when they tell about their work. In grades four through eight, field trips to institutions such as hospitals may show the wide range of skills that a hospital needs to be able to offer its services. Students should move from the more familiar doctor and nurse to a consideration of people such as the X-ray technician, the dietitian, and the nurse's aide. Visits to hospitals, stores, offices, or factories can also illustrate the division of labor that is necessary in our modern society. Do not visit a factory or business that is too complex or abstract for your students. Generally, visiting an office or computer center is not as useful as visiting a place that makes a single product such as soft drinks. Services that are more difficult to "see" such as banking and finance also may be poor choices.

Along with increasing your students' focus on the wide range of occupations that exists in our society, be certain to include the affective domain. By the upper grades of middle or junior high school, students can handle a variety of value exercises on what they like to do. Then they can think of how their individual abilities and values may lead to possible career choices. At the elementary school and middle school level, however, no student should feel that something is wrong if he or she does not have a career choice. Students should be encouraged to be tentative about career goals and to be aware that each person has the potential for success and satisfaction in any number of occupations.

5.3 SMALL GROUP WORK: THE ROLE OF CONSUMER AND CAREER EDUCATION

What role do you think consumer education and career education should have at the elementary level? Write down your ideas and compare them with those of others in your class.

Political Science

Knowledge about the key concepts of government is essential for citizens to participate in our democratic society. Instruction in civics or government has been part of the elementary public school program for a long time. Yet in terms of producing active citizen participation even at the simple level of voting, educators still have a long way to go.

The Center for Civic Education drafted exit standards for civics and government that all students should reach by the twelfth grade as well as exit and content standards for grades K–4 and grades 5–8. These represent the knowledge and skills that all students should acquire. The organizing questions for grades K–4 are as follows:

1. What is government and what should it do?
2. What are the basic values and principles of American democracy?
3. How does the government established by the Constitution embody the purposes, values, and principles of American democracy?
4. What is the relationship of the United States to other nations and to world affairs?
5. What are the roles of the citizen in the American political system?

The organizing questions for grades 5–12 are these:

1. What are civic life, politics, and government?
2. What are the foundations of the American political system?
3. How are the values and principles of American constitutional democracy embodied in the government established by the Constitution?
4. What is the relationship of American politics and government to world affairs?
5. What are the roles of the citizen in American democracy?

Compare the K–4 civic standards with grades 5–12 standards. Notice the similarities.

Of all the national efforts to set social studies subject area standards, the Center for Civic Education's probably will have the most impact both because of the conciseness of its standards and because of popular support for the position that more civics education is needed. The Center for Civic Education wants this area to receive more attention as a subject co-equal with other subjects and stresses the need for systematic treatment for civics and government from kindergarten through twelfth grade. This subject is too important to be left just to the last year of high school. The Center feels that students, especially those from less privileged socioeconomic families, need both the formal school curriculum and informal activities, such as practicing democratic procedures, to acquire the knowledge and skills necessary for informed and effective citizenship.

Again, as with other academic subject areas, teachers may question whether the content standards are too high and ambitious for most students to achieve. For example, for the first content standard, "What is government and what should it do?" students at the end of the K–4 grades should be able to provide simple descriptions of government. This standard seems reachable. Students are to describe people and groups who have the right to make, apply, and enforce rules and laws for others in their school, community, and nation. Thus, students should recognize that teachers and principals enforce school rules. This and similar topics, such as why is government necessary and what is the purpose of rules and laws, are commonly taught in the primary grades and the fourth grade.

However, within the same standard, students are asked the differences between limited and unlimited governments and why limiting the power of the government is important. Unless these ideas are made very concrete, concepts like limited or unlimited government can be abstract for many students. Would you like to teach these civic and government standards if you were teaching K–4? They are likely to have high public support although a few critics may think they reflect a conservative, law-related focus.

What teachers and the schools do about citizenship skills is related to their ideas of what a good social studies program is. Those who follow the citizenship transmission model described in Chapter 1 probably will not take as many steps to see that the social studies program is producing active and knowledgeable citizens.

In Chapter 6 we focus in detail on citizenship education, both in the school and beyond the classroom, and address topics such as teaching the Bill of Rights. But here we briefly discuss *law-related education*, a promising development to help improve the teaching of civics and government at the elementary level. Law-related education seeks to promote an understanding of society and its system of laws so that students learn how they may effectively function within the law. In addition, law-related education tries to teach critical thinking skills regarding laws and issues facing our nation.

Law-related education makes use of case studies that focus on fictional or simplified versions of actual cases. Case studies have been constructed from fiction such as William Golding's *Lord of the Flies*, in which boys isolated on an island by a plane crash deal with the problem of trying to govern themselves, with some unfortunate consequences. Case studies appeal to human interest since they show individuals caught between conflicting demands or facing a real crisis, such as a prison sentence. A good case study should illustrate some principle or concept; otherwise, students may miss the point of the exercise. In addition, students must accurately understand the facts in the case so they can make a good decision about what action should be taken.

Again, as in the teaching of history, geography, and economics, the local community can be an important resource in law-related education. Law-related education can use field trips or guest speakers from one or all of the following agencies: the local, state, and national justice agencies such as the local police, the state police, and the Federal Bureau of Investigation; the local, state, and federal courts; the offices of the public defender and the public prosecutor; and the various people and facilities connected with corrections, such as probation officers, work camps, and detention halls for juveniles. In addition, lawyers are always a good resource. The use of action-oriented problems in the community such as getting out the vote or cleaning a public park can also be promising.

Substance abuse in the school/community can also be used as a topic. The school has a responsibility for developing plans to deal with drugs in the school. Students can think about how to evaluate rules concerning illegal drugs in their own school. Can a principal or an administrator search student lockers and book-bags? Should students found having illegal drugs be suspended from school? These questions of protecting the welfare of the group while respecting the rights of the individual are an important topic of law-related education and can be related to the students' lives.

The use of field experiences and guest speakers can help enliven dry text-books. Speakers reflect current views. As always, using these resources effectively requires planning and helping students to observe and to ask good questions. De-briefing students and summarizing the experience are always worthwhile in assess-ing what students have learned. To make the social sciences and history meaning-ful in the context of a student's own interests and experiences, teachers need to be careful planners and use a variety of methods.

CURRENT EVENTS/CURRENT AFFAIRS PROGRAMS

What is the role of current events or current affairs programs in the elementary school? Part of the rationale for such programs is the assumption that all citizens must eventually be aware of current issues in order to vote and make intelligent decisions. One of the purposes of teaching current events, then, is to begin arous-ing student interest in what is happening in the outside world.

In your own classroom, current events can be the glue that binds all other so-cial studies elements together. A newspaper article about an earthquake in Costa Rica can bring together history (have there been earthquakes there before?), geog-raphy (where is Costa Rica and what region did the earthquake affect?), economics (what will be the long-term economic damage to the people who have lost their homes?), and political science (how are the relief efforts organized?). Frequently, current events can be related to whatever unit you are studying, or, in reverse, you might ask students to look for newspaper articles about the country or period you are studying. It makes sense, if you are studying China, to have your students be aware of what is happening today in China.

Current affairs programs are not limited just to the upper grades. Primary stu-dents can also be encouraged to become interested in current events. However, as reading and viewing abilities become more developed, older students are more likely to have the skills necessary to find and to locate information about current events. Because current events programs serve multiple purposes, different teach-ers use different formats for them, as the following cases illustrate:

Case 1. Barbara Carpenter, a fourth-grade teacher, has current events every
day after lunch. Students are encouraged to bring in newspaper articles

that are of interest to them to share with the class. There are no specific criteria for what should be brought in, so the items range from what is happening in South Africa to local crime reports. There is only coincidental correlation between current events time and what is happening in the social studies program.

Case 2. Maria Gomez, a fifth-grade teacher, has current events every Friday. She has a set of classroom newspapers, *The Citizen Edition*, published by Scholastic for the fifth grade, that is distributed and read during the social studies period. Ms. Gomez likes to use the Scholastic Junior classroom newspapers because many of her students come from families in which not much attention is given to current events. Few if any newspapers and magazines are delivered to their homes. In addition, the Scholastic series tries to coordinate some issues that are commonly taught at the fifth-grade level. Ms. Gomez thinks the students enjoy reading the junior newspapers and she finds the suggestions for the teacher helpful.

Case 3. Samuel Bronski, a sixth-grade teacher, has current events every Thursday. At that time he uses the previous day's local newspapers, which are delivered to the school free of charge. Mr. Bronski never forgets to have current events day on Thursday since the stack of newspapers becomes a nuisance if they are not removed. His last social studies class of the day gets to keep the newspapers. Sometimes Mr. Bronski finds that certain sections (e.g., the sports section) disappear before the last period of the day. Throughout the year Mr. Bronski has explained the different sections of the newspapers to the students. To be certain that they read more than just the comics, Mr. Bronski prepares a few questions for each student to answer during the current events class period. He thinks the students enjoy having and reading the adult newspapers.

Case 4. Andrew Oleson, a seventh-grade teacher, coordinates the current events program with the unit he is teaching. When the class is studying Russia, only items from newspapers or magazines that pertain to Russia can be brought to the class to be reported on. The items than are put on the designated bulletin board under the heading "Russia." Students get extra credit for the news items they bring as their class reports. Current events teaching occurs only within the regular social studies period.

Case 5. Ann Bronstein, an eighth-grade teacher, has current events every Friday. At the beginning of the year, five categories are chosen: international news, national news, state news, local news, and sports. The category of sports is a concession to students' high interest. At the beginning of each week, five students are given one of the above topics, which they report on in class on Friday. All students eventually have a turn, and every five weeks a new cycle is started. The students use the format of a television show, with each specialist reporting on his or her category. Students are encouraged to make use of magazines such as *Time* or *Newsweek*. Students are motivated to illustrate or use the chalkboard in their reports as they each receive a grade based on content *and* delivery.

5.4 ON YOUR OWN: YOUR VIEWPOINT ON CURRENT EVENTS PROGRAMS

Which of the above current events programs do you like the best? What appear to be the strengths or the weaknesses of each program?

Again, you see that your values make a difference in the teaching of current events. Regardless of your point of view, teaching current events requires a rich array of resources and materials.

Some teachers use current events as a separate subject with little or accidental correlation with the social studies program; other teachers use current events to supplement or reinforce what is going on in the regular program. Only in very rare cases would a teacher use current events as the basis for actual social studies units, since it is difficult to plan units around unpredictable events. However, a teacher could start a unit, especially on a given nation like the Japan or Israel, by focusing on that nation's current events.

A second area of difference among teachers is the sources used by both the teacher and the class to get current events data. This decision can be affected by the teacher's knowledge of the background of the students' families. Students from families that have a wide range of printed material probably do not have to use the junior newspapers prepared specifically for the schools. However, there are several advantages of using commercially prepared classroom newspapers published by Scholastic and Bruce Seide Publisher (*My Weekly Reader* [K–6], *Current Events* [7–8], *Scholastic News* [K–5] and *Junior Scholastic* [6–8], and *News-Currents* [3–12 and ESL, that is, students in classes teaching English as a second language]). If these newspapers are in the class, you are more likely to use them. Also they are objective and contain articles that are within the range of interest and comprehension of children. But some teachers do not use the commercial junior newspapers as a learning experience. Instead, they distribute them when there are only ten minutes left in the day. Students then get the message that current events are just a fill-in for killing time. It is little wonder that they learn to seek out the more enjoyable features of the commercial junior newspapers, like the comics.

Ideally, as they grow older, students should move into using adult sources of information. For this reason, the use of newspapers can provide an opportunity for learning valuable skills. Students can profit by exercises showing how an index like "Today's Contents" or "Inside" helps to locate specific features of the newspapers. Reading headlines is important, and it is especially helpful if your community has two local newspapers so that students can compare the headlines of the two newspapers on a given day. Occasionally, bringing in a well-regarded national newspaper such as the *New York Times* or the *Los Angeles Times* is helpful; compare them with local newspapers. Bringing in foreign newspapers as well as specialized newspapers such as the *Wall Street Journal* can also help students see the wide variety of newspapers available.

Distinguishing between an editorial and a news story is another important skill. Give students a news item that is accurate, fair, and objective and an editorial on the same topic. Ask them which article wants action to be taken; which article best describes what is happening; which articles tells the writer's feelings.

An increasing number of people depend on television as their source of news. It is likely that more of today's teachers will tape parts of current news programs on their VCRs to show to their students. Fax or on-line support is available for teachers from the CNN newsroom (at this writing, the informational number is 1-800-344-6219).

Current events may be related to the teaching of controversial issues, as many items of current events at the local, state, national, and international levels are controversial. Here again, the teacher as a decision maker must decide what role she or he will take in teaching controversial events. Having access to a wide variety of information sources such as newspapers and magazines will help students see the emotional impact of a division of opinion on a given issue as well as the differences in viewpoints. Many teachers encourage students to bring news items for a bulletin board. If this is done, students should change the news items frequently.

TEACHING CONTROVERSIAL ISSUES

As students become older, they become better able to discuss controversial issues. There is no shortage of controversial issues in our society; economics and government policy, for example, have always provoked differences among citizens. Drugs, AIDS, and abortion generate strongly held views among citizens. What should be done to improve the economic well-being of our nation? There is certainly a wide divergence of opinion among citizens as well as between groups such as business and labor. What should be our policy on foreign aid? Again, a wide difference of opinion exists.

Among social studies educators, there is much debate over what role teachers should assume in the teaching of controversial issues. Teachers' methods have been criticized in their communities. There have been court cases in which the question of academic freedom to discuss controversial issues for both teachers and students has been considered. In general, the courts have ruled that teachers can discuss these controversial issues if they are appropriate to the academic subject area. This means that a math teacher would probably not be protected by the courts if he or she discussed abortion during a math class.

Here are four typical roles that teachers play in presenting controversial issues:

Case 1. Gloria Young does not discuss any topics that she thinks are controversial in her fourth-grade class. She believes that the classroom must be a neutral place and does not like it when students argue and bicker among themselves. Ms. Young thinks it is best to shield students from unpleasant topics that may upset them. She believes children have a greater sense of security if they can think that all is well in their community and that they should not be unduly concerned about local or world events. Ms. Young also thinks that her principal appreciates her not posing a problem for parents who might be upset to learn that controversial issues are being discussed in the classroom.

Case 2. In the next room, teaching the fifth grade, is Carol Taylor. She is a civil rights advocate and a feminist and has a deep commitment to educating students on the injustices that women and other minority groups have suffered in the past. In her teaching of U.S. history she emphasizes how these minority groups were unfairly treated.

Ms. Taylor believes she knows the right position on controversial issues that come up in the classroom and made clear to the parents at an October open house how she feels. She argues that all Americans should have equal rights. Unlike Ms. Young, Ms. Taylor does not ignore controversial issues and actually welcomes their inclusion, especially as they relate to her teaching of U.S. history. Ms. Taylor is constantly bringing up questions on how the budgets of governmental units should be changed, with more emphasis on job retaining and antidiscrimination efforts.

If a student with a different viewpoint suggests another idea, Ms. Taylor calmly ignores it and proceeds to present her point of view. Ms. Taylor thinks that students hear and learn more in the media about accepting the status quo than making changes to improve the position of women and African Americans. She feels her job is to free her students from these "false" ideas.

Case 3. Marianne Ash teaches seventh grade in the same school. She believes that controversial issues should be discussed in the classroom. However, she also believes that she should be neutral and downplay her own views on certain issues. Even when students ask her how she will vote on a certain issue or what she thinks about a policy, Ms. Ash does not think it is appropriate for students to know. She is afraid that some students might accept her position without considering it carefully or that a few students who are not fond of her might immediately take the opposite position.

Ms. Ash encourages her students to present a variety of viewpoints on a given controversial issue. She tries to guide the discussion, toward which people will benefit from a given issue (e.g., rent control) and which people will be the losers. Ms. Ash believes that with rational discussion students can clarify their own positions after hearing a variety of viewpoints.

Case 4. Shirley Baker is a teacher in the eighth grade in the same school. Like Ms. Taylor and Ms. Ash, Ms. Baker believes that controversial issues should be discussed in the classroom. But unlike Ms. Ash, Ms. Baker gives her own point of view on issues. She tells students how she will vote on certain issues. On her car is a bumper sticker indicating her viewpoint on ecology. In her classroom, Ms. Baker thinks she should be a model of a politically active citizen. She tells the students about the organizations she belongs to that have a political focus. In the classroom, Ms. Baker brings in a variety of speakers with different points of view. She also uses a combination of other methods such as library research and group discussions to help students clarify how they feel on a given controversial issue.

5.5 SMALL GROUP WORK: VIEWPOINTS ON CONTROVERSIAL ISSUES

Which position do you think is the best of the four previously described for the teaching of controversial issues? Which one would you like to model? Give your reasons for your position.

As you can see, there are many opinions on the proper role of an elementary teacher in teaching about controversial issues. But in the previous four cases, there is another person whom we may have overlooked. That person is Dr. Jane Menshi, the principal of the school. She keeps hoping that the school district will issue some guidelines on the teaching of controversial events and the role of academic freedom for teachers and students. She knows that her teachers are handling controversial issues in many different ways. She has received a few complaints from parents about Ms. Taylor's strong position but was able to tell them that at least Ms. Taylor is open about her principles. If the parents want to bring up additional facts to teach to their own children what they think is right, they should do so. Dr. Menshi always points out to parents that the research on political socialization indicates that parents and the family are the most important factors in influencing what children believe about political issues. Dr. Menshi's discussions with parents have satisfied them and no parent has complained to a higher administrator.

Dr. Menshi, however, is a little concerned about the social actions that Ms. Baker wants to take. Ms. Baker believes that students need the experience of working in their community areas. She wants students to help support the local political candidates of their choice. The students would attend meetings of these political candidates and do tasks such as handing out political literature for the candidates for office. No student would be forced to do this community action, but students who want an "A" in the class probably realize that Ms. Baker is apt to look with favor on those who participate actively in community affairs. Ms. Baker even suggested to Dr. Menshi that students help in the political campaigns of school board members. What would the board members think of that? Dr. Menshi was very worried about this but did not know what she should do. What do you think would be the best position for the principal to take with regard to outside political action on the part of the eighth graders in her school? Can your class role-play some of the alternatives?

In looking over the four teachers' positions on teaching controversial issues, you can see that each has its advantages and disadvantages. The four positions move along a continuum from the teacher who does nothing about controversial events to the teacher who would like her class to take social action in the community. Social studies experts themselves disagree on the proper position for teaching controversial events, but most of them would not support Ms. Young's total avoidance of controversial issues in the classroom. This is simply an unrealistic position in an age in which students are bombarded by the media with news of their community, nation, and the world. Children are aware of problems and controversial issues outside the classroom, and sheltering them from these real problems, especially as they are growing older, does not make sense. The experience of the Persian Gulf War showed that in families and classrooms where the war was not discussed, children were more anxious and concerned about their well-being than when the war was openly examined. To become effective citizens, students need to be able to make judgments on issues. Furthermore, even if she does not realize it, Ms. Young is teaching values. Her stance as a person unconcerned about controversial issues is probably not a good model of what a teacher should be (see Figure 5.1).

Ms. Taylor is trying to get students to accept certain positions. In effect, this is a form of indoctrination. Viewpoints different from hers are not given much attention. In this case Ms. Taylor is supporting a liberal position; however, advocates of indoctrination can range from Marxists to conservatives, all of whom believe it is their duty to pass on their particular ideology. These true believers are really authoritarian teachers with regard to the teaching of their own value systems. They are not giving students the opportunity to hear other points of view.

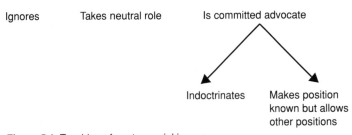

Figure 5.1 Teaching of controversial issues

The advantages of Ms. Ash's position are that students are exposed to a wide variety of viewpoints on a given issue, and Ms. Ash uses a variety of methods with which students can study the issue. Ms. Baker's position is similar to that of Ms. Ash, except that Ms. Baker gives her own position on issues. She makes her positions clear to the class.

Is this good? At least teachers like Ms. Baker let students know what the teacher believes. In many cases, students are perceptive enough to guess where teachers such as Ms. Ash stand by "reading" verbal and nonverbal clues. For example, without realizing it, teachers often do not write on the board the ideas suggested by students whom they do not like.

In effect, Ms. Ash and teachers like her want to play the role of a nonpartisan referee. This position probably receives the most support in the teaching of controversial issues. It is also a noncontroversial point of view with the community, which normally does not object if the teacher plays this role. Advocates of social action like Ms. Baker are likely to find themselves being attacked for pushing young "impressionable" students into political action. This is especially true when the action involves local issues. In some cases, however, teachers have been rewarded with praise and publicity, especially if the social action takes the form of doing something popular like cleaning up the local beach or getting out the vote.

The proper role of teacher in teaching controversial events is not likely to be settled in the near future since it is basically a values issue. Topics such as abortion are highly sensitive in many communities. Court cases on the rights of teachers and students continue to define the limits of academic freedom and free speech. Policy statements by local districts on the teaching of controversial events are helpful, as these statements generally support academic freedom. The National Council for the Social Studies has issued a position paper on academic freedom and the social studies teacher, which treats explicitly the teaching of controversial issues.[3] The guidelines outline the rights and responsibilities of teachers, the selection of educational materials, and visiting speakers. These guidelines also encourage teachers to introduce controversial issues in their teaching. But regardless of the position you take on teaching controversial issues, you need to recognize that ultimately all students as citizens will have to make decisions about these issues.

SUMMARY

Moving beyond the textbook in the middle grades means making the content of history and the social sciences (geography, economics, political science, etc.) more relevant to students. Oral history, family history, community history, children's literature, studies of shopping centers, and law-related education speakers can add zest to social studies programs. In addition, teachers must decide how they will teach current events/current affairs and controversial issues as well as considering how new discipline standards may change their teaching.

---

[3]National Council for the Social Studies. *Social Education* 55 (January, 1991): 13–15.

SUGGESTED READINGS

Bradley Commission on History in Schools. *Building a History Curriculum: Guidelines for Teaching History in Schools.* Washington D.C.: Educational Excellence Network, 1988. Suggestions of historians for teaching history.

Center for Civic Education. *National Standards for Civics and Government.* Calabasas, Calif.: Center for Civic Education, 1994. Report of the civics and government standards.

Cheney, Lynne V., and Shanker, Albert. "Mutual Suspicions." *The New Republic* 212, no. 6 (February 6, 1995): 4.

Jorgensen, Karen L. *History Workshop: Reconstructing the Past with Elementary Students.* Portsmouth, N.H.: Heinemann, 1993. Children create historical meaning as they interact with others.

Levstik, Linda S. "Teaching History: A Definitional and Developmental Dilemma." *Elementary School Social Studies: Research as a Guide to Practice.* Bulletin 79. Washington, D.C.: National Council for the Social Studies, 1986, 68–84. Discusses different approaches including Kieran Egan's ideas on the use of narrative as an aid to historical understanding.

Nash, Gary B., and Dunn, Ross E. "History Standards and Culture Wars." Social Education 59 (1), 1995, 57. Codirector and coordinating editor for the world history standards answer critics.

National Center for History in the Schools. *National Standards for United States History: Exploring the American Experience; National Standards for World History: Exploring Paths to the Present;* and *National Standards for History: Expanding Children's World in Time and Space.* Los Angeles: University of California, 1994. The three books reporting history standards.

National Council for Geographic Education. *Geography for Life: National Geography Standards 1994.* Washington, D.C.: National Geographic Society, 1994. Report of the geography standards.

Provenzo, Eugene, Jr., and Provenzo, Asterie Baker. *Pursuing the Past: Oral History, Photographs, Family History, Cemeteries.* Menlo Park, Calif.: Addison-Wesley, 1984. Good on past oral history.

Ravitch, Diane, and Finn, Chester, Jr. *What Do Our 17-Year-Olds Know? A Report on the First National Assessment of History and Literature.* New York: Harper & Row, 1987. A critical report on the poor achievement of American students in history.

Wronski, Stanley P., and Bragaw, Donald H., eds. *Social Studies and Social Sciences: A Fifty-Year Perspective.* Bulletin 78. Washington, D.C.: National Council for the Social Studies, 1986. Changes in both fields during the past fifty years.

Chapter

6

ELEMENTARY CITIZENSHIP EDUCATION

In this chapter we view citizenship education from a broad perspective. Not only is citizenship defined, but also the concept is related to the classroom, the school, and the community. These sections will assist you in gaining a broad perspective of the most fundamental goal of social studies education:

1/ Defining Citizenship

2/ Classroom Citizenship

3/ Citizenship in School

4/ Linking Schoolwide Citizenship to the Community

5/ Instruction in Citizenship

6/ Global Citizenship

What do you think of when you hear the term *citizenship education?* Does it sound abstract, adult, and far removed from the elementary classroom? It is true that children entering school have twelve years before they can exercise full citizenship rights. Even so, the experiences children have in elementary school can directly influence the attitudes and ideas they gain about citizenship. School and classroom events that involve seeking fairness under rules and cooperative problem solving can give students tangible contact with democratic values that they may not have opportunities to experience in other facets of their lives. More formal study of what democratic values are and how they evolve provides a context for critical thinking about how we can organize our lives for the greater good of all people. To better understand the power of schools in citizenship education, we need to explore two issues. First, we must consider what attributes or knowledge the citizenship role requires. Second, we must consider how children can best acquire these attributes.

DEFINING CITIZENSHIP

What does a citizen do? Often the answer we give depends on our frame of reference. Unfortunately, schools have often put into practice a narrow, almost authoritarian model of citizenship in their award and recognition systems. To be labeled "good citizens" in many elementary schools, children need only to obey and cooperate. By contrast, "good citizens" in our local communities are those who not only obey laws but also seek to conserve public property or come to the aid of someone in distress. They may strive to keep their neighborhoods drug free and raise issues of fairness in public, even when doing so is resisted by the majority.

For teachers, the orderly classroom frame of reference can lead to a focus that is entirely on the rule-following, obedient side of citizenship. In their anxiety to create environments where students can get on with the business of learning, teachers are prone to skip over the necessary step of exploring democratic values—fairness, equality, dignity of the individual, caring for each other, cooperation for the good of the group—that classroom order should knowingly uphold. We need to enact a definition of citizenship in classrooms and schools that promotes an active rather than a passive citizenship. We have to keep in mind the aspects of good citizenship that promote justice seeking and critical thinking: Good citizens protest misuse of authority by police and public officials. Good citizens seek new laws as a way of making desirable change. Good citizens complain when they see examples of government wasting taxpayer money. Active citizenship is not necessarily "orderly."

The active as well as the orderly component should be present in our definition of citizenship. We need to use the basics of democracy as guidelines for the system of school citizenship we devise. Some basics of democracy are that each person has one vote; citizens have equal protection under the law; decisions are made by majority vote; decisions and laws can be reviewed and amended by lawful process; decisions and government acts are based on law; and individual rights to religious beliefs, privacy, and speech are protected by the government. Classic democratic theory and practice as well as contemporary research support the centrality of the school's role in imparting these basic values and skills. Educational theorists such as John Dewey have demonstrated that children learn from experience to plan their own learning and consider how best to organize their classroom environments. The Lab School Dewey directed at the University of Chicago in the early 1900s promoted children's learning by projects and group planning and research.[1] Longitudinal data from the High/Scope preschool curriculum suggest that when at-risk children have experience in the area of planning and evaluation of daily activities, they achieve greater sociopersonal success as young adults and become contributing members of society.[2]

These two illustrations speak directly to the importance of developing citizenship in classrooms. They suggest that citizenship development based on democratic values should guide the way we organize our classrooms and learning experiences. Knowledge about the way children learn suggests that care must be taken in the way citizenship attributes are developed. The old adage about the futility of "do what I say, not what I do" is pertinent to acquiring these skills. Being told about democratic citizenship is not the best learning mode for children. Nor will they learn to be active citizens by following a set of rules and behaviors prescribed by the teachers or the school that requires absolute, unquestioning obedience.

Currently, several discipline, or classroom-management, systems are popular in classrooms. These systems, whether advertised as such or not, are versions of citizenship education. And each should be evaluated using the broader term *citizenship* rather than accepted under the apparently benign title *classroom management*. The Assertive Discipline Program and Jones's Classroom Management Training Program are two of the better-known systems. Each one has its own merits. Each can be helpful in making us think about and organize the way we handle our students so they can have an orderly and pleasant place in which to learn. However, when we consider adopting any classroom-management system we should ask ourselves citizenship education questions about it:

> Does it promote self-regulating behavior?
> Is it consistent with the way children learn?
> Does it promote critical thinking and decision making?
> Does it promote positive self-regard?

---

[1] John Dewey, *How We Think* (Boston: Heath & Company, 1993).
[2] W. S. Barnett, "The Percy Preschool Program and Its Long-Term Effects: A Benefit-Cost Analysis," *High/Scope Early Childhood Papers,* no. 2 (Ypsilanti, Mich.: High/Scope Press, 1985).

Affirmative responses to these questions are good indicators that the management system is consistent with the goal of developing democratic citizenship capabilities of children. Most teachers find that no one classroom-management system meets all their preferences and settings. Being required to adopt an entire system with little or no discussion of the type of citizenship education it implies should be resisted. Obtaining schoolwide consistency in discipline and management of behavior makes sense in a bureaucratic way; but rules should contribute more than consistency of student behavior. Does the rule have democratic value for the students? What is the decision-making role of teachers in enforcing it? To accept the principle that discipline and decision making both need to be taught consistently does not resolve the issues of how to obtain discipline while promoting decision making in a particular school or classroom.

When we consider how to organize citizenship education for the elementary grades, two components need to be included. Both are equally important. One is the more obvious and traditional instruction about the social institutions and procedures we have devised to maintain order as a large, diverse group of individuals in society. For this component, direct instruction *about* our system of government and its underlying values such as justice and equality continues to be an important responsibility in the elementary curriculum. A second component we need to organize is how to do, or the *process* of, citizenship. To acquire the attributes and commitment necessary for this part of citizenship, students must be involved in constructing, monitoring, and modifying rules and their application. Without experiencing, from the earliest school ages, the processes of self-governance, students will have greater difficulty in assimilating the "book-learning" about citizenship as well as putting into action as citizens the skills needed in decision making on controversial issues.

CLASSROOM CITIZENSHIP

The major task we elementary teachers have every new school year is teaching our classroom system to new students. Routines (for entering and leaving the classroom, for getting supplies, for getting information from the teacher, for keeping the classroom orderly) are modeled and practiced. In the first days of a new school year, teachers are "lawgivers." Children must learn to handle these routines for the business of the class to run smoothly. Once these routines are put into practice, the teacher needs to take the democratic step of helping children see that they are responsible for constructing the atmosphere of the classroom. This is easily done by leading the children in evaluating and changing or modifying the set of rules used to begin the school year. This process of evaluation, proposing change, trying it out, and evaluating again should continue until consensus is reached on rules that govern the class.

In addition to the ongoing plan for rule development, the following strategies are typically used to help children perfect these routines while fostering their active involvement with organizing their school day.

1. Begin a day or period by discussing and planning a schedule.
2. Reinforce children who perform the desired routines.
3. Conduct evaluation at the end of day or period that discusses "how we did with our routines," "what we need to finish tomorrow," and "how we can improve our work."

By following these steps students are learning to play the procedural, or disciplinary, side of citizenship in a classroom society. It is imperative, for everyone's benefit, that this discipline be taught and learned. Teachers should ask students why they think we plan and evaluate. How does this help us? Are we being fair to each other? How could we work together to get more done?

For children to develop active citizenship skills, the class system must allow them to make decisions. Some teachers build student choice periods into their daily or weekly schedule (Table 6.1). During these times students sign up for their choices. Teachers usually have a poster or bulletin board with slots where students may place their names to assist with traffic control and the negotiation of "equal access" to the most popular activities.

Organizing students to assume responsibilities for classroom duties is another important way to let children practice citizenship. Typically, duties include cleanup and leadership roles. The variety included in this array of tasks depends on the student age and classroom design. Figure 6.1 is an outline of fourth-grade jobs developed by Joan Elston and Barbara Mumma.

Elston rotates children through these roles. Her goal is to permit each student to have practice in both leadership and "followership," starring and supporting roles. All who visit this classroom sense the ownership and pride the system gives these students.

Classroom meetings are another essential strategy for modeling decision making. Decisions about real choices must be the agenda.

TABLE 6.1 STUDENT CHOICES OF PLACE/ACTIVITY

Kindergarten	*Third Grade*	*Fifth Grade*
Sand table	Computer	Typewriter/computer
Painting easel	Listening post	Experiment table
Bookcase/pillows	Filmstrip viewer	Art project
Typewriter/computer	Library corner	Media/library
Dress-up corner	Math games, experiments	Listening post
Block corner		

President
take attendance
pass lunch tickets
lead flag salute

Vice President
do daily checklist
substitute for president
take attendance to office
  messenger

Secretary
write thank you notes
keep field-trip checklist
fill paper drawers

Treasurer
record service points
collect, count money
distribute book orders

Room Maintenance
wash boards
open, close windows
empty pencil sharpener
empty wastebasket
scour sink

Technical Engineers
setup, operate equipment

Table Chairperson
lead group tasks
hand out supplies, handouts
collect papers
check desks for neatness

Figure 6.1 Classroom citizenship roles and responsibilities. Outline of fourth-grade jobs developed by Joan Elston and Barbara Mumma, Collins School, Cupertino, California.

Whatever the issue, the meetings should have the following criteria:

1. A signal for wanting to speak
2. A discussion leader (teacher for earlier grades)
3. A discussion of the choices that examines good and bad possible results of each choice
4. The possibility of seeking more information before voting
5. A way of voting secretly so that each child votes his or her own feeling
6. A way of following through to see that the vote is honored

Look for these criteria in the following transcript. As you read, think about the payoffs for the citizenship skills children can gain from classroom time spent this way.

SAMPLE CLASSROOM EPISODE 6.1

Looking in a Classroom: Classroom Decision Making

Mr. Cervantes wanted his first grade to thank the fifth grade class that had brought their puppet show on important U.S. presidents to the first graders. Mr. Cervantes opened the meeting with this question: "Who remembers some of the things we learned about the presidents from the fifth graders yesterday?" (Various children volunteer information they remember.)

Mr. Cervantes: What were some of the things you liked most about the show? (Various children describe what they liked.)

Mr. Cervantes: How could we thank the fifth graders?

Jesus: We could tell them on the playground.

Mr. Cervantes: Yes, that would be one way. Does anyone else have a suggestion?

Kerry: We could send them a letter.

Mr. Cervantes: Yes. Are there any more suggestions about how we could thank them?

Erin: We could go to their class and tell them.

Mr. Cervantes: Those are all suggestions I want us to think more about. What would be good about telling them on the playground?

Jake: It's easy to do.

Jenny: Not for me.

Mr. Cervantes: What are some problems with telling them on the playground?

Jenny: I don't know who the fifth graders are.

Mr. Cervantes: Well, let's think about the second suggestion. What are some good things about the idea of sending a letter? (Mr. Cervantes leads the discussion to cover all suggestions.)

Mr. Cervantes: You've given some good things for us to think about. Are you ready to decide? So that we each vote the way we think, I'm going to ask you to close your eyes and raise your hand when I ask for the choice you want. Are you ready? How do you show me?

POSTSCRIPT:

The class voted to go to the fifth graders and tell them, not Mr. Cervantes's choice. He wanted to use the event to write letters. Now he's thinking about how to honor the vote while capitalizing on the oral language opportunity presented by going to the fifth-grade class. What would you do?

Zooming our imaginary lens back into the classroom a few minutes later, we see that Mr. Cervantes is quickly taking them into preparing a choral reading "thank you" that will have all the children saying "we learned a lot from you," interspersed with individual children telling one thing they learned, such as "George Washington had false teeth made of wood."

6.1 *ON YOUR OWN: DECIDING THE BOUNDARIES OF COOPERATIVE PLANNING*

> How would you change the roles if instead of a first-grade class thanking a fifth-grade class, the fifth graders were thanking the first graders? Should Mr. Cervantes have manipulated the situation when the children did not prefer his choice? Or did he follow the spirit of the class? Would the same method work with a fifth grade?

There is a moral to this episode. Teachers should not embark on class decision making unless they are willing to abide by the decision the class makes. As the example showed, Mr. Cervantes structured the decision-making episode; he did not dictate the decision. He integrated language arts with the experience but not the element of language arts he had envisioned. As teachers, we choose issues that are appropriate to class decision making. How do you feel about allowing the class to decide whether to study math or social studies? We think that would be going too far. As teachers, our professional responsibility is to organize investigation in the different curricular areas. Making decisions about how to present something and selecting from a list of choices are appropriate for elementary students.

Conflict Resolution with Groups and Individuals as Citizenship Skill Building

The second part of learning ways to live together goes beyond organizing students to assume classroom responsibilities and procedures. Disagreements and conflicts between individuals and groups will arise no matter how imaginative and thorough the system for making classrooms and playgrounds run smoothly. Two strategies for helping students learn how to work through these incidents complete the well-rounded plan for citizenship development. One is conflict resolution, which engages individuals involved in a dispute in finding a mutually acceptable alternative. The second is the class meeting, which leads the whole class to work out a solution to a generally felt problem.[3] Study the steps for both strategies in Table 6.2 as a guide to evaluating the classroom incidents that follow. Ask yourself if you agree with the strategy chosen to address the conflict in each.

Bernie the Bully. A fourth-grade class is just returning from a recess during which Bernie reportedly shoved Sharif to the ground when Sharif came up to take his turn kicking in the dodgeball game. The teacher, Ms. Stearns, convenes a meeting to discuss better ways of sharing on the playground. Ms. Stearns asks Sharif what happened during the dodgeball game. Sharif hangs his head and says nothing. Penny, the original reporter, raises her hand and repeats that Bernie wouldn't let Sharif take a turn and pushed him down.

Bernie glares at Penny and grunts a noncommittal "Yeah" to Ms. Stearns's

---

[3]William Glasser, *Schools without Failure* (New York: Harper & Row, 1969).

TABLE 6.2 STRATEGIES FOR RESOLVING CONFLICT

Between Individuals	*Class Meetings*
1. Both individuals stop, cool off.	1. Leader asks whether anyone has problem group needs to discuss.
2. Both take turns talking about what is wrong.	2. When problem is volunteered, leader asks show of hands for agreement to hold meeting on problem mentioned.
3. Individuals listen to each other without interrupting.	
4. Each one tries to tell what he or she needs.	3. Leader asks group to define what problem issue is.
5. They brainstorm possible solutions.	
6. Individuals choose solution both like.	4. Group lists ways problem can be solved.
7. Individuals plan how to put solution into action.	5. Group evaluates and chooses solution.
8. Individuals "go" for plan.	

query for confirmation. Ms. Stearns turns to the class and asks, "How can we be certain that this type of problem does not happen again?"

Several children make comments to the effect that they don't have the problem, that Bernie has the problem. Ms. Stearns asks Bernie how he can change his behavior. Bernie screws up his face and spits out, "Let 'em play."

Dodgeball Dodgers.   Several children request to stay inside during recess. After the rest of the class goes out, Ms. Stearns asks the group why lately they have chosen to stay inside. They make comments that recess is boring and that if you're not a superstar, it's better not to play in the dodgeball game. After recess Ms. Stearns convenes a class meeting with the question, "What could we do to make sure everyone has a good time during recess?" Children suggest various ideas, some of which are about sportsmanship on the dodgeball field. Having listed their ideas, Ms. Stearns asks the children to vote for the two most important ideas to put into practice during recess. One of the most voted items is to "stop calling other people bad names during dodgeball." The other is "don't keep the same team members every recess."

After negotiating how to handle the team item, Ms. Stearns closes the meeting by charging everyone to put these ideas into practice next recess time.

Thinking about the Cases.   Did you agree with the strategies chosen in each case? Our reaction is that a class meeting was appropriately used in the second case, but that individual conflict resolution would have better fit the situation in the first case. It is true in the first case that Ms. Stearns may have helped Sharif get a chance to play, but she used a sledgehammer to kill a fly as far as Bernie is concerned. And Penny had better watch out for Bernie next time they're on the playground! We must be cautious to ensure that in our zeal to promote class resolution of problems we are not creating more individual problems. In other words, individual problems are not the best topics for group decision making.

It will always be true that individual students will require continuous and spe-cial attention beyond group strategies. Many schools are training students to assume arbitrator roles in conflict resolution between peers.[4] After learning to recognize conflict situations, these students form a "Peace Patrol" during out-of-class times. They try to stop conflict between two individuals before it escalates by applying the "win-win" approach of each party communicating what he or she needs to resolve the conflict and then negotiating a solution that gives something to both.

Students learn to assess their negotiations for the elements of a positive conflict resolution: Does the agreement meet the concerns of both parties and solve the problem? Do all the students in the dispute share responsibility to make the solu-tion work? Do the students know who is to do what, when, where, and how? Is the agreement realistically something the students can do? Teachers learn guidelines, too. By refraining from blaming or judging or lecturing or fixing, teachers give to students the responsibility for negotiating conflicts and arriving at agreements.

6.2 *SMALL GROUP WORK: MANAGING GROUP AND INDIVIDUAL CONFLICT*

Take turns describing a classroom conflict incident you have witnessed or expe-rienced that required the management of conflict by the teacher. Discuss which of these strategies could have best been used for each. Explore the limits and exceptions you sense in these strategies. How do you see them as part of citi-zenship building?

Emphasizing Values in the Classroom as Citizenship Development

In addition to the procedural approaches of daily student planning, choosing, eval-uating, and developing self-responsibility through class governance, class meet-ings, and specific training that gives students responsibility for conflict resolution, many parents and curriculum planners are calling for a more direct focus on teach-ing values. Figure 6.2 lists the values the Georgia State Board of Education has asked teachers to develop throughout all levels of the school programs. The intent is that these core values will pervade both the skill and knowledge components of citizenship education.

Procedurally, the strategy of values analysis can perhaps best serve as a way to focus on the intent of such mandates. Values analysis can seem almost identical

---

[4]Conflict resolution is commonly a component of districtwide programs for reducing violence in schools. Some sources for adapting aspects of this approach in individual classrooms and schools in-clude Naomi Drew, *Learning the Skills of Peacemaking* (Rolling Hills Estates, Calif.: Jalmar Press, 1987); Ruth Fletcher, *Teaching Peace: Skills for Living in a Global Society* (San Francisco: Harper & Row, 1986); William Kriedler, *Creative Conflict Resolution: More than 200 Activities for Keeping Peace in the Class-room* (Glenview, Ill.: Scott, Foresman, 1984).

Citizenship
  Democracy: government of, by and for the people, exercised through the voting process
  Respect for and acceptance of authority: the need for and primacy of authority, including the law, in given circumstances
  Equality: the right and opportunity to develop one's potential as a human being
  Freedom of conscience and expression: the right to hold beliefs, whether religious, ethical, or political, and to express one's views
  Justice: equal and impartial treatment under the law
  Liberty: freedom from oppression, tyranny, or the domination of government
  Tolerance: recognition of the diversity of others, their opinions, practices, and culture

  Patriotism: support of and love for the United States of America with zealous guarding of its welfare
  Courage: willingness to face obstacles and danger with determination
  Loyalty: steadfastness or faithfulness to a person, institution, custom, or idea to which one is tied by duty, pledge, or a promise

  Respect for the natural environment: care for and conservation of land, trees, clean air, and pure water and of all living inhabitants of the earth
  Conservation: avoiding waste and pollution of natural resources

Respect for Others
  Altruism: concern for and motivation to act for the welfare of others
  Civility: courtesy and politeness in action or speech
  Compassion: concern for suffering or distress of others and response to their feelings and needs
  Courtesy: recognition of mutual interdependence with others, resulting in polite treatment and respect for them

  Integrity: confirmed virtue and uprightness of character; freedom from hypocrisy
  Honesty: truthfulness and sincerity
  Truth: freedom from deceit or falseness; based on fact or reality
  Trustworthiness: worthy of confidence

Respect for Self
  Accountability: responsibility for one's actions and their consequences
  Commitment: being emotionally, physically or intellectually bound to something
  Perseverance: adherence to action, belief or purpose without giving way
  Self-control: exercising authority over one's emotions and actions
  Frugality: effective use of resources; thrift

  Self-esteem: pride and belief in oneself and in achievement of one's potential
  Knowledge: learning, understanding, awareness
  Moderation: avoidance of extreme views or measures
  Respect for physical, mental, and fiscal health: awareness of the importance of and conscious activity toward maintaining fitness in these areas

  Work ethic: belief that work is good and that everyone who can, should work
  Accomplishment: appreciation for completing a task
  Cooperation: working with others for mutual benefit
  Dependability: reliability; trustworthiness
  Diligence: attentiveness, persistence, perseverence
  Pride: dignity, self-respect, doing one's best
  Productivity: supporting one's self, contributing to society
  Creativity: exhibiting an entrepreneurial spirit, inventiveness, originality, not bound by the norm

Figure 6.2 Georgia core values. Source: List of Core Values from Georgia Board of Education, Office of Instructional Services Division for Student Support, Atlanta, Georgia, 1992.

to the class meeting procedures described in the second case about dodgeball. The difference may come in the elaboration of the problem situation: In the class meeting after the problem is defined, the teacher calls for suggestions for solving it; students discuss these and resolve the issue by voting for the best alternative to solve the problem. In values analysis, however, the steps in exploring a problem situation are more consciously elaborated to bring out the underlying values, or concerns, of the issue as well as those values embedded within proposed solutions. Further, in values analysis the possible consequences for each proposed solution are explored. The steps for values analysis are listed below.

Values Analysis Strategy

1. Identify the problem.
2. Clarify the value question(s).
3. Gather and organize evidence about the problem.
4. Suggest possible ways to resolve the problem.
5. Discuss the possible good and bad consequences of each solution.
6. Decide among the solutions proposed.
7. Take action based on solution chosen.

Reading about another classroom case will highlight the values analysis strategy (see Sample Classroom Episode 6.2).

SAMPLE CLASSROOM EPISODE 6.2

Looking in a Classroom: "Starters" and Uniforms

Several fights over fashion-statement clothes have broken out on the elementary school grounds. Drive-by muggings, even a shooting incident, have occurred at the neighboring high school over the desire of some students for clothes that others have. Mr. Tolliver, "Mr. T.," a sixth-grade teacher, challenges his class to do something about the problem. Holding up a Starter jacket, he asks, "What does this mean to you?" Students volunteer responses that go from describing the fashion to the violence that has occurred over such clothes.

Mr. T. then asks, "What is the problem with Starters?"

Initially, students say there is no problem, that they all like these jackets.

Mr. T. goads them, "Then, we don't have a problem? What about the fight before school today? Is that good?"

He lets students vent their concerns about being the object of a violent act, or being caught near someone who is the object of an attack, leading them to affirm that the problem with wearing some kinds of clothes to school is that many students want to be stylish but cannot afford the necessary clothes.

Mr. T. asks, "Do you think this boils down to wanting to get respect by dressing a certain way and not having an easy way to get the right clothes?" Students nod in agreement.

Next, Mr. T. asks students to suggest possible ways they could solve the problem.

Many students supported the proposal of having fund-raisers so everyone would get a Starter jacket until Mr. T. had them calculate how much they would have to raise, and think about what they could do to raise the money. Someone else ventured that at Mother Elizabeth Seton Elementary there was no problem because everyone dressed alike.

Mr. T. asked, "What solution does this suggest to you?"

"School uniforms," the class moaned.

Mr. T. then said, "Let's talk about this a little. How would uniforms solve our problem?"

Amid side comments of "No way!" "I'd rather quit school," "That's like prison," Mr. T. keeps the discussion from closing down by bringing students back to the problem. Finally, they conclude that Starters are a status symbol that give some students status and that kind of status seeking might be avoided if everyone dressed in the same way. In other words, students are beginning to see that the value of reducing clothes choice may result in a greater amount of security, another value, for all.

After twenty minutes, students' interest begins to wane. Mr. T. tells the class that they have made a good beginning at solving a problem. He challenges them to talk about the proposed solutions with each other and at home and be ready to continue discussing the issue the next day. He asks them to have some ideas of what they can do as a class.

Reflecting on the session later, Mr. T. is disappointed because the idea that a person's value should not be defined by clothes was not discussed. He resolves to try introducing this more basic value in tomorrow's discussion.

Even though the session may not have arrived where Mr. T. would have wished, it can be seen as a successful beginning. The class did not dwell on the explicit statement of the values in conflict, nor did the students come up with the underlying value of respect for the individual. The session can be counted as successful, however, as it did get students to pose the problem and initiate the step of taking action toward a solution. The class did not dwell on the explicit statement of the conflicting values, but this is not necessary to the analytical process.[5] Some solutions for this problem might include the following: organize a school convocation to discuss the subject, convince kids not to wear expensive clothes to school, make a school dress code, pass a school uniform code. Mr. T. needs to be sure that whichever alternative his students choose, they will outline the ways they will work toward implementing it in specific acts. He must also see that they keep the issue in focus by following up on the process and amending it as they work toward resolving the original problem.

CITIZENSHIP IN SCHOOL

School student councils help a few students gain active citizenship skills. Those students who are bold enough to run for office and lucky enough to get elected will gain leadership practice. Typically, these students meet with an administrator and bring messages about schoolwide functions back to their classrooms. Children in such groups gain experience by participating in meetings and presenting messages to their classmates; in some schools, they vote on issues at the meetings. The rationale for having a student council is that learning by doing promotes growth in active citizenship. The issue is how to extend the benefits of student council participation to more than one individual student from each class.

Beyond classroom responsibilities, some schools organize schoolwide positions and announce them in want ads. These positions include street and building traffic patrol, school lunch helpers, checkers for distribution and collection of noontime and recess equipment, librarian helpers and media center technicians, office helpers, playground cleanup patrol, and student council officers. These positions are mostly for middle graders. Students are not elected to these places but rotate through them periodically. Children apply for their positions by signing up for interviews. Teachers in charge of each job category check to make sure children understand the responsibilities involved. Children not selected for the first six weeks usually get a chance to serve during the second six-week period.

---

[5]Not all experts would agree that values analysis can be conducted this way. Thomas Licona of the State University of New York at Cortland's Center for the 4th and 5th R's (Respect and Responsibility) argues that central values, or virtues, need to be directly defined. Called by varied titles—values education, moral education, character education—the concern for guaranteeing that virtues be part of public school curriculum is gaining momentum. See "Who'll Teach Kids Right from Wrong?" by Roger Rosenblatt in *New York Times Magazine* April 30, 1995, pages 36–41, 50, 60, 64, 74.

By giving of their time and talents, children are contributing to making their school a place they own and can make better. Children can learn cooperative skills and see the benefit of working for a common cause when they participate in schoolwide campaigns. Fund-raising and cleanup drives are common to most schools. Class and individual awards for accomplishment help children recognize the value of their achievements and have pride in group effort.

Encouraging the expression of opinions about school events is a positive technique for building a sense of civic efficacy among students. Primary-grade classrooms can reserve a bulletin board with the heading "Citizenship: Success and Needs." Children can be encouraged to draw or write on the board about acts or situations they wish to compliment or ones they wish to improve by offering suggestions. Periodically, during sharing time, these contributions should be commented on and then removed to make room for new additions. Extending this idea is an effective strategy for focusing attention beyond individual classrooms. Directing students' attention to needed improvements in the school or local community can lead students to find out who is responsible for such things as repainting the traffic crosswalk or replacing the worn playground equipment. Students can write a class letter to comment on the needed change. Teachers and classes have been amazed to learn that such letters are read at school board and city council meetings.

We should not underestimate the power of student letter-writing campaigns. One middle-grade teacher, Mr. Garske, devised a system for counting the number of drivers not coming to a complete stop during school hours at the four-way stop crossing near the school. These data were used in a letter to a city councilperson as part of an argument for erecting an electric stop light at the crossing. The city councilperson contacted the teacher and came to the class to discuss the problem. Children were involved later in the conversation between the councilperson and representatives from the city departments of transportation and works. Some students attended the council meeting when the request was first proposed. The children involved continued to follow the process after they left Mr. Garske's room. Two years later when the light was installed, these first-year high school students returned for a class photo taken around "their" stoplight. The photo will remind them of the power of citizen opinion and of the patience and persistence required to move a bureaucracy through the process of change.

LINKING SCHOOLWIDE CITIZENSHIP TO THE COMMUNITY

Providing children access to the community outside school is an important element in the development of citizenship. One way to guarantee these links is by integrating a community strand into the curriculum at each grade level. If the school staff will decide jointly which public agencies will be linked to each grade level, they can ensure that children have a broad foundation for understanding how community business gets done (see Table 6.3). The agencies and activities are interchangeable, especially within the primary grades. The crucial element for citizenship is that the activities are based on children's firsthand exposure to real institutions and situations. Partnership schools, where local/regional firms and agencies agree to get involved with local schools, provide exceptional citizenship opportunities. Cooperating volunteers can be asked to help students develop ways of solving problems they jointly identify, such as before- and after-school activities, cleaning up and making school neighborhoods safer, improving school resources, organizing community participation activities in the school, and improving school health care programs for students. In many schools, cleaning up the school grounds has been used as a punishment for students who have misbehaved. Schools with such traditions need to find ways of making the volunteer jobs attractive. Learning to serve deserves positive recognition in every school and extra doses of it in schools where serving was seen as "doing time" or punishment.

A second means that schools traditionally have used for linking children to the world of citizenship happens at election time. In some schools children read campaign literature and hold mock elections. Social scientists tell us that children replicate their parents' political orientations and choices. Even though the results of school mock elections may be interesting to teachers, the child receives little concrete citizenship development from such an exercise. In fact, the contrary is true. In voting for candidates, children typically get little information on which to make their decisions. They probably do not know what the candidate stands for or what the important issues are in the campaign. They are generally forced to rely on media images and home orientations. School elections then can take on the aspects of a horse race, where winning is the only issue. We must ask ourselves if

TABLE 6.3 COMMUNITY CURRICULUM LINKS

Grade	Group	Activity
Kindergarten	Police	Visit police car and traffic crossing; practice emergency reporting.
First	Fire	Visit station; practice safety routines and emergency reporting; have fire hazard home inspections.
Second	Sanitation	Visit dump and recycling sites; organize cleanup campaign.
Third	Transportation	Visit bus-maintenance yard; take traffic and road surveys.
Fourth	Health	Visit hospital and retirement home; adopt patients.
Fifth	Courts	Visit municipal and traffic courts; survey local statistics.
Sixth	Social Service	Visit children at homeless shelter; conduct campaigns for food and clothing.
Seventh	Environment	Visit animal control or wild life refuse; conduct ongoing observation and cleanup.
Eighth	City/County Council	Visit council session; survey agendas for issues and media for facts; debate issues.

this is the substance about elections that we wish to have the school propagate. Elections need to be studied and given attention in the classroom, but we should keep voting in perspective. Voting is the last act in a long process of making choices. It is the process, not the vote itself, that must be emphasized.

Middle- and upper-grade children are capable of following political campaigns. They should be encouraged to do so. Keeping track of candidate statements over time and collecting facts about issues to display and analyze are essential current events activities. Analyzing the way candidates portray themselves and the issues on television, counting the number of times the candidate's name is mentioned, and noting the main and underlying messages alert children to how the media are used to shape our opinions and ideas.

Some teachers fear that students will become less patriotic as adults as a result of analyzing issues and questioning candidates. As teachers, we need to examine what we mean when we say that our goal is creating future patriotic citizens. We have all been taught that patriotism is a good and necessary value for our nation to survive.

In most public schools, love of one's country is instilled. We learn to revere national symbols—the flag that flies in front of the school; the reproductions of historical scenes and individuals, such as George Washington; the Minutemen's fife and drum corps; and the signing of the Constitution—and we continually repeat the rituals of loyalty in the Pledge of Allegiance and singing of the national anthem. Most of us believe that these symbols and rituals are appropriate, even essential, elements of school culture, as the activities create a sense of national identity and pride essential for young children living in this country.

6.3 SMALL GROUP WORK: PERSPECTIVES OF CITIZENSHIP AND IDENTIFICATION WITH PLACE

patriot	foreigner	citizen	tribe member
native	nationalist	immigrant	naturalized
undocumented	alien	refugee	bi-national

At first glance these terms seem not to connect with the topic of ritual procedures of citizenship as practiced in many elementary classrooms. This exercise is meant as a provocation for you to think about the wider societal issues concerning the relationship of citizenship to place. Should citizenship be directed to a community, a nation, a church; to all humanity; to the environment, to the planet; or to all these places? Do you have positive and negative feelings about these terms? How do these terms relate to culture? To religion in general, or to a specific religion? Discuss to what institution(s) we owe our allegiance(s) with your colleagues. Is there only one boundary of citizenship or loyalty for you? What is the purpose of boundaries or frontiers? How do your loyalties relate to living as a citizen in the United States of America? What do these considerations mean to you as a teacher?

Indeed, children seem to depend on these rituals in school as a necessary part of their daily routine. But what are our objectives in incorporating them? What are we looking for when we repeat these rituals every day? Do they accomplish our purpose? What are young children learning as a result of participating in these rituals?

Jean Piaget demonstrated that young children have great difficulty with the concept of country as an entity that is also part of, yet different from, community and surroundings they know. In the late 1960s, Wallace Lambert and Otto Klineberg found that by the age of seven, children were specific about their own national identification.[6] Furthermore, they had internalized an international pecking order that included derogatory national stereotypes. At that time children of other nationalities tended to see Americans as a high-status group, as did the Americans themselves. More recent surveys find that American children see Japanese as the current high-status nationality. Other studies have found that by the age of ten children internalize an attitude about their own power within the political system. This sense of power was related to the socioeconomic status of the children's families. Teachers were found to modify their approach to citizenship-related activities according to the socioeconomic status of children in their schools. Teachers emphasized obeying laws and fulfilling responsibilities to children of poorer, blue-collar families. In contrast, teachers of middle- to upper-class children tended to emphasize problem-solving approaches to citizenship topics.

We have no evidence that the pledge to the flag, singing a patriotic song or voting in a mock election is harmful to children's positive regard for national identity and citizenship. If, however, our purpose is to develop a love of our nation and a feeling of belonging to it, these activities are just the first step. To be effective, these rituals need to be accompanied by cognitively engaging activities that help children build their own positive connections to their schools and local communities. Without the practice of participating according to democratically oriented classroom procedures, we cannot assume that bridges of meaning and citizenship skills are built through the repetition of prescribed rituals. As we have seen, activities that can assist in this bridge building are planning and evaluating the school day with children, involving children with the responsibilities and decision making of running the class and school, and organizing exposure to public institutions. To reinforce links between symbols and rituals and understanding the ideals and functioning of civil society, children need direct instruction in the basics of citizenship under our system of government.

INSTRUCTION IN DEMOCRATIC CITIZENSHIP

Functioning effectively in our modern, complex society requires sophistication. We must understand what our rights and responsibilities are. We must be able to locate and deal with a myriad of public institutions. We must know how to seek and use in-

---

[6]Wallace E. Lambert and Otto Klineberg, *Children's Views of Foreign People: A Cross-National Study* (New York: Irving, 1967).

formation we need from the mountains of information that are available but not always easy to find. We must understand the rules of the game as they exist under our system of government. Beyond the classroom, school, and community arenas, children need instruction in three general topics—the rule of law, our system of justice, and the global nature of citizenship. This section suggests how to organize these three topics.

The Rule of Law

Typically, the "formal" aspects of learning what the law is and how it can be extended or changed are reserved for segments of the fourth, fifth, and eighth grades. The basis for understanding our formal system needs to be constructed, as we saw in the preceding section of this chapter, by a link to community functions at every grade level as well as citizenship activities that become part of the daily classroom life. Young children, as well as middle graders, can profit from formal consideration of the need for rules.

Young children are socialized rule followers by the time they reach kindergarten. They need to discuss the rules they have at home or in the classroom, why these rules are important, and what the consequences are when rules are not followed. Questions such as "Why do we have to raise our hands in class?" or "Why do we have to put garbage in the garbage cans?" are essential beginnings to discussions in later grades about the documents that define our society's rule of law.

Middle-grade children need to translate into everyday language the documents that establish the basics of citizenship in our society. Documents that should be discussed in this fashion are the *Declaration of Independence,* the *Constitution of the United States of America*, and the *Universal Declaration of Human Rights.* For example, asking fifth graders to read the Preamble and give six main reasons that the representatives to the Constitutional Convention stated they needed a constitution can help to define the historical context as well as make the content of the rest of the document more meaningful.

> We the people of the United States, in order to establish a more perfect Union, establish justice, ensure domestic tranquility, provide for the common defense, promote the general welfare, and secure the blessings of liberty to ourselves and our posterity, do ordain and establish this constitution for the United States of America. (*Preamble to the Constitution*)

Unfortunately, not all the Constitution is as easy to decipher as the Preamble. Middle-grade children need an overview of the structure that the Constitution creates for governing our society. One way to outline the main ideas contained in this document is through use of a visual outline or advance organizer such as that illustrated in Figure 6.3. Bulletin boards depicting main ideas about our system of government, such as the separation of powers and how a bill becomes a law, are keys to unlocking the lines of printed text for many students.

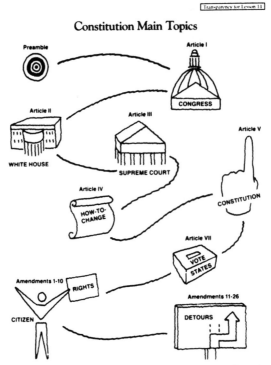

Constitution Main Topics

Figure 6.3 Advance organizers as instructional aids: Learning how the Constitution can be changed. *Source:* Reprinted by permission from page 62 of *You and the Constitution*, by June R. Chapin and Rosemary G. Messick. Copyright © 1987 by Addison-Wesley Publishing Company. All rights reserved.

Making the Bill of Rights live for middle graders requires involving them in relating the document to hypothetical situations. Through lessons, such as the following fifth-grade example, students gain a knowledge-level awareness of their citizen rights.

This lesson requires critical thinking and discussion. When students examine situations that are familiar to them, they can readily see the relevance of the Bill of Rights to their daily lives. They may not be, and should not be, required to remember every detail of the first ten amendments to the Constitution. They will, however, gain a sense of the importance this document has. Pedagogically, note that small groups should read and discuss *before* the whole class discusses the lesson. Without the small group step, most children will miss the "opportunity" personally to read and discuss, thereby short-circuiting real contact with the material. The small group step is crucial to this lesson.

SAMPLE LESSON PLAN 6.1

Bill of Rights: Can This Be Done?

OBJECTIVE:

Students categorize hypothetical situations as being protected or not protected under the Bill of Rights.

MATERIALS:

For a class of thirty, one copy for each student of the Bill of Rights, one transparency of "Am I Protected?" and a chalkboard or butcher paper chart for recording answers.

PROCEDURE:

1. Explain that the Constitution gives each citizen certain protections or guarantees that the government may not take away. "Our task in this lesson will be to discover what our citizen rights are and to decide whether certain situations interfere with these rights."

2. Divide the class into groups of three and assign an amendment to each.

3. Distribute the amendment list, giving groups a minute to read their amendment and skim the others.

4. Explain that you will show a situation on the transparency and each group must decide whether (a) their amendment relates to that event and (b) whether the event interferes with their rights according to the amendment.

5. Show the events one by one, recording student decisions in category columns by event number (see recording chart).

6. Conclude by asking students to list what they learned about the Bill of Rights through this exercise. Ask how these events relate to real life.

7. Assign "I Learned" statement to be written and handed in within five minutes.

EVALUATION:

Did students relate the acts to the amendments? Could they generalize from the amendments and acts to make statements about their citizen rights?

continued

SAMPLE UNIT PLAN 6.1 (CONT.)

TRANSPARENCY:

"Am I Protected?"

1. You own a hotel. The president calls and asks you to keep ten soldiers there because they are on duty in the neighborhood and have no place to stay.

2. You are opposed to a Supreme Court decision. You write a letter to the editor of your local paper stating your opinion.

3. You were freed by a jury decision from charges of robbery. Now, five years later, the bank that was robbed brings charges against you.

4. A policewoman knocks on your door. She shows you a search warrant and wants to come in to search your apartment.

5. You own a hunting rifle. Your neighbor says you have no right to have it at home.

6. You are asked to give evidence about a traffic accident you were involved in while you were under the influence of alcohol.

7. Arrested for driving while drunk, you are put in the county jail for a year and fined $10,000.

8. You are fourteen and want to get married.

9. The public school now begins each day with Bible reading.

SAMPLE RECORDING CHART: "*AM I PROTECTED?*"

Permits	Does Not Permit
1.	
2.	
3.	
etc.	

The Justice System

Formal instruction is necessary to supplement the real and vicarious contact children have with our system of justice. They may have had real contact by riding in a car with a parent when a highway patrol officer pulled their parent over to issue a traffic ticket. Or they may have testified in a divorce hearing concerning child custody. Television provides them with a barrage of vicarious contact. These kinds of contacts need to be supplemented with classroom instruction. Increasingly, news coverage and reenactments of crimes cause children to become fearful. They need to have a forum that permits them to discuss their fears as it extends their knowledge of the ideals of the justice system: that a person is not guilty of a crime until proven so in a court trial and that people who become involved in crime still have civil rights.[7]

As citizens living under the justice system and as consumers of televised programs that deal with criminal justice issues, children need an overview of what the steps and requirements of law are. Reviewing a televised episode of a prime-time show such as "Picket Fences" or "The Commish" or "NYPD Blue" while they look at a copy of Figure 6.4 would permit middle graders to become more critical of what they see.

Upper-grade students need specific instruction in the justice system. This instruction should include textbook study and classroom discussion. Possibilities for bringing textbooks to life include visiting courts in session, interviewing officials of the justice system, reading and dramatizing case studies, and participating in mock trials. Local bar associations and law school students are another resource for bringing the justice system to life. Associations are usually eager to send representatives to classes. Without getting into the finer points of contracts and torts, attorneys are able to illustrate how civil disputes as well as criminal charges are resolved. Teachers should take advantage of the resources law-related curriculum projects offer. These projects provide sample lessons and resource units that are available free or at minimal cost.[8]

Instruction about the justice system is a necessary complement to direct experiences that schools can provide young citizens. To round out their instruction in being citizens, children need to consider their roles as citizens of the world.

GLOBAL CITIZENSHIP

As our world community contracts to become a global village with nearly instantaneous communication and certainly eventual interconnection between all spheres of endeavor, our definition of citizenship must also change to fit this new reality. Children in our classes are, in fact, citizens of the world. As such, they need to develop a loyalty to and identity with Earth's fellow creatures.

---

[7]Ava Seigler's *What Shall I Tell the Kids?* (New York: Dutton, 1993) is a guide for teachers and parents that would be useful as discussion material in staff meetings and parent groups.

[8]Following are law-related education centers: Center for Civic Education, 5115 Douglas Fir Drive, Suite 1, Calabasas, CA 91302; Constitutional Rights Foundation, 601 S. Kingsley Drive, Los Angeles, CA 99005; National Street Law Institute, 605 G. Street N.W., Washington, DC; Special Committee on Youth for Citizenship, American Bar Association, 1155 East 60th Street, Chicago, IL 60637.

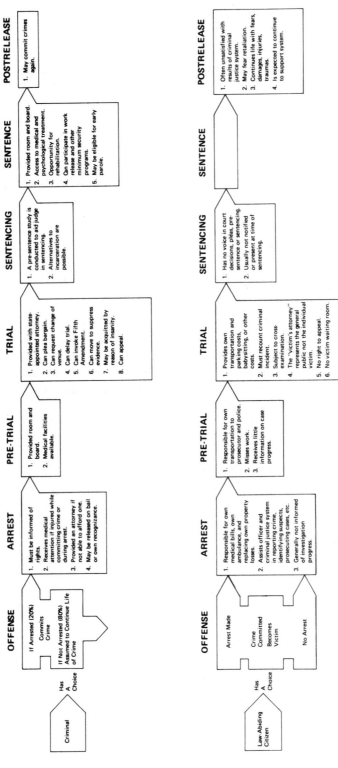

Figure 6.4 Criminal and victim in the judicial system. Demystifying the judicial process can be furthered by placing what is portrayed on a prime-time police drama in the context of prescribed judicial processes for both criminals and victims of crime. *Source:* Reprinted by permission from pp. 170–171 of *Excel in Civics: Lessons in Citizenship* by Steve Jenkins and Susan Spiegel; Copyright © 1985 by West Publishing Company. All rights reserved.

Three Themes of a Universal Curriculum

1. We are all global citizens who share a responsibility for solving the world's problems and for creating the world we desire.
2. We are all members of the family of humankind. We are responsible for understanding and caring for people of cultures different from our own.
3. We are stewards of Earth, which is our home and life-support system.

Instruction that incorporates a global perspective on ecology, resources, cultural variety, and human choices is a challenge. A favorite topic easily adapted to a global dimension is the study of endangered species. Rather than limiting the species in the sample from which to choose to local or national examples, animals from the whole world can be included. From research about animals that are endangered and where their habitats are located, children should be led to deliberate about what strategy they can take to help save their favorite animals. To do this they will need to do further research into what is causing the animals to disappear. They need to search for connections between human and environmental change. The next step is to decide what kind of action to take based on this further information. Children can become effective lobbyists by letter even in the international arena. The last process that evolves from this global approach is valuing. (Recall that we detailed this strategy earlier, using the classroom discussion about Starters to exemplify it.) Children should be prompted to state what they have learned from this process about their relationship to the planet.

The ecological principles of balance and relatedness present endless opportunities for value analysis in this era of global citizenship that asks us to focus on the bumper sticker slogan "Think globally; act locally." It is easy for children, and adults, to thrill to the warm, protective sentiments of faraway campaigns to preserve environments and protect species as presented in films such as *Free Willy*. Bringing these feelings to bear on issues closer to home is crucial for helping children to see the complexity and interrelatedness of defending the Earth. Every region is replete with "acting locally" environmental issues; see the following list.

Sampler of Ecological Conflicts

Hazardous waste dump sites versus acquiring attention and funds for removal
Logging economies versus endangered species
Species overpopulation leading to environmental degradation versus animal rights
Ranchers and sheep herders versus survival of predators such as wolves
Housing development versus protection of green space or wetlands

Domestic animal birth control versus animal and individual owner rights
Species extinction and ozone depletion versus airborne pollutants and
    pesticide- and herbicide-bearing agricultural water runoff

When teachers involve their students in local environmental issues by organizing learning about these issues through observation, sampling, and other scientific processes, they are exhibiting the most responsible kind of global citizenship education. Long-term teacher and school involvement with a specific site can reap not only the rewards of student enthusiasm and learning but also a school role in community improvement. Global citizenship truly begins at home.

Using a children's trade book such as the *Riverkeeper* as a storyline prompt that can lead to acting on local environmental concerns can be organized for any location by adapting the following lesson plan in a middle grade.

SAMPLE LESSON PLAN 6.2

The Riverkeeper and Me[9]

OBJECTIVES:

Students will

1. Identify five facts about the Hudson River.
2. Understand the term *estuary*.
3. Brainstorm a list of places or things to care for around school, home, or neighborhood.
4. Analyze ways they can be keeper of a small part of the world.
5. Select an area or object to care for.
6. Create a mini-journal of their activities as keepers of their special sites.

TIME:

Two forty-minute periods, plus a variety of other times throughout the school year.

---

[9] Adapted from Vicki Weiss, "Adopting Exit 109: Literature Promotes Action," in *Children's Literature and Social Studies*, Myra Zarnowski and Arlene F. Gallagher, eds. (Washington, D. C.: National Council for the Social Studies, 1993), 42–46.

RESOURCES:

George Ancona, *Riverkeeper* (New York: Macmillan, 1990).

Kids for Saving the Earth Guidebook (one for each student). Available free from Target department stores to teachers working with groups of students; chart paper.

SUGGESTED PROCEDURES:

1. List items students care for, save, or keep such as baseball cards, stuffed animals, stamps, letters, photographs, or pets. Have students list how they care for or keep these things. What is needed to provide proper care or attention for keeping them in good condition? Write these items on chart paper and hang on the classroom wall.

2. Introduce the book *Riverkeeper* by telling students that they will hear about an individual who keeps something, too. Suggest that they listen for the definition, the mission, and the ways that John Cronin cares for the things he keeps. Read the book aloud. At the end of the story, have students recall significant and interesting details.

3. Locate the Hudson River on a classroom map so that children can identify where the story occurs. On a chart or transparency, trace the path of the Hudson River and write some of the details from the story. This will assist in story mapping.

4. Discuss the network estuary, which means an arm of the sea at the lower end of a river. Be certain students understand that the Atlantic Ocean actually rolls into the Hudson River.

5. Write the definition of "riverkeeper" on the chalkboard or a transparency. List environmental places the children could care for around their school, home, or neighborhood. Add these suggested places to another chart and post it in the room. You might develop catchy descriptions such as "sidewalk saver," "trail trooper," or "pond protector."

6. Visit the places mentioned around the school or neighborhood. If possible, have students clean up the areas mentioned or beautify them in some way.

7. Have students select a site for which they will be the keeper for a specific duration of time. They can work individually, in pairs, or in small groups. Allow time for students to care for their adopted property. If students do this off school property, periodically have them visit their sites and write in a mini-journal about the experience.

continued

SAMPLE LESSON PLAN 6.2 (CONT.)

EVALUATION:

1. Can students see ways they can improve the environment?
2. Can students write five facts about *Riverkeeper?*
3. Can students write a comparison between their efforts and what John Cronin did?
4. Can students locate the Hudson River and define *estuary?*

EXTENDING THE LESSON:

1. Have the class write a letter to John Riverkeeper.
2. Create a mini-journal of what students accomplish each time they care for their site.
3. Record in sketches, photographs, or video the activity and changes in the area.
4. Place a sign to identify that the area is being cared for by class members.
5. Visit a nature center or preserve to talk to caretakers.
6. Analyze improvements in the sites through graphing techniques.
7. Make contact with local environmental groups and agencies to learn about protection and restoration plans.

Another approach to global citizenship focusing on the environment is to explore the general theme of ecology and environment through a literature set. The following list presents a starter set that could be used in a classroom organized around an integrated language approach. Through small group and individual reading, discussion, and journal keeping, students can gain a broader perception of environmental settings and issues that they can use as a foundation for selecting targets for environmental activism.

Trade Book Resources for "Thinking Globally and Acting Locally"[10]

Ancona, George. *Turtle Watch*. New York: Macmillan, 1987.

————. *Riverkeeper*. New York: Macmillan, 1990.

Elkington, John; Hailer, Julia; Hill, Douglas; and Makower, Joel. *Going Green: A Kid's Handbook to Saving the Planet*. New York: Penguin Puffin Books, 1990.

---

[10]Weiss, "Adopting Exit 109," pp. 39–40.

Elting, Mary. *Volcanoes and Earthquakes*. New York: Simon & Schuster, 1990.

George, Jean Craighead. *One Day in the Tropical Rain Forest*. New York: Harper-Collins, 1990.

Huff, Barbara A. *Greening the City Streets: The Story of Community Gardens*. New York: Clarion Books, 1990.

Lauber, Patricia. *Seeing Earth from Space*. New York: Orchard Books, 1990.

Patent, Dorothy Hinshaw. *Yellowstone Fires: Flames and Rebirth*. New York: Holiday House, 1990.

Pringle, Laurence. *Restoring Our Earth*. Hillside, N.J.: Enslow, 1987.

van Allsburg, Chris. *Just a Dream*. Boston: Houghton Mifflin, 1990.

It is not enough to provide children with information about global problems. You must also show them avenues to personal efficacy in relation to these problems as part of the instructional sequence.

6.4 *SMALL GROUP DISCUSSION WORK: BUILDING A CONTEXT FOR GLOBAL CITIZENSHIP*

Read the following lesson asking yourself where it might be used in a sequence of instruction and how you could add personal efficacy to this topic. Discuss possible techniques with your colleagues.

SAMPLE LESSON PLAN 6.3

Feeding the World

OBJECTIVES:

Students gain relative perspective of global population groups and food supplies.
Students suggest ways to respond to problem situation.
Students see global situation from simulated, foreign pespective.

MATERIALS:

World map, colored chalk, baguette of French bread, and regional identification cards with following data:
Asia — 54 percent of population, 5 percent of food supply
Africa — 10 percent of population, 1 percent of food supply

---

continued

SAMPLE LESSON PLAN 6.3 (CONT.)

Latin America — 8 percent of population, 15 percent of food
  supply
Middle East — 2 percent of population, 5 percent of food supply
West (United States, Canada, Western Europe) — 26 percent
  of population, 74 percent of food supply

PROCEDURE:

1. Tell class that for today they are going to represent all the people
    that live on Earth.

2. Divide them into five groups proportionately—for example, for a
    class of thirty, Asia would have sixteen students; Africa, three; Latin
    America, two; Middle East, one; West, eight.

3. Show or have member of each group come forward and identify its
    space on the world map. Have each group move to its own seating
    area, which should be roughly proportionate to its geographical
    occupation of the planet.

4. Bring out a baguette, explaining that it represents the food available
    on Earth and that you are going to divide it according to how much
    each region actually has.

5. Tell class that their groups are to discuss three questions once they
    get their part of Earth's food supply. Distribute bread.

6. Show questions previously written on chalkboard:

    How does your group feel about its food supply?

    What could your group do about this situation?

    Are your responses like those of people in the real world?

7. After groups have discussed their answers to the questions, call on
    each group to share its information with the whole class.

EVALUATION:

1. Ask large group what they learned in this short experience. Ask
    what questions they have now about world hunger and write
    questions on butcher paper for future reference.

2. Ask individuals to write a paragraph or draw their feelings about the
    lesson.

Students probably will have heard of voluntary groups that work to improve environmental and global problems. Organizations such as the Sierra Club, Greenpeace, and Amnesty International are willing to send representatives to school in an effort to gain support for their causes. Before inviting guest speakers into our classrooms, however, we need to review our responsibilities toward citizenship education. Are we providing the children with an opportunity to experience data from a variety of opinions about the issue we are studying? Do we ask them to question the opinions and data they hear and gather? We need to explain these responsibilities to representatives invited to present their group's perspective.

Learning about human rights programs and goals is another vital part of global citizenship education. Many states require study of genocide and the Holocaust. By bringing knowledge of past atrocities into the curriculum, we can hope that children see themselves as having a responsibility, as world citizens, for trying to prevent such tragedies from happening again.

Guidelines for Instruction about Human Rights and Genocide[11]

1. To help students understand that prejudice, intolerance, and hatred of other people are the seedbed for violations of human rights.
2. To make students aware that acts of genocide do not happen randomly; they are purposefully planned and occur with government sponsorship.
3. To help students understand that attitudes that permit seemingly small violations of human rights could pave the way for the acceptance of genocidal actions.
4. To demonstrate through historical and contemporary examples the variety of ways in which human rights can be violated.
5. To help students understand the calamitous effect of human rights violations, including the loss of rich cultural traditions through the crime of genocide.
6. To make students aware of the *Declaration of Independence* as a statement of the natural law philosophy of human rights.
7. To make students aware that human rights are best protected in a democracy where there are limits on the power of the state and all people have full civil rights and political liberties.
8. To make students aware of the human rights guarantees contained in the Bill of Rights and subsequent amendments to the Constitution of the United States.
9. To help students understand the responsibility of governments, including the U.S. government, for protecting human rights.

---

[11]*Model Curriculum for Human Rights and Genocide* (Sacramento: California State Department of Education, 1986).

10. To help students understand that there is a pattern and a clear story about how rights have been lost and how they are protected.

From time to time, American leaders ignore or criticize the United Nations. This organization, however, remains the principal structure that facilitates communication and sponsors programs that attempt to address global needs. Older children should compare the similarities between the Bill of Rights of the U.S. Constitution and the Universal Declaration of Human Rights of the United Nations. Younger children should have exposure to both lists and discuss what, for example, freedom of opinion and expression means. One way to make the rights vivid for children is to relate current events to them. What human right, or rights, are refugees from the Caribbean area seeking by coming to the United States? What rights are denied in such nations as Iraq, Saudi Arabia, or Israel?

Universal Declaration of Human Rights (1948)

Equality before the law
Protection against arbitrary arrest
Right to a fair trial and freedom from *ex post facto* criminal laws
Right to own property
Right to political asylum
Freedom of thought, conscience, and religion
Freedom of opinion and expression
Freedom of peaceful assembly and association

International Covenant on Economic, Social, and Cultural Rights (1966)

Right to work and choose one's work freely
Right to earn equal pay for equal work
Right to education
Right of all peoples to self-determination
Right of ethnic, religious, and linguistic minorities to enjoy their culture

6.5 SMALL GROUP WORK: DEVISING A WORLD WATCH CHART

Read the activity described below. Then discuss these questions with your colleagues: What positive and negative outcomes could this activity generate? Does the activity promote global citizenship? How? How does the activity relate to current event awareness, critical thinking, and citizenship efficacy?

An ongoing current events bulletin board that involves middle-grade children in analyzing world events is to have posted on it the *Universal Declaration of Human Rights*, with each item arranged on the vertical side of a chart. Children write in names of countries and dates of instances where a right has been denied as they watch and read about world events.

As events unfold, there is class discussion about each, led by a pair of students assigned to it. The pair is responsible for presenting why each side feels justified. Then the class decides what the conflict means and what action the class may want to take.

Discussion about how current actions of all governments fall short of the ideals of human rights can provoke feelings of impotence in children. Unless you are prepared to take citizen action steps, such as letter writing, discussing current events using a human rights context is not recommended. However, to ignore this important avenue to providing positive direction for the moral concerns of children is to ignore our responsibility for world citizenship education.

Global citizenship is a complex, contradictory, and often controversial notion. Many Americans argue that global education activities undermine our national interests. Indeed, this may be the case if we define American interests as different from or antagonistic or superior to those of other countries. Nations, ours included, tend to see resource issues according to their own perspectives. Learning more about our connections with what may happen anywhere on Earth will help us evaluate both the costs and the long-term benefits resulting from seeing ourselves as citizens of Earth.

SUMMARY

To summarize our exploration of citizenship education, we need to recall that it is one of the major historical goals of public education in our country. Traditionally, young children have been prepared for citizenship by ritual inculcation of loyalty and formal instruction in our system of government with the addition, in some schools, of citizenship action programs. We agree with Morris Janowitz, University of Chicago sociologist, who claims that we must reform our citizenship education. He said that old-fashioned, simple-minded patriotism is not effective in our current interdependent world. He believes that civic consciousness is a more relevant approach to creating a persistence of love or attachment to a country—a territorially based political system.[12]

As national affairs become more relevant to our daily lives, we realize that the vitality of democratic citizenship cannot be maintained by the existing range of political forms. Voting turnouts grow smaller. People feel they are not getting enough service in return for their tax dollars. The number of residents who are not citizens

---

[12]Morris Janowitz, *The Reconstruction of Patriotism: Education for Civic Consciousness* (Chicago: University of Chicago Press, 1983).

grows. Politicians and political parties appeal less and less to the public. New ventures in citizenship are needed. Schools can do much to meet this need.

In this chapter, we have suggested that concrete, direct experiencing of decision making as well as learning about our system is necessary to prepare responsible citizens. To guarantee that children have opportunities for civic observation and participation in decision making, we suggest specific planning across the grades and schoolwide curricula. As an element of culture learning, citizenship development needs to be integrated into the processes we use to organize our classroom communities. Beginning instruction about the rights and responsibilities and procedures of the various governmental levels is an essential building block, as well, for citizenship development. The key to internalizing the citizen role, for most elementary students, is active, personalized involvement.

SUGGESTED READINGS

Dinwiddie, Sue A. "The Saga of Sally, Sammy and the Red Pen: Facilitating Children's Social Problem Solving." *Young Children* 49 (July 1994): 13–19. Detailed presentation of social problem solving with young children that, with other articles in same issue, amply illustrates the connection between building a culture of responsibility in school and preparing children for citizenship in an expressive, not repressive, society.

Engle, Shirley, and Ochoa, Anna. *Education for Democratic Citizenship*. New York: Teachers College Press, 1988. Broad-based, learned presentation of civic role as central in public education and the derived relationship of social studies.

Hanvey, Robert C. *An Attainable Global Perspective*. Denver: Center for Teaching International Relations, 1976. Seminal outline of five dimensions necessary for a global perspective useful for thinking about global citizenship.

Heller, Carol, and Hawkins, Joseph A. "Teaching Tolerance: Notes from the Front Line." *Teachers College Record* 95, no. 3 (Spring 1994): 337–368. Thorough and inspiring contextualization of citizenship goals through review of diverse educational programs that build bridges toward racial and ethnic unity by appreciating diversity and seeing similarity.

Isaac, Katherine. *Civics for Democracy: A Journey for Teachers and Students*. Minneapolis: Free Spirit Publishing, 1993. Book-length discussion of necessity for linking goals of citizenship development with action in larger community, recounting broad range of actual school-based programs.

Lewis, Barbara A. *Kids with Courage: True Stories about Young People Making a Difference*. Minneapolis: Free Spirit Publishing, 1993. Stimulating annotation of citizenship efforts that may begin in school but extend far beyond and return to change student lives and visions.

Kaplan, Dan; Taylor, W. Frank, Jr.; and Soldy, Ann. "We the People." *The Instructor*

96 (October 1986): 94–96. Teaching ideas about the Constitution for younger children.

Kniep, W. M. "Global Education in the 80's." *Curriculum Review* 25 (November–December 1985): 16–18. Urges need for more global view in curriculum.

Miller, F. Gene, and Jacobson, Michael G. "Teaching for Global Mindedness." *Social Education* (March–April 1994): 4–6. Uses Hanvey's dimensions to argue global view as extension of multicultural perspectives.

National Council for the Social Studies. *Mission Statement.* Washington, D.C., 1992. Official statement by content area professional organization of centrality of citizenship to this subject and totality of schooling.

Parker, Walter C. "Assessing Citizenship." *Educational Leadership* 48 (November 1990): 17–22. Argues centrality of citizenship in curriculum and presents ways to organize for assessing citizenship.

Shaheen, J. C. "Participatory Citizenship in the Elementary Grades." *Social Education* 53 (October 1989): 361–363. Suggests projects and activities.

Chapter 7

CULTURE LEARNING

As a result of reading this chapter, you should have a broad view of the ways that schools influence children's learning of culture and how we can pursue social studies goals as we organize culture learning. *Multicultural education* is the term most frequently used to refer to this aspect of social studies. Part of what multicultural education discusses brings a new emphasis to social studies. Part does not. Social studies tradition includes learning about other cultures and democratic values. Insights from multicultural education broaden the more traditional social studies scope of learning about cultures and citizenship; this expanded scope includes conscious and positive learning of how to relate to and get along with individuals and groups of differing backgrounds while becoming more aware of the strengths to be recognized in one's own cultural heritage. Specific objectives for the chapter are for you to be able to describe how culture is learned in three spheres of schooling and to suggest various strategies for creating positive classroom cultures, for learning about cultures, and for resolving intercultural conflicts in a classroom. To help you toward these objectives, the chapter is organized in four sections.

1/ Describing Culture Learning

2/ Classroom Organization and Culture Learning

3/ Classroom Instruction about Cultures

4/ Classroom Intergroup and Multicultural Problem Exploration

DESCRIBING CULTURE LEARNING

Culture learning as part of the social studies can be seen from a variety of perspectives. To get a sense of these perspectives and discover which ones you share, respond to these multiple-choice items.

7.1 *SMALL GROUP WORK: DEALING WITH CULTURE ISSUES IN THE CLASSROOM*

With others in your group, take turns sharing your responses to these multiple-choice questions and the text commentary at the end of this section. Do you have personal experiences to share that these questions remind you of? What are your ideas about the teacher's role and responsibility for this aspect of schooling?

1. What is the most significant goal children can gain from learning about their own culture and other cultures?
   a. Knowledge about how peoples of various cultures live and what they value
   b. Appreciation for the diversity of peoples and their ways of life
   c. Ability to accept people from different ways of life or of differing appearances
   d. Ability to communicate and work together with others toward common goals
2. What is the best strategy for improving the ability of children from diverse groups to live together in a positive way?
   a. Present lessons about different ethnic and racial groups
   b. Celebrate holidays of significant ethnic and racial groups
   c. Structure classroom tasks so that children must learn by working together
3. What is the best strategy for resolving differences between racial or cultural groups in the classroom?
   a. Prohibit discussion about racial or cultural clashes in the class
   b. Read stories about conflicts that have "happy endings"
   c. Discuss racism, stereotyping, and scapegoating with the class
   d. Invite adult members of different racial and cultural groups to the class to present their points of view
   e. Role-play conflict situations that lead children to practice resolution

Did you have difficulty choosing one best answer? Clearly, each item has more than one acceptable answer. Part of the difficulty you experience in this forced-choice exercise may be due to your uncertainty about the term *culture learning.* You may not be accustomed to the definition we use. From our perspective, culture learning occurs at every grade level in two ways. First is instruction. Traditionally, we have concerned ourselves with culture and culture learning as content we learn about. From the academic discipline of anthropology, social studies programs have incorporated facts and generalizations about peoples of various times and places as significant instructional information for transmitting the concept of culture. For example, children learn that Chinese cultures exist in many locations outside the People's Republic of China and that family loyalty is one of the most important elements in understanding Chinese ways of being.

Immersion is the second way that children learn culture. Children absorb unconsciously what will become their culture through the close contacts of their daily living. They may learn that their school values quiet behavior whereas their family values lots of verbal communication. They may have conflicting feelings about associating with some groups in school that are not held in high esteem by their home culture. Culture learning, both positive and negative, occurs in schools as naturally as breathing. Anthropologists call this learning *acculturation* when a child is acquiring the culture of parents. They distinguish acculturation from culture learning known as *assimilation*, when an individual, usually from a cultural minority, assumes attitudes and practices perceived by the larger society as more powerful than those of the individual's original culture. Both these processes are part of culture learning. Assimilating the official curriculum of the school and becoming acculturated to the ways and rules of daily living there as well as at home are both types of culture learning.

From our perspective, it is important to remember that there are many kinds of home life. Further, there is not one superior culture, but many, often competing ones, each with its own values and history. Both kinds of culture learning—becoming culturally knowledgeable with positive self-esteem and developing the ability to get along with "different" others—are essential and integral to social studies. We need to plan how to honor both ways of culture learning—to keep the virtues of our social studies tradition of transmitting knowledge about culture and cultures, and to add to this tradition a consideration of the way we live together in classrooms. These can be among the most powerful culture learning experiences a child has.

CLASSROOM ORGANIZATION AND CULTURE LEARNING

You can plan for culture learning by examining the following three aspects of classroom life: *motivation*—the way you introduce, organize, and reward academic performance in your classrooms; *instruction*—the content you offer about the ways of life of groups of people; and *problem solving*—the ways in which interpersonal and intergroup problems are observed, discussed, and resolved.

Motivation and Classroom Organization

Classroom interaction teaches children more than the content of lesson plans. Children learn from the way a class is organized to get work done, from the way the teacher calls on students, and from the way students are seated and prompted to move about the classroom. Unfortunately, what they learn from these aspects of classroom life may not be what the teacher intends or would wish. Students may learn that being quiet and compliant earns them more teacher approval than when they ask uncalled-for questions or want to discuss fairness issues. They may learn that to get ahead in school they must behave like the majority community, assuming its language and culture while repressing or denying their own. This kind of assimilation is known as learning the hidden curriculum. The culture of the classroom is the hidden curriculum. If the classroom culture serves to promote one group while ignoring others, the hidden curriculum amounts to institutionalized racism, contradicting the formal, pro-justice curriculum of social studies. To use the power of the hidden curriculum in a way that is beneficial to all students, teachers must examine their assumptions about how to help children learn in positive ways.

Comparing our beliefs to what actually happens in classrooms is one way to uncover this curriculum. Teachers and future teachers agree that our basic goals are to guide children to realize their potentialities and to learn to live and work with others in a rewarding way. Yet the organization and management of many classrooms often denies the second goal. We use individual rewards for learning and group rewards for behaving. We give stars to individuals who complete work successfully and top grades only to those who do better than others. The message children may get from this situation is that learning and working hard are not related, that children who do not shine academically have reduced value. School routines are criticized as granting almost exclusive recognition and value to children who excel at individual academic achievement. In classroom settings with various cultural and ethnic groups represented, the children of "less value" are often members of social or economic minority groups that have less status in the outside community. Thus the reward systems of our school and classroom often reinforce the divisions and inequities of the adult society. We do not help children attain our basic goals of realizing their individual potential as they learn to work together.

There is new research on what can be accomplished in classrooms toward our goal of educating children to relate positively to all people and groups and to improve their own academic performance. More students can develop a positive relationship with learning if teachers alter the ways learning is organized. Researchers concerned with intergroup relations and minority-group achievement have begun to verify that the way we structure expectations in our classrooms can have a positive effect on intergroup relations and achievement. Basing their procedures on Gordon Allport's earlier theory that "prejudice may be reduced by equal-status contacts between majority and minority groups in pursuit of common goals," researchers organized nonsuperficial, noncompetitive, equal-status contact in classrooms.[1] These structures are known as cooperative learning groups, as described in Chapter 3.

7.2 *ON YOUR OWN: TERMINOLOGY REVIEW AND CONTEXTUALIZATION*

The glossary indicates the crucial, yet elusive nature of preparing for culture learning in the classroom. There is societal disagreement about the relationship of these terms to instruction in schools. You will develop your own unique perspective about how these concepts relate to learning and instruction as you work with children. Our purpose here is simply to alert you to the pervasiveness and complexity of the issues of culture learning.

Review these terms. Do they have specialized meanings to you? Do you disagree with these definitions? Can you give examples of each term? Note any additional terms that you believe should be included in a glossary about culture learning and discuss them with your group.

Afrocentrism: values and perspectives flowing from the continent of Africa, typically used as guides for organizing curriculum for African Americans.

assimilation: person of one culture merging his or her ways of living, or culture, into another, usually dominant culture.

bias: acts or attitudes that favor an individual or group over others.

bigotry: acts of intolerance based on an individual's belief in a particular creed or practice or opinion.

culture: way of life and belief of a group passed from one generation to the next.

Culture: examples of "high," or "capital C," art and literature esteemed by "educated" individuals of a shared culture.

discrimination: favoring or rejecting an individual because of his or her group identification.

diversity: typically used in contexts that seek to value individuals and groups for their uniqueness; those holding this view argue that not all need to be alike in order to form a viable social group.

ethnic group: group that shares a distinctive culture for racial, religious, or historical reasons.

ethnic studies: units or courses that present the history, culture, and contemporary issues of an ethnic group.

ethnocentrism: belief that one's group or culture is inherently superior, leading to contempt for other groups or cultures.

---

[1]Gordon Allport, *The Nature of Prejudice* (Reading, Mass.:) Addison-Wesley, 1954.

empowerment pedagogy: instructional strategies that recognize and capitalize on or make a strength of minority-group cultures that come from
differences in language, ethnicity, disability, sexual orientation, gender, or religion.

Eurocentric: values and perspectives flowing from the European point of
view, such as using the westward movement to present the settlement
of North America, or Columbus's voyage to present the discovery of
America.

institutionalized racism: accepted, often unquestioned, organizational
practices or regulations that function as discriminatory norms against
individuals with traditionally ostracized social characteristics.

multicultural education: multiperspective knowledge and processes of
positive interaction between individuals of different groups that lead
them to value their similarities and honor their differences.

nationalism: ideas that seek to bind individuals to an identity with a political institution based on symbols, myth, shared history, and usually a
geographical territory.

pluralistic society: society composed of multiple ethnic and cultural groups.

politically correct: descriptive of a person or group that aligns itself with a
predictable point of view on issues that keep within a perspective
condoned or revered by the group in power.

popular culture: activities and beliefs of everyday people that may not be
recognized by political or cultural authorities as "the" best or most significant representation of that culture.

prejudice: unfavorable feeling about members of a group formed without
knowing individuals of the group.

scapegoat: a person who is blamed and made to suffer for acts of the
group to which he or she belongs or is seen to belong.

stereotype: unchanging idea about a group that defines members of that
group without regard to their uniqueness as individuals.

Cooperative learning apparently improves intergroup relations when it is used
in ethnically and culturally mixed classroom groups. Furthermore, there is evidence that when cooperative learning is used, students' average academic achievement improves also. Although this strategy can be employed productively with any
school subject, cooperative learning can have special relevance for the social studies. A major purpose of the social studies is to help children become active, critically thinking citizens capable of working together toward their common welfare,
and cooperative learning offers a positive approach to constructing a cultural mi-
lieu crucial to this process.

Cooperative learning strategies create a classroom culture based on mutual assistance, equality among group members, and role diversity in learning tasks. In

other words, this process itself teaches one of the social studies' major goals—learning to live positively with each other. But the content of cultures we teach about is important and requires our careful thought. How shall we organize what we want children to learn about a culture?

CLASSROOM INSTRUCTION ABOUT CULTURES

When we prepare to study a culture that may be foreign to us, we have sensitive decisions to make. Shall the traditional aspects of the culture be highlighted? Shall the aspects of a culture that are presented to tourists by representatives of that culture be questioned? When we focus on American immigrant cultures, shall we present the memories of the places of origin as immigrants prefer to recall them, or shall we examine a more objective contemporary version of the culture? Shall the culture study be coordinated with a cultural celebration of holidays as we know them? Does the historical background of the group in the United States matter? Should groups be studied separately?

To address some of these questions, put yourself in the shoes of a parent whose culture the school plans to study. Would a Mexican-American parent, for example, want her children and other children to know about Cinco de Mayo? Hanukkah? St. Valentine's Day? The Day of the Dead? Would that same parent prefer that children experience some of the food, music, and folk arts and crafts of her culture? What would that parent want us to know? For what purpose would that parent want to have her culture studied in the classroom?

Possibly a Mexican-American parent would want us to include study of her culture as an integral part of the curriculum so that her children might feel their group is valued as a regular component of the school and society. Possibly not. This particular parent may be upset with our labeling her as a Mexican American. We have defined her as Mexican American, a one-dimensional category, when in fact, she may also be divorced, a medical doctor, and a fifth-generation American whose ancestors had been ranchers in Arizona long before it became part of the United States. Any one of these facets of her identity might be far more significant to her than her ethnic background. Obviously, we cannot know how all parents feel about the elements of their own identities they wish to have included in the classroom curriculum. What we can do is acknowledge an individual's preference about how he or she wishes to be identified. And always remember that most individuals prefer not to be labeled according to only one aspect of their background.

Each of us is culturally multifaceted. Look at yourself. Identify who you are in each of the concentric rings of the cultural identity diagram in Figure 7.1. Which of these rings best defines the way you live your life? Elements of our culture are related to who we are sexually, how old we are, and our religious background. The interaction and conflict between these various facets, or microcultures, of our lives continually redefine and reshape our cultural identities. We also, to one degree or

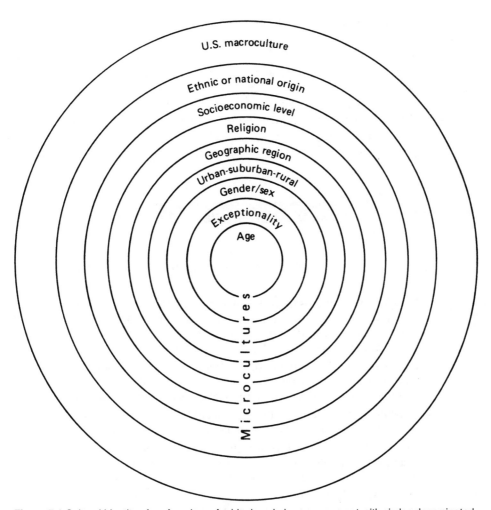

Figure 7.1 Cultural identity of an American. A widening-circles arrangement with circles denominated from center ("Age") to outer ring ("U.S. macroculture"). *Source*: Reprinted with permission of Merrill, an imprint of Macmillan Publishing Company, from *Multicultural Education in a Pluralistic Society* by Donna M. Gollnick and Philip C. Chinn. Copyright © 1986 by Merrill Publishing Company.

another, are shaped by and share in the national culture. Acknowledging our own many-layered reality should guide us away from presenting material that prompts children to draw stereotypic conclusions about people and groups they study. Children need to learn about themselves and others as complex, changing cultural beings. They need to learn that although the larger society may categorize individuals as part of a group, people in any group differ widely from each other.

The process of cultural becoming begins with self-naming. Exploring our own names invites us to confront openly what labels mean. At the beginning of each school year, teachers need to assist students in their continuous process of self-representation. Simply asking each child to tell the name he or she wishes to be called assists this process. At every age, students appreciate the self-affirming opportunity activities focused on finding out more about the names associated with them offer. The research-sharing starters in Sample Activities 7.1 can serve the dual purposes of helping students get acquainted with one another and of affirming students' home culture in any classroom.

Beyond exploring their own names, middle-grade children need guided experi-

---

SAMPLE ACTIVITIES 7.1

Exploring Our Names

1. Request that students do research at home asking parents to tell why students' first and middle names were chosen. Draw a picture that incorporates student name and tells the story of how they were named for a class display.

2. Does student's first name have another meaning? What does the name mean in other languages? Make a class roll of names and definitions and names and their equivalents in other languages.

3. What do your students' last names mean? What part of the world do they come from? Make a class name dictionary and atlas.

4. How do different groups order names and pass them along? (Order examples: Hispanic: given name, father's last name, mother's last name; Chinese: surname, given names; Russian: given name, patronymic, surname.

5. Do you prefer a nickname? What does it mean?

6. Students use one of these reference books to find something to share about their names:
   Meltzer, Milton. *A Book about Names*. New York: Thomas Y. Crowell, 1984.
   Dunking, Leslie. *The Guinness Book of Names*. Enfield, Middlesex, England: Guinness Superlatives, 1984.
   Hook, N. J. *The Book of Names: A Celebration of Mainly American Names, People, Places, Things*. New York: Franklin Watts, 1983.
   Hook, N. J. *Family Names: The Origin, Meaning, Mutations, and History of More than 2000 American Names*. New York: Macmillan, 1982.

ences in name-calling? The typical admonition "We don't use names that hurt" needs to be turned inside out. Rather than prohibiting name-calling with no discussion, many brave teachers have discovered that a good technique for defusing the explosiveness and pervasiveness of name calling is to study the negative slang words students are using that year (see Sample Lesson Plan 7.1). In one class, even after all the sensitizing about name-calling, a student suggested that the class develop a book based on their experience and call it *Our Black Book of Names*. Of course, the teacher then had to ask the students to think critically about why this list would be

---

SAMPLE LESSON PLAN 7.1

Confronting Name-Calling: Names We Call

OBJECTIVES:

1. Students define name-calling and its effects on the name-caller and the person named.
2. Students bring examples of name-calling and stereotyping to discuss in class.

TIME:

One to two 40-minute sessions.

MATERIALS:

Paper bag, slips of paper, chalkboard, or chart paper.

PROCEDURE:

1. Tell students they are going to have a real-life vocabulary lesson. Ask them if there are names they know about that they feel should not be used in the classroom. Why do we censor these names? Why do people use these names sometimes? "Let's act like linguists and see whether we can uncover the semantics and attraction of names we call each other." Ask students to write on slips of paper names they use or hear used that refer to groups of people.
2. Collect the anonymous slips in a box or paper bag.

continued

SAMPLE LESSON PLAN 7.1 (CONT.)

3. Draw a slip and write its contents on the chalkboard, pronounce it, and ask the class to volunteer a definition.

4. For each, ask students to volunteer their thoughts about how a person feels when called by this name.

EVALUATION:

After exhausting the slips of paper, ask, "What have we learned about name-calling?"
Conclude by asking for individuals to take turns coming up and erasing a name they wish they would never have to hear.

---

called "black." A precocious student commented, "Using *black* is not politically correct!" Taken by surprise but excited by the teachable moment, the teacher challenged the class to further investigate the ways they heard words used to classify or stereotype individuals and groups before they started their book. In two more sessions of sharing, this class developed their own ideas about what being politically correct was all about and titled their book *Hurting Names*. Two caveats are in order for teachers as they use this strategy: Do not censor names students contribute. Prepare the class for this session by having the students recall how they act when they discuss topics that can hurt them or their friends. Providing a forum in which they can discuss their feelings is especially meaningful to students of mixed heritage. Often they need to articulate the cross-pressures they feel about being categorized into any one of their antecedent groupings. Exploration of these experiences is a real-life study of the changing sociology of groups!

SAMPLE ACTIVITIES 7.2

Developing Multiple Perspectives

1. Conduct naming research about the names groups give themselves and what they mean. Starter examples: Navaho — *Dineh*;

Cheyenne — *Tsistsista*; Salish — *Sle'lign*; most American Indian self-names mean "the humans," "the people."

2. Select any historic event—the beginning of a town, building of an interstate highway, development of a suburban mall — and have students decide which of these names apply to people of different groups involved in the situation: *native, indigenous, nomad, displaced refugee, pioneer, colonist, squatter, homeless, exiled, immigrant, legal alien, illegal alien, migrant*. Discuss how this exercise changes students' ideas about the past and history.

3. Consider what the act of naming a place means. Find meanings and/or linguistic origins of local names of streets, neighborhoods, towns, counties, rivers, mountains, and swamps. What do these names tell about the history of a place? Have the names changed? What did the name change mean?

4. Local history projects need not be confined to a particular grade level. Pursuing local history inevitably leads to uncovering multicultural roots. Good source books for project and process ideas include the following:

   Cooper, Kay. *Who Put the Cannon on the Courthouse Square?* New York: Walker, 1985.

   Jungreis, Abigail. *Know Your Hometown History: Projects and Activities*. New York: Franklin Watts, 1992.

   Wertzman, Davis. *My Backyard History Book*. Boston: Little, Brown, 1975.

   Westridge Young Writers Workshop. *Kids Explore America's Hispanic Heritage*. Santa Fe, N.M.: John Muir Publications, 1992.

Learning from Each Other

Each school year brings a new cultural configuration to many of our classrooms. Informal culture learning can be promoted if we take advantage of the cultures of children in our classrooms throughout the school year. Finding out who we are and where we come from serves to instruct us about others as well as make us feel valued for who we are. Promoting the children's exploration of who they are does not directly address the "learning-about-culture" issue; but by valuing individual children for who they are, we hope the self-esteem messages children internalize are "I am worthy and welcome," "My classmates are like me in many ways," "My classmates like me," "My classmates are different from me and that's interesting," "I have something from home that is worth teaching my friends about."

Kim Anh Vu is a social studies teacher at Steinbeck Middle School, an urban magnet school in San Jose, California, that has many limited-English-speaking students of many nationalities. She devised a multicultural unit that engaged every student in culture teaching and learning. Her objective was that all students should experience teaching elements of their own culture and learning those of another. To begin the unit, Ms. Vu gave each student this unit overview handout (see Sample Unit Plan 7.1).

SAMPLE UNIT PLAN 7.1

Unit Overview of Cross-Cultural Teaching/Learning

STUDENT GUIDE FOR "CULTURE VULTURE CLUB" MEMBERSHIP:

Over the next two weeks you and your partner will be given some time during each period to work together on becoming eligible for the Culture Vulture Club. You will each be tested orally by an examiner of your partner's choice on your performance of the following tasks. Partners are expected to earn perfect scores and will be awarded Culture Vulture memberships at the Cultural Exchange Evening we will plan and hold on October 15, our Back to School Night for parents. Teach your partner how to do these things:

1. Say and write his or her name, or a name similar to it, in your language and script.
2. Greet properly a friend, a parent, a teacher, a grandparent, a new person in your language.
3. Thank someone for a favor in your language.
4. Describe the right foods for various times during the day.
5. Tell how to prepare a simple dish using proper ingredient names.
6. Write an invitation for your parent(s) to attend the Culture Exchange Evening.

The Plan involved pairing each student with a culturally different partner based on the students' dominant home language. The tasks each pair had to perform were apparently simple. As students became involved in the tasks they discovered that things may not be as simple as they look. They also learned (especially the American partners of the learning pairs) to respect the knowledge their partners had, which at first had not seemed to be an asset. Parents attending the exchange evening were amazed and touched at what their children had learned and what they had taught a "foreigner." Most of all, students felt bonded to each other and to this teacher, who had honored their cultures and languages in this manner.

Children of single-parent or blended families, or families in varied relationships with immigration and naturalization laws and in various phases of the assimilation process, often make up the majority of our classes. Classrooms are populated with children of families with same-gender partners, children in foster care, and children from families defined as dysfunctional by outsiders. Assignments requiring children to research their family connections need to be presented to parents in a nonthreatening, flexible manner. The last thing we want from a school assignment is to have it create dissension at home, insecurity, or even shame for the child. We need to inform parents and caretakers about forthcoming assignments that might involve family sensitivities and ask that they alert us if there are activities that might be uncomfortable for their child.

SAMPLE ACTIVITIES 7.3

Promoting Self-Esteem and Cultural Awareness

PRIMARY GRADES

"Profile of the Week": Post paper silhouette or photo of child with "Things I like about..." comments from classmates about spotlighted child. You can collect and write statements during a sharing time.

"The Way We Were": Put up baby pictures of class members, with birth information, favorite toy, and first words.

"Our Gang": Display current Polaroid photos of children with name and favorite things such as color, food, activity.

Our Gang variation/extension: Number photos and have children draw a number. They write "What I like about..." sentences to display under the picture they wrote about.

Culture Cooking: Collect simple culture-related recipes and schedule parent to assist classroom-cooking session on monthly basis. Have parent describe ingredients and where to get them. Compile a class cookbook.

Body Prints: Have children trace each other on butcher paper. Outlines are colored by each child, cut out, and displayed in classroom. Discuss how we are alike and different.

Self-Portraits: Have children make and sign crayon drawings or tempera paintings of themselves. Display the drawings.

continued

Sample Activities 7.3 (Cont.)

INTERMEDIATE GRADES

"American Rainbows": Make a bulletin board featuring a rainbow with seven colors. Write "food," "homes," "religions," "families," "styles," "languages," "appearances" on different colors. Have students collect or draw pictures that illustrate diversity and place them on the appropriate rainbow color.

"We're Here": On a world map, connect student names or pictures to place of birth.

"What's in a Name?": Put up a research bulletin board with each student telling what she or he discovered about her or his first name — why parent chose it, its meaning, origin.

"Book of Origins": Have students do individual research on family that can include stories starting with grandparents' detailing where they lived and what they did, illustrated with timeline and map of origins.

"Our Resumés": Have students identify their favorite things, abilities or talents, and future goals. Collect these into a class book.

Learning from the Community

Other sources of learning about cultures are parents and grandparents, sources we often hesitate to tap. We may feel that because of language barriers or social inhibitions, some parents would not come to our classrooms to share their cultures. Breaking down these inhibitions might be easier if we gave choices of times and tasks for parents and other relatives to come to the class to share. The sharing can be simple and brief. It can be a picture, religious object, game, song, story, newspaper. Accept anything and offer suggestions if a parent does not know what he or she has to share. The payoff of parent presentations is multiple. Parent and child feel valued and included. Other children begin to see similarities between their ways and those of their classmates. Having parents in the classroom provides face-to-face contact between parents and children from different groups. We know that this kind of contact reduces fear of the unknown for all involved.

Basic Ideas for Primary Grades Instruction in Cultural Diversity

1. There are many kinds of families.
2. All kinds of people live in our community.
3. There are some ways in which we are alike.

4. There are some ways in which we are different.
5. We work together in our community.

Excursions into the community, such as field trips and walking tours, can also be used to highlight learning about local cultural or ethnic groups. As the children study their community, they should give attention to the stores, restaurants, theaters, churches, cemeteries, and clubs that are ethnically or culturally identified.

Often, local ethnic organizations are willing to send a representative to classes to tell children about their group and share some of its local history. Children can get more from these visits if they discuss why the visitor is coming before the day of the visit. They should list the questions they would like to ask and decide how they will make the visitor feel at home in the classroom. Following the visit is a fine occasion for the practice of thank-you note writing and the further study of group issues that the visitor initiated.

7.3 *SMALL GROUP WORK: MATCHING ACTIVITIES TO BASIC IDEAS*

Categorize the activities in the following list according to the basic idea of cultural diversity each one fits best. Then develop two more activities for each category and share with a colleague or your class. When you have finished, you will have a good beginning for integrating the affirmation of cultural diversity in your social studies program.

_____ Make a class book of individual pictures and stories of people in activities of different cultural heritages.

_____ Celebrate holidays honored by various cultures.

_____ Gather pictures of all kinds of families from different cultural groups. Ask children to find a family with a grandmother, two brothers, and so on.

_____ Talk about what children do when they are with their families. Make a chart story about the discussion.

_____ Take walks or trips to see community workers on the job; include a variety of ethnic or racial groups in your selection.

_____ Have children categorize pictures of people according to basic activities of eating, working, playing, worshiping, and homemaking.

_____ Share a book with children that shows a child cooking, making music, celebrating a holiday, carrying out a daily routine, or communicating in a culturally identifiable way. Ask students to point out how the activity is different from and the same as the way they would do that activity.

When teachers take their classes to a culturally related community celebration such as Chinese New Year, Greek Festival Days, Japanese Obon, or an Indian Powwow, they need to secure the assistance of a member of the group whose celebration is being visited. This person should serve as a cultural interpreter. Children should learn what the costumes, foods, music, and dances represent. They should discover how that group came to the community and learn something of the local history of the group. They should find out what activities the group organizes to teach its children their traditions. Furthermore, the students should discuss why the group chooses to keep these traditions and whether the traditions are the same here as they are in the group's country or region of origin.

The excursion should be followed by a review and discussion of the event visited. Further interviews with the cultural interpreter may be needed to answer the questions children have about what they saw and experienced. Individual pictures or stories or newspaperlike accounts of the experience are appropriate ways for children to integrate the event into their experience.

Incorporating the language and culture of students in our schools tends to empower students. Teachers need to see their roles as adding a second language and culture to a student's repertoire rather than subtracting the primary language and culture. Some further ways we can promote a child's pride and proficiency in a primary culture include ideas that extend beyond our individual classroom to the entire school:

1. Provide signs in the main office that welcome and inform people in their own languages.
2. Encourage students to use their primary language in school in such settings as cooperative groups, during assemblies, and in other functions; let them use the language in some writing assignments.
3. Recruit people who can tutor students in their primary languages.
4. Create units of work that incorporate other languages in addition to the primary school language.
5. Acquire books and reading materials written in various students' primary languages for classroom and school libraries.[2]

Some of us come from regions and communities that are not currently nourished by the arrival of new groups or immigrants. Unless we have personal contact with someone of contrasting ways or appearance, we may grow up thinking of ourselves as not having a distinct culture. We say, "Oh, I'm just an American," or "I'm so mixed that I don't claim any ethnic group," or more sadly and erroneously, "I don't have a culture!" Our task as teachers in such settings is to help every child uncover the unacknowledged and taken-for-granted ways in which he or she is a

---

[2]Adapted from New Zealand Department of Education, *New Voices: Second Language Learning and Teaching: A Handbook for Primary Teachers* (Wellington: Department of Education, 1988).

cultural representative. All the strategies for self-naming and naming others that were discussed earlier are viable in communities that identify themselves as mainstream American. In addition, these students need to explore their own ideas about what they do and believe that makes them American. Some topics to pursue are listed in Sample Activities 7.4. It is probable during the course of this kind of exploration that every student will discover group connections that he or she can prize; students also should be able to identify some of the many ways we express our Americanness. Participating in class activities that affirm multiple ethnic, racial, or linguistic backgrounds helps many students feel that they belong to the larger society. Our goal is to find a balance between honoring distinctiveness and prizing what is shared and common.

SAMPLE ACTIVITIES 7.4

"Being American" Bulletin Boards

1. Collect pictures for an "American Culture" that can be categorized into sections on food, clothes, homes, shopping, churches, government, schools, entertainment, transportation.

2. "America Keeps and America Lends and Sells" can serve as a theme for reconfiguring any of the cultural categories — food, music, architecture, words — used locally that have come from or gone to another culture. Use a world map and different-colored labels to identify "keeping," from "exporting." Food examples include pizza, taco, gyro for "keeping" and hot dog, Coca-Cola, cookie for "exporting." "Keeping" architectural examples include pillars, Romanesque circles within arches, kiosks, and for "exporting" tepee, glass and steel, freeway; "keeping" words— *schlepp, ciao, cheri* — are legion, as are "exports" such as *jazz, jeans, basketball, weekend.*

3. Divide an American map into regions — New England, Midwest, East Coast, Southeast, and so on. Periodically change the focus for the regions using natural resources, common foods, expressions, ethnic composition of population, favorite sports and events. Have the students collect pictures that illustrate each focus, and locate and compare geographic regions.

4. Display an American map labeled "American Name-Calling" that locates state nicknames, regional nicknames, city nicknames, different names for the same foods, favorite expressions, or greetings.

Learning about Cultures from Secondary Sources

Learning about a culture from books and films or other materials is like learning another language from a textbook and tapes. Being where the language is spoken makes all the difference, just as firsthand contact is the best way to learn culture and learn about culture. Because we are not usually able to take our students to live with other people, we are forced to rely on books and mediated images as sources for learning about cultures.

Selection of authentic and contemporary materials about cultures is a sensitive task. In recent years, publishers of major textbook series have made substantial efforts to include in their books a greater variety of cultural and racial group representations as well as to make those inclusions authentic, nonstereotypic portrayals. We must go beyond textbooks, however, if we want to gain a depth of understanding about a particular group. Most texts are organized as factual surveys, and children need more material than a text provides to investigate a specific culture. Teacher's editions may give us some leads to enrichment materials about cultures they include, such as trade books and films. Other sources of materials about various cultures and ethnic groups are listed in the bibliography of this chapter. To give students critical practice in analyzing information to which they are exposed, teachers should prompt students to find out when the source they use was published and, if possible, something about who wrote and published it. Asking whether the pictures would be the same if taken today and whether the author was a native of the culture being described should become part of social studies instructional routines.

Whatever secondary sources they select to study a culture, teachers should use several themes and questions to guide students in exploring them. Teachers can help students examine how the group being studied uses the resources around them and how these resources shape the culture. In other words, what do resources have to do with clothing, housing, and eating styles? Another watchword to observe in selecting and using secondary materials is perspective. Good history instruction causes students to try imagining how an event such as the Civil War or the Gold Rush would look and feel to the different groups involved in it. Using a book or video that portrays one point of view is acceptable so long as the teacher helps students imagine how the story might have been portrayed if told from another perspective. Looking at cultural practices to discern how they serve to bind the group together can move students beyond fascination with what is exotic or perhaps distasteful. Reflecting on changes groups suffer as a way to discover what group members do to help their cultures survive can assist students in understanding practices as diverse as Amish separatism and the African-American use of kente cloth. Asking these reflective questions over time will work toward building the students' critical sense that automatically prompts them to question either-or concepts and unchanging answers when learning about the social world. All these suggestions can be woven into a multicultural frame of reference that teachers can use in instruction aimed at learning about other cultures.

SAMPLE ACTIVITIES 7.5

Correcting for Stereotypes Bulletin Board

IMAGES OF JAPAN: HOW DO WE KNOW A CULTURE?

Our Stereotypes	Traditions	Japan Today
kimono	kimono times	kimono times
cherry blossoms	spring festival	spring festival
hard work	duty, loyalty	work and play
tea, rice	tea ceremony	coffee, tea, soft drink
manufactured goods	calligraphy	revere art, technology
look alike	geisha, coman	Western, traditional dress

Have students use these three themes to categorize pictures cut from magazines focusing on a single culture or national group or combination of them. They should find some pictures that fit all three categories and discuss how we develop our images of groups or nationalities. Do we get our ideas about groups within our own society in the same ways? Do our textbooks portray a culture's traditional way of life?

Using Holidays as Critical Thinking Times

Another source for teaching about cultural diversity is holidays. Consider how we might celebrate them using a multicultural frame of reference. Examining the possible motivations behind our traditional holiday art activities can provide clues. For our national culture, why was it important for Americans to remember President Washington as a young boy who always told the truth? Once children have explored the cherry tree chopping as a morality tale, making cherry-festooned hatchets of construction paper can have more meaning for them. Showing connections between the holiday and children's lives necessarily takes us into the religious realm. For example, children might discuss preparation for giving up something as a way to remember what Jesus Christ gave up as an initial understanding of pre-Lenten celebrations known as Mardi Gras or carnival in Catholic cultures. They can examine the Jewish Passover, Pesach, as a celebration of the Hebrew exodus from Egypt that recalls the hard times the Jews experienced while enslaved by the Pharoah. Jews commemorate these times by serving such ritual foods as *matzoh*, unleavened bread that reminds them their ancestors left Egypt with such haste they could not wait for the bread to rise; *moror*, bitter horseradish recalling the horrors of slavery; and *haroset*, a mixture of chopped apples, nuts, cinnamon, and wine recalling the mortar the Hebrews used to build cities for the Pharoah. Learning such symbols and their meaning can show students how people of other religions recall difficult or important times of their faith. The Muslim holiday *Eid al-Adha* requires that an animal such as a lamb, goat, sheep, cow, or camel be sacrificed and cooked; then part of the meat is eaten at home, and part is given away to the poor or the needy or to friends. This holiday ritual commemorates God's command to the Prophet Abraham to sacrifice his son Ishmael, and God's subsequent release of Abraham from this awful duty by giving him a lamb to sacrifice in place of his son.[3] Hearing this story allows children to learn that sacrifice for a belief plays an important part in holidays of many faiths. In exploring reasons behind religious holidays, we help children learn about other cultures and, possibly, gain experience teaching others about their own cultures and beliefs. In teaching about culture, include examples that help students understand the importance of ritual and celebration in all our lives.

The approaches to instruction about cultures presented here can help you move your students toward the multicultural goals of seeing multiple perspectives, expanding their worldview and their knowledge about their own cultures, and learning to value cultures as visions of how groups can survive and adapt to changing circumstances. Ideas and strategies described under the subtitles of learning about ourselves and naming can strengthen a cultural sense of self. Activities and ideas generated around the categories of learning from each other and community sources serve to recognize and include all locally represented cultures in the classroom learning community. Using bulletin board themes can spotlight collections showing how an American can be recognized. Questioning stereotypes helps students visualize what they all have in common and assists them in recognizing stereotyping that may be done for the purpose of excluding certain groups. Extending and enriching instruction about cultures with secondary sources helps to encourage the critical thinking we want students to cultivate when they consider other cultures as well as their own.

CLASSROOM INTERGROUP AND MULTICULTURAL PROBLEM EXPLORATION

Are we doing all that is required to prepare children to live in our culturally and racially pluralistic society when we structure more equitable learning settings in our classrooms, celebrate ethnic holidays and heroes, and incorporate multiple

---

[3]An explanatory *Calendar of Religious Holidays and Ethnic Festivals* updated biannually is available from the National Conference of Christians and Jews, Inc., 71 Fifth Avenue, New York, NY 10003, c/o Maurice Bozarth, Calendar Edition. Other curriculum materials dealing with intergroup conflict resolution are also available from this source.

perspectives in our presentation of the American experience? Each of these categories of classroom and social studies instruction opens vistas to the realities of our society. None, however, *directly* instructs children about ways to live and interact positively in situations where power, prejudice, stereotyping, and status create conflict in personal and group interactions. Bringing problematic and conflictual situations into the classroom for controlled explorations adds a direct, real-life dimension to preparing children to live in our multicultural society. Learning to deal with new situations and people takes practice. Viewing alternatives is a learnable critical thinking skill, and looking at a situation from another point of view is an attitude we need to model.

To many of us, the idea of intentionally including conflict in our classrooms is threatening. We may be highly adept in conflict avoidance; we may prefer not to recognize conflict when we see it. By controlling the situation, we hope the reasons for the conflict will disappear. And sometimes they will. Or we hope that we can prevent conflict by instructing children to treat one another with respect. Surely, we need to communicate this message in the hope that conflicts will be averted. Still, conflicts will always arise. Our task is to decide what to do about the conflict we see that emerges from individual and intergroup interaction. Lessons in conflict resolution can assist us with this task.

7.4 *ON YOUR OWN: INTERGROUP CONFLICT IN SCHOOLS*

Examine your feelings about conflictual classroom situations by choosing the one response that best matches what you would prefer as a response. These sample conflict situations are designed to prompt your thinking about where you stand intellectually and emotionally.

Situation 1

Anton, an African-American child, comes to you after recess and tells you that Chad, a white child, called him a "nigger" while they were standing in the third-grade line.

1. You tell Anton to ignore Chad.
2. You get the children to work and call Chad and Anton to the hall to have him explain why he would "name-call," asking him never to do it again.
3. You seat the class and give them a "lecture" on words we do not use in polite society.
4. Later that day you use the event as a situation for the class to explore

through two puppets, one black and one white, without mentioning the boys who provoked this role play.

Situation 2

Your fifth graders are buzzing about the new second-grade teacher, Mr. Todd, who is a dwarf.

1. You discuss the term *stereotype* with the class.
2. You tell the class that they should treat others as they would like to be treated.
3. You invite Mr. Todd to your class to tell them how he feels about being a "little person" teacher.
4. You ask the children to write about how they would feel if they were suddenly transformed into dwarfs.

Situation 3

A newly arrived, adopted Korean child enters your kindergarten. Chungsoon cannot speak English. This is a novelty to all the other English-speaking children. They are laughing and pointing.

1. You ask children to think of ways they can make Chungsoon feel at home in the class.
2. You appoint Angeline to be Chungsoon's special friend.
3. You read the book *I Am Here: Yo Estoy Aqui* about Luz, a Spanish-speaking kindergartener who learns to communicate with the other children through a Spanish-speaking classroom aide.
4. You create a special place separate from the other children for Chungsoon to work and give her special, individual attention with gestures.

Examine Your Choices

If you selected number one in the first situation, number two in the second situation, or number four in the third situation, you need to examine why you are more comfortable ignoring the conflicts involved in these situations. Conflict can be turned into a learning experience for you and the children only if it is examined. If it is ignored it will not go away; it will become part of the hidden, nonpositive classroom culture. If you chose number two in the first situation, you should consider the effect of this method. It may keep Chad from name-calling in your presence, but it also may inspire Chad to call Anton "tattletale nigger." If you choose to lecture the class, you are in effect, telling them what not to do. Yet they need to know why. They need to explore how it would feel to be called a similar name. The choices that involve presenting the conflict as an exploration using different characters requires extreme readiness on your part to "seize the moment of teachability." Can you be that alert? Ready? Adroit? What if you do not observe situations that are auspicious lead-ins to these vital issues?

There is no course that can prepare you completely for the decisions you will have to make in handling individual and intergroup conflict. What you can do is discuss with colleagues the situations in this self-check and other situations in which you have been involved or that you have observed. Be assured that as a teacher you will have issues of stereotyping and name-calling and prejudice. Only experience, informed by your attentive eyes and ears and tempered by your sense of social justice, can give you the self-confidence and courage to handle this kind of culture learning in a positive manner.

Teaching about Interpersonal and Intergroup Conflict

Techniques and materials for the exploration of conflict usually fall into the bibliographic categories of role playing, problem solving, and critical thinking. Typically, more than a verbal prompt is used to initiate this kind of classroom episode. The initiators can take many forms: staged incidents, photographs portraying children in dilemmas, puppets that get into conflict situations, filmstrips that lead into a crisis point, and trade books that portray social, racial, or cultural dissonance.

Using dolls dressed as people who have come to the classroom is another effective way to involve children in the experience of living with people who are different from them or people who have disabilities to overcome. "Persona dolls" are introduced by the teacher as people who have come to join the class, as portrayed in the following transcript.

SAMPLE CLASSROOM TRANSCRIPT 7.1

Looking in Classrooms: Exploration of Differences

Mrs. Lever introduces Brian, an orthopedically handicapped third grader, to the class one morning during opening exercises. She brings in Brian, a doll dressed as a third grader seated in a wheelchair.

Mrs. Lever: Class, we have someone who will be joining us. His name

---

continued

SAMPLE CLASSROOM TRANSCRIPT 7.1 (CONT.)

is Brian. He comes to us from Children's Hospital where he has just learned to use his new wheelchair. His mother tells me that Brian is eager to be in our class. He was hurt in an auto accident. He cannot use the lower half of his body. He will need our help to do certain things. Do you have any questions about our new classmate?

Melissa: Can he talk?

Mrs. Lever: For now, Brian will talk through me. Later, some of you may learn enough about Brian to talk for him.

Vito: How come he's coming to our class?

Mrs. Lever: He lives in our neighborhood and finished second grade last year.

This line of questioning continues until children have discovered that Brian will need help with bathroom visits, with getting a drink of water, and with moving in and out the doors. Mrs. Lever then sets up a buddy schedule for Brian for the rest of the week.

A few days later, Mrs. Lever asks the children to share what they have learned now that Brian is in the class. Brian's buddies tell about their troubles in bathrooms and with doors. Mrs. Lever leads them to explore how they would feel if they were Brian. Finally, Mrs. Lever asks them to think about what they could do to make their classroom and school an easier place for Brian to be. She fully expects that the group will begin a campaign to prepare the school for children like Brian. She expects that they will speak with the principal and write to the school board about their concerns.

Under the guise of fantasy you can introduce explorations of real-life problems and conflicts. Classrooms can accommodate more than one persona doll. In settings where children would not have contact with certain "different others," the dolls can provide opportunities for empathy-building experiences that lead children to think critically about human variety that is outside their life spheres.

Staging classroom incidents is one of the most effective avenues to open discussion and to generate more personal insights about the effects of prejudice and stereotyping. Here are five classic ideas that have proven adaptable to a variety of ages and settings.

SAMPLE ACTIVITIES 7.6

Understanding Prejudice and Stereotyping

BLUE EYES AND BROWN EYES:

This is a teacher-instigated experiment in social control and prejudice. Separate children according to some observable trait. Do not use skin color, since this experience is intended to be analogous to the real experiences that happen as a result of prejudice based on skin color. Treat representatives of one trait, such as brown eyes, with great favor. Allow them to sit in the front of the class, have more privileges, be first in line, have all the recess equipment, and so on. Treat the blue-eyed children with disdain. When they make an error, call attention to it and say, "Well, that's what I expect from a blue-eyed person." After a day, or less for younger children, of this kind of teacher treatment, hold a class discussion on how each group felt. Extend the discussion to whether this kind of thing happens in the real world. Discuss what children have learned from this experience that they can use for the rest of their lives.[4]

THE MUSEUM:

This experience is to help children recognize their stereotypes and consider where they came from. It is appropriate for middle graders. Ask children to discuss the purpose of a museum. Ask them to tell what would be in a museum about people. Ask children to close their eyes and imagine that they are in an ethnic museum. Their purpose is to imagine a display in the African-American Room of the museum. Allow some silent time before proceeding.

After silent imagining time, ask children to describe what they put into the African-American Room.

Then suggest that children move to another room. Use a group that has significance for the class for the next mental display. Repeat the same recording process followed for describing the African-American Room.

Discuss whether members of the group being portrayed would decorate their room the same way. Record corrections or deletions on lists

continued

[4]Jane Elliott and William Peters, *A Class Divided: Then and Now* (New Haven Conn.: Yale University Press, 1987). PBS video also available.

---

using another color marker or chalk. Now ask students to visit the museum again as though they were members of the group represented in each room.

Finally, ask students to tell what they learned from their museum tours. Record their contributions. Conclude by asking students to write ways to use what they have learned. Collect statements and display around original "Museum" lists.

WHAT DID YOU SEE:

This is a dramatic illustration of how selective memory distorts the way we remember events and individuals or groups. With no warning, stage a classroom interruption that will be witnessed by the children. You could have two children from another class, preferably from differing ethnic or cultural groups, chase each other into your room shouting at each other, using derogatory names, over a playground argument that you end by sending them to the principal's office.

Once calm is restored, ask the children to write about who they saw, what the people said, what happened first, and what the scene was about. Then have them compare their stories. Are they the same? What kinds of differences are there? Are there differences related to mixing facts with conclusions or inferences? Are there differences of interpretation that stem from the racial or cultural identity of the players?

This experiment is much broader than intergroup relations. It should inspire more critical thinking about what we see and read in the news.

STEREOTYPES: GENERALIZATIONS THAT HURT PEOPLE

Ask students to identify behaviors they do not like and write them across the chalkboard. Next invent a fictitious name and have the group make up a sentence that connects the behavior to the name. For example, "Ximena always wants to be first" or "James stole someone's baseball glove."

Next, add a sentence that further identifies each character. "Ximena lives in East Los Angeles," "James comes from a poor family." Then, ask students to compose a third sentence for each that puts the two previous sentences together in a way that says something general about the people identified in the first sentences. Various possibilities for each may be listed: "All girls want to be first," "Mexicans have to have their way," or "Poor kids steal."

Ask students to tell why these groups of sentences do not make sense. Explore how the individuals in these examples would feel if they heard them. Ask students to recall whether they have ever heard people making judgments about individuals that sound like the ones they have just invented. Discuss how they can learn to analyze this kind of thinking in their own lives. Teach them the categories — religion, race, ethnic or racial group, gender, age, mental or physical ability, amount of wealth, family situation — that are used when people make stereotypic comments. Practice making more examples and discussing why they are and are not true.

ADVICE COLUMN:

Cooperative groups can act as though they were editing answers to the following letters written to a newspaper advice column:

Advice Editor:

I am worried that I will not be able to make friends in my new school. My family is Muslim and when I told the class that I did not want to eat snacks during Ramadan, the kids just laughed and called me a dirty Iraqi. I feel that the kids in my fourth-grade class think all Muslims kill people. What can I do?

Sincerely,
Selina

Dear Advice Editor:

I feel that being Haitian is bad. No matter how hard I try, the kids in my building treat me mean. They call me names and tell me to get a boat and go back to where I came from. What can I do to make them understand that we cannot go back? How can I be more American?

Your friend,
Marcel

Each group should compose a letter giving Selina and Marcel suggestions. After reading the responses to the class, let students analyze the positive and negative elements of each response.

The composition of our classrooms and the consequent interplay arising from the differences between individuals presents us with a built-in curriculum. Differences each child brings represent potential contributions for the growth of the other children of the group. The challenge is learning how to take advantage of these opportunities. Curriculum guides, with lesson ideas such as the ones outlined above, can initiate but not complete your curriculum planning. Each class will bring you a new configuration of cultures to explore and incorporate into your daily activities. Business as usual will come to mean changing and adapting your approach to include and incorporate elements of your students' cultures as part of the curriculum. A wise immigrant grandmother, when asked by a teacher how to respond to the needs of her grandchild, gave this advice: "You must give her roots to grow and wings to fly!" Explaining, she continued, "I want her to know who she is and where she came from. These are her roots. But she must have knowledge about the American culture so she can go where she wants and become who she wants to be."[5]

SUMMARY

In this chapter we have reviewed three ways that culture learning can occur in the elementary classroom. The way we organize learning is potentially a positive culture-forming process. Cooperative learning modes appear to offer a powerful tool for building positive interactions between children who may perceive themselves as different from others in cultural ways. We may learn about cultures by taking advantage of the cultures that children bring with them to school. Recognizing that each individual identifies with a variety of microcultures can guide us in the way we orient children's study of groups of people. We may learn about dealing with differences in our own and others' cultures by practicing the skill of seeing a situation from another perspective and exploring alternative resolutions of conflicts. Finally, we clear a path for creating new ways to behave in our culture by seeking solutions to real problems related to individual and group identities.

SUGGESTED READINGS

Banks, James A. "Multicultural Education: Development, Dimensions and Challenges." *Phi Delta Kappan* 75 (September 1993): 22–28. Clear, concise statement of this influential educator's definition and prescriptions for multiculturalizing schooling.

---

[5]From "Addressing Needs of Immigrant Students," an address by Laurie Olsen, Director, California of Tomorrow Foundation, given in Santa Clara, California, March 15, 1991.

Bennett, Christine. *Comprehensive Multicultural Education: Theory and Practice*, 3d ed. Boston: Allyn & Bacon, 1994. Broad conception of multicultural education in updated college textbook.

Boutte, G. S., and McCormick, C. B. "Avoiding Pseudomulticulturalism: Authentic Multicultural Activities." *Childhood Education* 68 (February 1992): 140–144. Presents set of authenticity checks teachers can use to evaluate their attempts to multiculturalize curriculum.

Byrnes, Deborah A. "Teacher, they called me a _____!" *Prejudice and Discrimination in the Classroom.* New York: Anti-Defamation League of B'nai B'rith, 1987. Practical defintions and activities for classroom teachers.

Cohn, Amy L., ed. *From Sea to Shining Sea.* New York: Scholastic, 1994. Multicultural collection of stories and songs related to all periods of American history.

Coles, Robert. *The Spiritual Life of Children.* Boston, Mass.: Houghton Mifflin, 1990. Respected child psychologist explores children's feelings and thoughts about spiritual issues.

Derman-Sparks, L. *Anti-Bias Curriculum: Tools for Empowering Young Children.* Washington, D.C.: National Association for the Education of Young Children, 1989. Almost instant classic as positive source assisting teachers wanting to incorporate multicultural approaches to instruction.

Grant, Carl A., and Sleeter, Christine E. *Turning on Learning: Five Approaches for Multicultural Teaching Plans for Race, Class, Gender, and Disability.* New York: Macmillan, 1989. Contrasting approaches according to philosophical orientation; excellent analytic matrix with ample practical examples of each approach to multicultural pedagogy.

Hakim, Joy. *The Story of Us.* New York: Oxford University Press distributed by D. C. Heath in U.S., 1994. Groundbreaking series that employs storytelling approach to U.S. history, highlighting interplay of conflicting cultures and connecting past to present events in ten volumes for elementary and middle levels.

Howard, G. R. "Whites in Multicultural Education: Rethinking Our Role" *Phi Delta Kappan* 75 (January 1993): 36–41. Elaborates difficulties and misgivings of "majority-culture" teachers in adopting multicultural approaches.

McCracken, Janet Brown. *Valuing Diversity: The Primary Years.* Washington, D.C.: National Council for the Education of Young Children, 1993. Up-to-date sourcebook for resources and activities beginning with preschool years.

National Council for the Social Studies. "Guidelines on Multicultural Education." *Social Education* 56 (September 1992): 274–293. Statement by professional association listing ways pluralism can be integrated in social studies.

Ogbu, John U. "Understanding Cultural Diversity and Learning." *Educational Researcher* 21 (November 1992): 5–14. Disagrees with widespread approaches to school reform efforts of core curriculum and multicultural education arguing that they do not address real difficulties of minority group students who have traditionally not done well in public schools.

Pilger, Mary Anne. *Multicultural Projects Idea Index*. Englewood, Colo.: Libraries Unlimited, 1992. Indexes sources that detail craft, holiday, food, game, and historical projects.

Teaching Tolerance. 400 Washington Avenue, Montgomery, AL 36104: Southern Poverty Law Center. Free periodical for teachers, replete with multiculturally related teaching ideas and experiences. Fax 205-264-6892. See especially Spring 1994 number containing interview with historian Ronald Takaki, "Reflections from a Different Mirror," pages 11–15, defending a pluralistic view of multicultural instruction and the opportunity schools have to "hold up a different mirror" in teaching students about our society.

Chapter 8

LANGUAGE LEARNING in the SOCIAL STUDIES

This chapter explores issues of language and literacy learning within the social studies. The pedagogy of delivering social studies content through a variety of language-rich sources is addressed, as is content-driven development of expressive language skills. Opportunities and limitations of language and literacy learning in the social studies units are delineated. These issues are discussed in the following sections:

1/ Relating the Social Studies and Language/Literacy Learning

2/ Language Development in Social Studies Units

3/ Trade-Offs in Social Studies-Language Integrated Instruction

All instruction requires language and, ultimately, is about language. Social studies instruction presents special language considerations for many students. They often consider the required content reading to be lengthy, dull, abstract, and lacking in story-line interest. Students may not express their distaste or difficulties in these terms. Instead, they typically object to the following strategies we have traditionally relied on to help them "get through" the material:

- Take turns reading orally in class from the social studies textbook
- Fill in workbook exercises that may or may not have been connected to what had been discussed in class
- Learn a traditional form for outlines without having previously developed a need to use an outline
- Reread textbook chapters and write out answers to end-of-chapter questions
- Hand in note cards filled with main points and supporting details from outside reading
- Answer the confusing test items that were part of the publisher's package

If your social studies instruction in the elementary grades consisted primarily of these activities, you probably thought of them as drudgery. As a teacher you may have a mixed perspective on these same activities. You may agree that they are less than scintillating, but you may not see how they can be avoided. To help students overcome these language hurdles common to most social studies instruction, the whole-language approach to instruction is being recommended. Advocates argue that using literature-based input and strategies from reading-writing workshops[1] will offer students a human interest, plot-stimulated access to social studies. This approach should help to overcome the common lack of interest students experience when they have to read typical social studies textbook writing, with its expository style, high idea density, technical words, and long sentences.

Most teachers, therefore, must find a way to make content accessible to students. Often, difficulties of access to social studies content are related to concepts that are beyond student experience and to reading materials that are above student ability to decode. Conversely, by moving away totally from the textbook as a guide to content, teachers may lose the continuity that texts offer by their chronological organization and thematic interweaving of the issues inherent in the larger context of history study. The goal of this chapter, then, is to explore different ways instruction can address important social studies goals and understandings while

---

[1]General writing workshop procedures include cooperative planning of ideas often based on reading and possible outlines or structures, individual or team writing, peer editing, and individual or team refinement and revision.

still helping students overcome language and literacy barriers so they can get at social studies content. To pursue this goal, we risk repeating some material presented in earlier chapters on lesson and unit planning as well as overlapping content from your language and literacy curriculum classes. However, we believe that the relationship of language and literacy development to social studies content and goals deserves this additional focus.

Recall the importance of language as a social studies goal. The major aim of social studies is to prepare students to become critically active citizens. Consider the language and literacy requirements of citizenship in our country and world. We must listen, read, and view with understanding to keep up with what is happening. To respond to our own and our community self-interest, we need to be able to explain what we think and to support our positions. Equally important are the writing demands of conducting our affairs. We order goods and services, make consumer complaints, fill in all kinds of forms, keep minutes, formulate agendas, submit proposals, and write reports and letters and memoranda for the businesses and organizations with which we are associated. We complain about the paperwork we must wade through, but without it our lives would become even more frustrating. The old American custom of "putting it in writing" is here to stay.

Thomas Jefferson understood well that only if the gentleman farmers of the new republic were educated would they be able to become critically informed and involved as citizens. The need for educated, critical thinkers is even more crucial in our time. Citizenship for us has expanded to include wider, more diverse segments of society and a global range of social issues. The security and enhancement of our way of life hinges on the citizen's ability to think about critically and to express himself or herself on the issues of the day. To thrive in our society, children must become critical readers, logical thinkers, and concise, persuasive speakers and writers.

RELATING THE SOCIAL STUDIES AND LANGUAGE/LITERACY LEARNING

Advocates of the whole-language approach to literacy learning are helping us to see that good thinking and writing skills flow from well-developed oral language. They understand that good literature read by the teacher and discussed by the children builds a rich foundation for oral fluency essential to growth in literacy. A sharing or collaborative approach to these language experiences between the teacher and students and among the students seems to lead to increased learning and heightened feelings of efficacy. This insight is as illuminating as it is demanding to social studies planning and instruction. Philosophically, whole-language advocates remind us of the centrality of student participation and of starting instruction with what students know as the basis for further learning. The whole-language approach can help us see that, from a psychological perspective, covering what is in a textbook by reading and rote recitation may not lead to greater student comprehension. Politically, we can see that whole-language strategies require students to participate and collaborate in their own construction of knowledge; therefore, these tactics offer one means by which to progress toward one citizenship goal: engaging students in working toward solutions for issues that concern them.

Pedagogically, whole-language specialists suggest that we think of listening/viewing/reading-speaking/writing connections as transactions with texts.[2] By expanding the definition of text to include all the linguistic arenas, we can see more clearly the demands this redefinition makes on social studies planning and instruction. To engage students better, social studies instruction needs to incorporate a variety of textual transactions. Initially this may seem to be an overwhelming additional planning task. On more careful analysis, we can see that textual transactions have always been embedded in social studies instruction. Carefully exploiting them and becoming more discerning about how they are sequenced will help us overcome some of the frustration we feel when planning social studies instruction. To test this assertion, examine the following classroom episode and find the language opportunities inherent in this informally developed social studies theme. Read the vignette and look for these aspects: What social studies knowledge and skills were developed? What language/literacy skills were being developed? What sequence did the teacher use to develop them?

SAMPLE CLASSROOM EPISODE 8.1

Looking in Classrooms: Global Education in Kindergarten

Veteran kindergarten teacher Barbara Schubert, tired of the inanity of most sharing times, decided to introduce a global slant to the routine. She added a globe and a package of red stick-on dots. Children continued to bring in toys and other significant objects to share. Ms. Schubert directed them to look for where the toy, or object, had been made.[3] Quickly, children learned the words *Korea, Taiwan, Japan,* and *Hong Kong* by sight and by location on the globe. After the children told about the objects they had brought, they placed a stick-on dot marking the place on the globe where the item had been manufactured.

---

[2]Although it is beyond the scope in this book to detail the whole-language approach, we include aspects of it that are crucial to integrative social studies instruction.
[3]Barbara Schubert, Blackford School, Campbell, California, permits the use of this teaching episode.

Through initial structured questioning, each child was prompted to include the usual information of what I brought (naming and describing) and how I got it (sequencing), in addition to the extension of where it came from and where that place is on the globe (identifying origin).

Then serendipity entered! One morning a child asked, "What are we going to do about all the volcanoes?" Uncertain of the child's meaning, Ms. Shubert responded, "What volcanoes?" The child brought the globe to the circle and pointed to the mounds of red stick-on dots on Japan, Hong Kong, Taiwan, and Korea, which reminded him of red mountains about to explode. Astutely, Ms. Schubert moved into questions about what the dots meant. The students then were off and running, at their level of comprehension, on the implications of the balance of trade.

After some discussion, the children dictated the beginning of a chart story, with Ms. Schubert asking the children to tell what described most of the toys they shared. After listing several ideas — "mine has batteries," "it transforms," "from Japan," "orange and black" — they decided that none was true for all their toys.

Ms. Schubert: Then what is true about all? Think about the location of the volcanoes.

   Children: Asia!

Ms. Schubert: Can we begin our story with a sentence about toys and Asia?

The children directed Ms. Schubert to write "Most of our toys come from Asia." Then Ms. Schubert asked them to tell her more details about the first sentence. They added: "Our toys are made in Korea, Hong Kong, Taiwan, and Japan. They are imported."

Ms. Schubert asked the children to talk about these facts with their parents and to come to school the next day ready to tell more facts and feelings about the significance of the red dots. Again, posing questions that follow the Taba model of concept formation (see Chapter 4), which substantiates expository writing, she led them to compose a paragraph starting with one general statement followed by two more sentences that added detail to the topic sentence.

As they wrote more about their investigation, Ms. Schubert had them find statements of fact and feeling in their writing. Every child could locate and name numerous countries as well as place them relative to continents and oceans. Beginning understandings of economic pro-

continued

---

duction, consumption, and trade were emerging. Many children brought their parents in to see the "volcanoes." The topic extended into looking at labels so the children could see where their clothes had been made. (At this juncture, had Ms. Schubert been working with a more formal, planned way, she might have led the children into a new line of investigation about where cotton, rayon, polyester, ramie, and wool come from and the processes involved in transforming some of these materials into clothing.) Then Ms. Schubert asked the children to talk to their parents to learn of things other countries bought from the United States. The informal theme of global trade and interdependence produced several pages of chart stories that year. Children continued to bring parents into the classroom to read the results of the students' investigation into world trade. Parents were astounded that kindergarteners could become articulate about a topic that is usually part of a college-level economics course.

This vignette illustrates our contention that young children can investigate apparently sophisticated social studies topics with great interest and profit. Further, their language learning was strengthened, not by rote oral pattern exercises and routinized phonics drills taken from a teacher's manual, but by a horizon-expanding topic that generated opportunities for language skill development. To extend their oral exchanges about things within their experience, the teacher guided them toward the formation of concepts and generalizations while teaching them an expository paragraph composition form. By orally describing, categorizing, and drawing conclusions, and then putting the results into a group-written story, "reading" the story, and performing further oral activity followed by further writing and reading, the children developed language/literacy skills as a natural outcome of the integration of language practice with social studies content. This kindergarten episode also shows that through writing the results of their study, children are led to consider more consciously what they are learning. Ms. Schubert accomplished this by approaching the topic using concrete and emotionally meaningful objects and experiences. For young children, and most of us, topics that best prick our interest are those with which we are familiar. Topics that build from the familiar to the unfamiliar are motivating as they permit us to sense our connection to a wider world.[4] The

---

[4]Learning theorists call this *proximal development*. It involves capitalizing on what is known and bridging from that to more sophisticated understandings by contact with more knowledgeable students or adults. Planning instruction that creates verbal interaction between more and less knowledgeable students is applicable to every age and subject, but is particularly important when you are planning for English-as-Second-Language learners.

teacher built on the children's contributions and gave them a reason to explore further by involving their parents in the process of investigation and its findings.

Her strategy facilitated the children's development of expressive skills. She gradually helped them to make the transition from telling to writing, from idiosyncratic recall to recall based on facts, from stream-of-consciousness recall to a more logically considered relation of observations. All these are facets of thinking. Writing the charts was, in essence, a thinking exercise flowing from prolonged oral exchanges. Collaborative learning, always a keystone of primary-level large group investigation, is increasingly seen as a language/literacy vehicle for older children as well. Small group work in social studies unit study and investigation, by virtue of the language activities required, generates collaborative learning opportunities important at all levels. If viewed from an integrative perspective then, social studies, and other subjects too, while focusing primarily on the knowledge and understandings of the content pertinent to the subject, automatically serve to enhance language and literacy learning.

Expressive Goals and Basic Instructional Strategy in Social Studies

We know that children who read and write with ease usually have previously developed oral-language facility. Recognizing this, a primary concern in our instruction is to provide all students with a rich oral-language environment. Children must be exposed to oral language from a variety of sources ranging from the teacher's own inventiveness to hearing stories read to them or watching and listening to media. Immersion in a content-rich environment supplies children with expressive ammunition from which they draw when they have opportunities to re-create their knowledge. Every time they recite rhymes, sing songs, assume roles in dramatic enactments, tell experiences, retell stories, discuss how to resolve problems, or make decisions, they are enlarging their language and thinking potential.

Experts list three major purposes for oral language and writing that are most related to social studies. One is informative or investigative, a second is interpretive, and the third is persuasive. Narrower, more behavioralistic statements of these goals include recalling facts about topics, listing characteristics or properties of topics, creating categories based on properties, relating events in sequence, and stating opinions and supporting them with facts. Can primary children as well as older children pursue these three purposes? They can, if we keep in mind the whole-language focus on the broader definition of expression that includes oral, pictorial, and kinesthetic as well as written modes. Typically, these purposes, or goals, are not developed when we limit expressive tasks to answering questions from a textbook or other book read to the class, doing fill-in-the-blank items, or matching items in workbooks.

Developing young children's expressive ability is an ongoing, multifaceted, overarching goal. A good learning environment will have various and simultaneous expressive activities related to all curricular areas. The basic strategy, or method, used in social studies to develop these abilities is applicable to other content areas as well.

The following list outlines this basic set of steps. At every step in the strategy the verbal exchanges between teacher and students and among students enhances both social studies and language learning.

Basic Strategy For Prompting Language Expression

Step 1. Eliciting student experience with topic to be introduced: concrete experience—exposure to picture, story, other information, experiment, visit, event

Step 2. Discussing: making terms clear, outlining sequence, findings, questions

Step 3. Motivating: considering purpose for using information, establishing need to organize information

Step 4. Defining expression: deciding form for expression, making structure explicit, developing samples of structure

Step 5. Providing time to develop expression: assisting expression development, providing time to share expression

8.1 ON YOUR OWN: ANALYZING STRATEGIES IN A CLASSROOM EPISODE FOR LANGUAGE EXPRESSION

You may find it useful to read the kindergarten vignette again to identify the basic strategy steps in the list above as Schubert employed them. What do you think was important in this episode for keeping the children's interest, enthusiasm, and expressive productivity going?

When children produce less than adequately in expressive tasks, the difficulty can often be traced to a faulty instructional strategy. Teachers may omit or fail to develop sufficiently one or more of the basic steps—finding student connections to the topic, providing adequate input, framing the task, defining a motivation for the effort, providing models of the task, or supporting the process of development. Children who are enthusiastic about a task usually have an audience for their efforts in mind. Children who make a speech to tell why they favor or oppose letting pets roam freely in the community usually have been instructed about the form a persuasive talk should take. A class in which most children complete expressive tasks successfully has usually been provided instruction in all the steps in the basic strategy for developing expression.

LANGUAGE DEVELOPMENT IN SOCIAL STUDIES UNITS

Beyond the basic strategy for prompting language expression, whole-language experts are providing us with ever more insightful keys to developing language. From their discussions we can make connections from the overarching issues of language and literacy development to social studies unit instruction. Texts, whether oral, viewed, or written, are events that promote students to construct meaning. We can help students unlock meaning from "textual" transactions by the kinds of guiding questions we ask and the kinds of integrated planning we organize in the social studies units. As students become aware of the different purposes they have in their transactions with texts—reading for pleasure, deciding whether an article has information they need, learning how to do something, gaining a sense of place or time, answering a specific question—they can consciously frame their own questions to guide their interaction with texts. Students can use their questions as previewing or prereading prompts to help them structure a focus for their interactions with text and to access the meaning of what they read. These skills can be practiced with any kind of text. The content of a textbook section can be more readily unlocked when instruction begins by establishing a relationship between the student reader and the text. All kinds of texts—video clip, photograph, diary entry, news item, or story—can become more personally relevant to the student by instruction that consciously attempts to build a bridge to the information source. Teachers can introduce a unit through a brief examination of a sample of the text. From this introduction, students can learn how to formulate the questions they will need to study the rest of the unit. Table 8.1 illustrates guiding questions and reactions students can use to explore text.

One way to use a whole-language approach to social studies is through literature sets. An ambitious version of this strategy has students pursue individual readings of books related to a theme. They communicate with themselves and each other using a variety of expressive activities. Teachers incorporate books that represent different genres as well as varying levels of readability within a literature

TABLE 8.1   STUDENT TRANSACTIONS WITH TEXTS AND GUIDING QUESTIONS

Type of Anticipated Reaction	*Guiding Student Question*
personal, emotional	How does this relate to my experience? How do I feel about this?
connective	What does this remind me of? How does it connect with what I know?
descriptive, analystic	What does it say? What is happening?
interpretive, elaborative	What does this mean? How could it be changed?
evaluative	Does this make sense? Do I agree?
self-reflective	Do I understand? What questions do I have?

SOURCE: Lytle, S. L., and Botel, M. *PCRPII: Reading, Writing and Talking across the Curriculum*. Harrisburg: Pennsylvania Department of Education, 1988.

collection on a unit theme. Taken as a set, the works should portray a period in history, a historical event, or a social issue such as civil rights or past and present immigration. Subtopics of the theme might be pursued simultaneously. Students can work individually and in small groups on a subtopic or large question that relates to the broader theme. Teachers incorporate these general procedures taken from writing workshop strategies to keep students motivated and progressing.

1. Teacher introduces each item of literature set; students choose one.
2. Students spend individual time daily reading and writing in journals—facts and feelings or other questions a group wishes to pursue.
3. Several times a week group activities are scheduled allowing students to share journal entries, settle on words to study, and discuss how topics concerned them.
4. Teacher skims each set of books and student journals to learn where to add depth by instruction on social studies content such as a timeline or to add basic questions for the group to pursue. By listening to student talk, teacher raises additional questions, suggests sources, and helps to connect different sources.
5. Students share with entire class and/or some larger community: rereading journal entries, recalling significant discussions, applying skills from study of opinion-editorial pages of newspapers to write appropriate community groups and representatives; inviting leaders to discuss issues with class.

Research and practice in the teaching of writing has supported the value of writing as a way of knowing. This research further suggests the value of having the teacher model the act of writing as well as share, as an equal, parts of his or her effort with students.[5] When students see that teachers are learners and employ techniques to learn similar to those students are asked to follow, the effect on the classroom is powerful. By sharing the adult application of writing as a way of knowing, teachers become part of the classroom community of learners. Integrating journal and other kinds of writing with social studies units offers students and teachers a collaborative forum. Teachers and students often make similar kinds of statements when they discuss the personal effect of sharing their writing: "When I tell someone else, I understand it better myself." Both telling and writing force us to organize our listening, reading, and thinking in a way that we can understand better; with practice and editing, we can help others to understand us also.

There is general agreement that we can devise literature-based experiences around any theme. Our challenge when adopting some of these strategies is to take advantage of their more holistic appeal while keeping the development of social studies understandings and skills as the principal guide in selecting and organizing themes or topics for study.

---

[5]See especially publications about the Bay Area Writers Projects and volumes produced using the University of New Hampshire writer workshop approach for teachers that was inspired by Donald H. Graves.

Organizing Literature in Social Studies Units

If we consider the teacher role in planning language-integrated social studies units, the previous section may have put the cart before the horse, giving you a guide for exploring texts without exploring what happens before you begin instruction.

You can integrate literature into social studies in various ways. Textual transactions can be exploited within a unit that relies entirely on literature sets, or they can be pursued within units that use one novel to enrich a social studies textbook. In fact, newer social studies series are infusing literature samples, and sometimes whole novels or nonfiction works available in boxed kits, as integral elements in their grade-level packages. Teachers can import literature exploration to extend any unit that is built around a textbook. Questions suggested in Table 8.1 are appropriate to guide student transactions with a diary entry or a newspaper excerpt that is included as a textbook sidebar or material that must be copied and passed out to the class. These literature extensions can help humanize the general topic or period being studied by offering a flavor of the times. By exploring our reactions to these materials and taking seriously the questions students raise about these excerpts, we help students personalize their connection with the content. Selecting one novel as a whole-class assignment is a less demanding way to take advantage of the illumination and engagement a personal story can bring to a social studies unit. It is easier to orchestrate input from textbook study, pertinent reference works, and visual materials when one novel is read by the whole class.

Selecting one novel to represent a unit topic may simplify instructional planning, but we need to recognize and account for the limitations this choice implies. An example for a unit on settling the American West is Scott O'Dell's *Sing Down the Moon*. It depicts from the Navaho perspective the Native Americans' displacement, enforced by the United States Cavalry, as settlers from the East begin to move into the Southwest. If this is the only novel read, we must be sure to discuss other points of view about the same event. To diversify the way an event is interpreted, we need not feel constrained to give equal time by also reading a settler's story and a soldier's story, but when we choose a point of view for our literature selection that is typically understated in textbooks and popular culture sources, we need to ensure that we are multiculturalizing our study. In the Navaho removal example we should further multiculturalize our study by helping students imagine how the story would have been told by settler or a soldier in the cavalry. Year-long planning that intentionally diversifies perspectives by choosing samples that give voice to a variety of age, gender, ethnic group, social status, religious, and geographic backgrounds can also serve to overcome any bias or narrowness arising from whole-class reading of single novels in one unit.

In the actual planning sequence, you need to assemble sources and make decisions about themes and subthemes. Many lifetimes could be spent investigating the theme we introduced earlier about past and present-day immigration! We need to consider how much of the school year we want to or can afford to spend on this theme. Can student interest be sustained for the amount of time this theme would require? Are there other social studies goals and strands that need to be pursued? Dividing and limiting the initial broad topic or theme will be a necessary part of your preinstructional planning.

Let us look again at the immigration theme as a way social studies units can be organized to include language and literature strands.[6] Assume that this topic is part of a middle-grade program that includes the major historical events of industrialization, economic depression, migration from rural to urban areas, and world wars that have shaped individual lives in this century. Other social studies goals for the year include conducting a community involvement project and extending awareness of and concern about global events. Language and literature goals include enrichment and extension of all language-skill areas with the expectation that reading will include whole books representing fiction and nonfiction genres, and language expression that will generate varied public products ranging from debates to drama to documentaries.

With the broad topic of immigration, you can have individuals and/or small groups read biographies about people who arrived in this country during the first half of the century and those who continue to arrive. This strategy can help the students understand the larger theme, especially if you encourage individual data gathering and significant language activity, leading to reports and large group formulation of the historical context of the people studied. The theme may need to be limited or divided into subthemes to keep it manageable and to allow for activities that develop the other major social studies goals. Some possibilities might include limiting the biographies to one for each of two or three subthemes and scheduling them into month-long segments interspersed throughout the year. Another possibility could be to devote one semester to in-depth study of one subtheme, such as World War II.[7] Blocking out topics in the school-year calendar can bring social studies unit planning into focus.

In addition to the general sequence followed in planning and instruction in social studies, once goals and topics have been defined, some specific additions need to be considered to account for language/literature-based instruction in social studies units. Increasing communication opportunities through activities requires that you plan in two areas: how to subdivide a topic and how children can choose to present their findings. You need to ask whether the library has sufficient materials for each group to use and whether the topic has enough subdivisions for group work. Often social studies textbooks suggest topic subdivisions that are appropriate for group work. The primary topic called "types of communities" is a good example. Group work can be done according to the kind of community—urban, suburban, rural—or according to the way different life activities—transporta-

---

[6]We are aware that most school districts adopt programs and textbook series and many now include literature selections as well. We include the following exposition, however, to alert you to the processes involved in this kind of instructional planning.

[7]See the excellent overview and analysis of such a unit in the end-of-chapter reference to Kornfeld.

tion, getting food, working, housing—are organized in each community type. Table 8.2 illustrates the steps in planning an activity sequence.

As another example, perhaps a unit on Latin America, groups might select different countries or regions to explore. Within each group, individual children would be responsible for subtopics such as geography and climate, people and customs, products and trade, and history. In a shorter investigation where the topic was school cleanup, different children would contribute ideas for each of the subtopics—restrooms, playground, halls, cafeteria, classroom—to be organized in a group product.

Another factor in choosing a topic for group investigation is its potential for community involvement. Jane Rowe, a fifth-grade teacher in Provincetown, Massachusetts, reported how her class, and the entire school, integrates language/literacy development through the theme of community problems by simulating the town meeting process. Each year, teachers, in conjunction with local government, announce a "situation" based on real community concerns. As they work through the year-long problem-solving process of preparing for the town meeting, groups of students assume special-interest identities. They develop questions for interviewing to gather information, make phone calls and write letters to get further information, discuss existing laws and regulations with city officials, visit sites pertinent to the problem, develop positions and proposals for the town meeting, and practice parliamentary procedure. By the time of the mock town meeting, every student has acquired greater facility with the whole range of language/literacy skills on the way to gaining an indelible impression

TABLE 8.2　TYPICAL ACTIVITY SEQUENCE IN SOCIAL STUDIES PLANNING AND INSTRUCTION

1. Planning	*2. Instruction*
Select and schedule topic.	Introduce topic with concrete experience.
Collect, analyze, select student sources.	Give overview of unit topic, expectations, options.
Devise activity options.	
Project specific unit schedule.	Organize students for gathering data.
Anticipate areas for direct skill and content instruction.	Set goals, timelines for investigation
Structure student assessment processes, timelines, products.	Teach research, literacy skill as data-gathering producers need to know.
	Continually monitor group/individual progress.
Schedule use of unit materials, equipment, contacts, resources.	Instruct about, discuss contextual framework of topic.
Prepare student materials for distribution.	Have individuals and small groups present to class.
	Conduct culmination activities that draw together and make conclusions about topic; assess individual learning.

of the decision-making processes necessary to make a democratic organization function.[8]

A third consideration is designing collaborative group projects that foster oral language. Children in primary grades need projects they can accomplish in one or two work sessions. Collaboration may be limited to initial communication, preceding individual activity, about how to share materials. Primary-grade children can also work with a partner when the roles are defined and the task is an activity to produce a product, such as drawing a story sequence. Children in intermediate grades can work together on a project over several sessions. They can work well in cooperative groups in which role responsibilities are taught and posted for reference.

Part of the preinstructional phase of language-integrated social studies planning includes anticipating the skills students will need in order to have successful transactions with texts they encounter as part of the unit. The next section describes some strategies for assisting students through one of the classic roadblocks they must navigate in gaining meaning from texts. Successfully integrated language–social studies instruction does not dismiss direct teaching of skills. Rather, the skill instruction evolves as a consequence of what is needed to develop the content of the unit or project. The following classroom episode illustrates how one teacher prepares her students to conduct their searches for information. This fourth-grade class is studying cultural diversity in their state. Notice how Ms. Ishikawa prepares the whole class for individual work. She is prompting them with a structure that can direct their purpose for reading.

SAMPLE CLASSROOM EPISODE 8.2

Looking in Classrooms: Structuring Reading Purpose

Ms. Ishikawa: We've been studying about diversity in our state. In addition to our general reading and study, we are going to do some personal investigation. One part of the investigation will be to interview people in our families. The part we want to begin work on today is our library research about our immigrant roots.

---

[8]Jane W. Rowe, "To Develop Thinking Citizens," *Educational Leadership* 48, no. 3 (November 1990): 43–44.

	Before we begin, we need to decide what kinds of information we all need to look for, even though we will be learning about different places. I will keep track of your ideas on the chalkboard. Who can get us started?
Cathy:	My family came from Ireland and England. What do I do?
Ms. Ishikawa:	I suggest you make one choice, but if you have time, you may want to research both. If Cathy chooses Ireland, what should she try to learn about it?
Lloyd:	Maybe where it is?
Ms. Ishikawa:	Good start. What else?
Cathy:	What they wear.
Ms. Ishikawa:	(Writes and uses body language to call on other children; different children add items such as language, kind of work the Irish do, the climate, the way the country looks, etc.). This is a good list. Now we need to look at it and see if there are certain things that could go together. Let's do some clustering. If I write *land* (she moves to another chalkboard segment), what would go with it? (She supplies *population* as a second category and asks students to supply others; they come up with *population, resources, famous places, way of life,* and *why people left.*) Tomorrow when you find your country in the encyclopedia, how can you use these categories?

Students tell how they can write down information they need to recall under each category as they read. Further preparing them, Ms. Ishikawa instructs each student to fold a blank sheet of construction paper into six parts and write one of the topical headings at the top of each part.

By exploring together what they need to look for before they read, these students defined a purpose for reading that will give them a structure for recalling what they find. This careful guidance will provide students a structured transaction with information-bearing texts. Giving students a teacher-made list of questions to answer as they read is a quicker but probably less effective method, as it does not involve students in its formulation.

Let us return to Ms. Ishikawa's fourth-grade class to see how she further prepared the students to gather information. This time we follow her lesson plan. Ms. Ishikawa wants the students to practice looking for details and main ideas before she asks them to work independently. She knows her students can find encyclopedia entries, but she wants them to learn to paraphrase and summarize the information they find. Here is the lesson she used to follow the first project session.

SAMPLE LESSON PLAN 8.1

Direct Teaching Lesson: Using Encyclopedias for Main Ideas and Details

OBJECTIVES:

Students will skim encyclopedia article for specific details. Students will read encyclopedia paragraphs and state main ideas.

MATERIALS:

Tape next to overhead projection screen a sheet of butcher paper with six sections on which categories are labeled (land, population, resources, famous places, way of life, why people left). Have at hand a magic marker, set of encyclopedias, transparency of Iceland encyclopedia entry, highlighter transparency pens, overhead projector.

PROCEDURE:

1. Move students to carpet facing overhead projection screen.
2. Tell students: "We are going to practice using an encyclopedia to gather information for our roots reports. There are two kinds of information we will need. One is specific numbers and facts. The other is more general ideas. Who knows how we go about looking for specific facts?" (Students review skimming.) "Who knows how we go about looking for general ideas?" (Students review process for getting main ideas.)
3. "Let's look at our category sheet. Which of these call for specific facts? Which seem to call for main ideas?"
4. "Now, let's pretend that my grandparents came from Iceland. What volume do I go to?" (Have students find Iceland entry.)

5. "So we all can work together, I have a copy of the Iceland entry on this transparency." (Lead group to entry overview by asking questions about subtitles.)

6. "We should read the whole entry for our report. After the first reading we should look at our papers and see which of the sections to return to for information we want to write down."

7. Take turns orally reading entry, pointing out along the way when paragraphs contain information pertinent to categories on sheet.

8. Have volunteers highlight detail sections of transparency while you record in appropriate category on sheet in front of class their rephrasing of facts and information. For "way of life," review entry for ideas and have students come up with and highlight main idea phrases. Discuss how reading for general ideas is slower than skimming for facts.

9. Use thumbs up or down to check for understanding: "First thing I do is look for details" (down). "As I do the first reading, I make mental notes about what parts to come back to" (up). "Main ideas must be copied word-for-word" (down). "For the second reading I skim subtitles looking for places that should give me details" (up).

10. "Tomorrow we will begin our own encyclopedia reading. Who can review for us the steps for finding information from the article on our country?"

11. Continue independent practice using encyclopedia next session.

This direct-teaching lesson assumes that students will not take extensive notes and will work individually on this phase of the project. If the students had had earlier practice in this kind of task, the teacher might have incorporated the use of individual note cards. There is no one correct way to take notes that works for everyone on every kind of topic. What does work is exploring the categories of information that need to be collected before beginning the information-gathering process.

Gathering information independently may not be the best way to approach this kind of task. Some children are more successful when reading of this nature is presented as a team or collaborative task. Often students working in pairs can actually write together whereas alone or in a larger group they cannot produce. During the skill acquisition phase of information gathering from reading or listening/viewing, direct-teaching techniques are essential. They should include a teacher-initiated probing and purpose structuring followed by student work with teacher-led verification. For primary grades, teachers use webbing or clustering as a way to brainstorm questions to answer or to organize information students already know about the topic to be investigated. For intermediate grades, the same techniques are appropriate. Reading experts urge direct assistance that includes these steps:

1. **Predicting** what is in the content to be read or what questions will be answered, led by the teacher.
2. **Reading/listening/viewing** done by pairs of students to look for confirmation or rejection of predictions or answers to questions.
3. **Confirmation** of predictions or responses to questions as an entire class or group activity directed by the teacher that leads to further predictions or questions, thus renewing the predict-intake-confirm cycle.
4. **Resolution** when longer topics or textbook chapters are summarized orally and decisions are made as a group. These are decisions such as whether notes need to be taken about specific sections, or whether a general summary needs to be written that answers questions like these: What are the most important points? What are the parts you liked best? What should we learn from this?

No one technique works with all students for every kind of textual transaction. Information-gathering activities led by the teacher are essential structuring or scaffolding devices for English learners as well as native English speakers. Verbal exploration of pictures and graphics is equally important as a means of concept/vocabulary development. In general, when children are involved and able to talk about the content they hear, view, or read, they will comprehend more.

Classifying or organizing is another step in social studies unit learning that works well with strategies often associated with language learning. Children need practice to gain confidence in developing their own categories and organizing information. They are assisted toward these skills when they have a structured purpose for viewing or reading as well as a technique for getting the main ideas from information sources. A simple approach that combines brevity and tangible results is writing a paragraph about a single picture by responding to teacher-made questions. An example could be a textbook reproduction of a historical incident, such as the W. D. Cooper engraving entitled *Boston Tea Party*. After briefly telling the story of the Boston Tea Party, ask students to respond orally to these questions about the engraving: What kinds of boats do you see? To whom do they belong? Who are the groups of people in each of the boats? What kinds of clothes are they wearing? What is each group doing? Who are the people on the shore? What are these people doing? What made these people destroy the boxes of tea?

First, students orally answer these questions in a large group. Then, by composing answers to each question using key words, the pairs of students will compose paragraphs about the event.

Short exercises that incorporate intake and retelling of information within a single lesson serve as building blocks for longer assignments. This strategy permits nonnative English-speaking students to have immediate success. It teaches all children the importance of asking questions, or setting purposes, for information gathering, and gives students experience in transposing the information into a personal product. Ms. Ishikawa could have used this strategy in her Iceland lesson.

Gradually, reading and writing purposes can become more complex and demanding. Most teachers involve students in daily journal keeping. Extending the personal reportorial voice toward different themes and purposes is a natural outgrowth of this practice. Students become more engaged in journal keeping when they are prompted to assume a historical identity and to react to the unfolding historical fiction they're reading, or to tell how they feel about a current event discussed by the class. Other forms for organizing and presenting information need to be practiced. By varying the purposes for gathering information, you can integrate instruction about presentations for different goals. Basic presentation outlines are shown below.

Outlines for Three Kinds of Presentations

1. *Descriptive Outline*
   Introduction tells what will be described.
   Major quality or event.
       Two or more sentences that tell more details about topic.
   · Additional major quality or event (as many paragraphs as needed).
       Two or more sentences that tell more details about topic.
   Summary tells how major qualities or events fit together.
2. *Persuasive Outline*
   Introduction tells what issue is.
   State position about issue.
       Two or more sentences supporting position.
   State argument against position.
       Two or more sentences telling why argument is not good (as many
           paragraphs as needed to cover reasons for position).
   Summary restates position and major reasons and why others should agree.
3. *Comparison Outline*
   Introduction tells what is to be compared.
       Two or more sentences describing what is to be compared.
   Describe major point of comparison.
       Two or more sentences describing how topics compare on this point.
   Describe another point of comparison.
       Two or more sentences describing how topics compare on this point
           (as many paragraphs as needed to cover major points).

Summary states conclusion about how two topics are the same or different. Two or more sentences supporting conclusion.

These basic outlines will be modified as students gain greater facility of expression. There is nothing sacred about these particular outlines. However, using such an outline will help students organize their ideas according to the purpose of their presentation.

Sample Writing Outline

Introduction: Georgia was one of the colonies most similar to British society.
Major point: Landowners lived like aristocrats.
Major point: Plantation owners were interested in cash crops.
Major point: The upper class of plantation owners organized society to suit themselves.
Conclusion: The upper class of plantation owners had power and economic resources in Georgia.

Better results usually come when you work through a topic familiar to the whole class before asking individuals or small groups to put together a presentation. Initially, you will need to supply the main points of the report or presentation. If, for example, the general topic was to describe life in the American colonies, you could pick a colony such as Georgia and lead the class in the development of it by supplying the major points and leading the group in the elaboration of these points. After several projects have been developed in this manner, students can be asked to come up with the major points as part of the prewriting or preparation for an oral presentation.

8.2   ON YOUR OWN: INTEGRATING REFERENCE BOOKS WITH SOCIAL STUDIES

Match these reference books with the topics listed below:
encyclopedias, *Guinness Book of World Records*, world almanac, telephone book, world atlas, historical atlas, card catalogue, dictionary, textbook, *The Book of Lists*.

_____ 1. When the first Olympic Games were held
_____ 2. What the zip code is for Indianapolis, Indiana
_____ 3. How far it is to Anchorage, Alaska, from where you are
_____ 4. Who the richest people in the world are
_____ 5. Where the Mason-Dixon line is
_____ 6. What people thought of the Constitution in 1787

Discuss how you recall using reference books in your elementary school. What should be guidelines for using them in your teaching?

As a spin-off from integrated contact with reference books, students may learn to use the books with more facility through trivia contests. Once a reference book has been introduced, students can be invited to submit questions on index cards based on using that reference. Answers to the questions are written on the back of the cards. The cards are signed and deposited in a "trivia contest" box The students can earn trivia points in their free time by correctly finding the answer or adding questions to the box. Students earning an agreed-on number of points over, perhaps, a two-week period can be rewarded with ribbons or privileges.

For students, skill building in structuring their reading, knowing where to look for information, finding main ideas, putting information into categories, and organizing information according to a presentation purpose is a lifelong learning project. To grow in these language/literacy areas, students need constant engagement with units that require them to practice in a meaningful context. We need to provide students with models of how to perform these skills through content-driven projects that enable them to apply the models.

You have studied the whole-language approach to language and literacy instruction. You need to employ these strategies as you see them helping students learn how to refine and present the knowledge they gain in social studies units. It is beyond our scope to review the steps in the prewriting and writing process or list the suggestions and self-prompts that we can develop with students to help them prepare and practice reporting orally and in writing. As you work with integrating these strategies in social studies, you will help students overcome most of the problems that lead them to lose interest in and not understand social studies content. To be sure, the writing process requires more in-class time to undertake, but the additional time this process entails is well worth the investment. Through it, students are acquiring a procedural structure that helps them build confidence and independence in their written expression. Another advantage of the process is that your role in correcting written work is reduced because of improved student editing and proofreading. Further, the structure and content of student work gradually improves as the children gain practice and skill in offering alternatives or clarifying what they do not understand in another child's written expression. Perhaps the highest recommendation for the process is that it teaches students they can help each other learn.

TRADE-OFFS IN SOCIAL STUDIES–LANGUAGE INTEGRATED INSTRUCTION

The term *trade-off* usually refers to a problematic situation in which the consequences of making choices are not all positive or all negative. The decision to capitalize on language and literacy development through the subject of social studies involves a series of trade-off issues.

On the positive side, when traditionally defined language arts skills are integrated with social studies instruction, the motivational appeal of learning both subjects is enhanced for students. Early childhood specialists insist that instruction begin with the child. According to this perspective, successful instruction will take into consideration life settings and experiences and connect them in ways that permit students to see their own connections to the wider world. Social studies teachers can help build this bridge by taking care to assess where students are in relation to prescribed social studies curricula. Social studies topics become more accessible for students when the topics are presented in ways that assist students to unlock abstract language and participate in constructing their own knowledge through oral, written, and expressive activities.

A possibly negative trade-off that must be made if you adopt the child-centered perspective is reduced coverage of prescribed social studies materials and content. On the other hand, it may be impossible for us to imagine how some historical topics usually covered in a chronologically organized book are important, at least at this point in students' lives, for any reason except to say they have been covered. Additionally, defining social studies as part of a broad field that includes language arts almost certainly means that the teacher must select fewer social studies topics to develop during a year if adequate attention to a language-rich construction of knowledge is given within each topic. Still, exploring fewer topics in greater depth may not be an automatically accepted option in states and school districts that are strongly committed to an ambitious grade-level list of social studies/history topics and where state assessment is in place.

Another trade-off issue involves matching teacher preparation and school schedules with student learning needs. Teachers often feel caught in the middle of these crosscurrents. On the one hand, they wish to meet students' needs. On the other, these needs may be so diverse, each requiring specialized knowledge, that only a multitrained super specialist could begin to respond to their individual needs. Most teachers agree that the fragmented lives some students lead outside school recommends learning approaches and school days that help put together the pieces.

Critics of middle-level schooling feel that greater integration of subjects decreases time lost for students in switching between rooms, teachers, and subjects as it increases the relevance of subjects for students. Student attitudes toward school and their engagement with learning can be increased, the critics argue, by a more holistic approach that focuses attention on fewer discrete subjects and requires adjustment to fewer teachers, thus extending the primary-grade mode of one teacher responsible for multiple-subject teaching. Even though this may be a position with which they can sympathize, many middle-level teachers are educated as subject specialists and feel inadequate when they are made responsible for multiple-subject instruction. To address this issue, some schools use team teaching. This trade-off requires teacher investment in planning time and instructional collaboration that school schedules often do not adequately support.

Another trade-off issue in literature-based instruction is the possibility that so much attention and time may be required to digest the particular novel that students lose the larger picture of social studies content. Unless a teacher is alert to the social and historical and geographical context of a novel, he or she may fail to tap the richness of a personalized example carried by a plot line. Literature-based instruction requires more of a teacher than textbook-organized instruction. If teachers claim that social studies content is being addressed, they must prepare activities that develop that content by constructing timelines, conducting additional investigations from various sources about famous events and people, and integrating map and visual information. In addition, some versions of literature-based social studies tend to lose sight of the citizenship strand of social studies. They become book-bound literary exercises that leave no time for crucial exploration of community issues.

Further, the kinds of student materials needed to successfully initiate whole-language, literature-based, broad field instruction may not be readily available or affordable. To take advantage of the whole-language approach, teachers need assistance in integrating literature and writing workshop materials and activities, and they need the assurance that there will be a consistent year-by-year program for teaching social studies content and skills. With increased attention to subject standards in assessment, especially in geography and history, we must be careful that in our eagerness to adopt whole-language ideas we do not lose sight of the need to provide for the continuous development of social studies content and skills. Shifting toward literature-based social studies instruction cannot be done without time for curriculum development and money to support it.

SUMMARY

Language and literacy skills are intimately tied to social studies instruction. Without content to give their writing real purpose, most children see little reason to practice their skills in letter writing, narrative, or explanation. To access the language-learning potential of social studies, children need instruction and guidance in gathering and communicating information. They also need continued teacher instruction about the larger social context, chronology, and issues of an era. Otherwise, in their concentration on literature-based social studies, students can lose sight of social studies content and skills. If insights from whole-language, writer-workshop, and literature-based approaches are to be integrated into social studies instruction, a school or district must be willing to commit to a long-term investment in curriculum development and staff development. Rethinking many of our traditional approaches to social studies instruction can result in more powerful, holistic social studies learning for students.

SUGGESTED READINGS

Book Links. American Library Association. 50 E. Huron Avenue, Chicago, IL 60611; ph. 800-545-2433. Up-to-the-minute source for children's literature book plots.

Farris, Pamela J., and Cooper, Susan M. *Elementary Social Studies: A Whole Language Approach*. Madison, Wis.: WCB Brown & Benchmark, 1994. Multiple-author methods text detailing social studies instruction from the whole-language perspective.

Graves, Donald H. *The Reading/Writing Teacher's Companion: Investigate Nonfiction*. Portsmouth, N.H.: Heinemann, 1989. This and the following book by Graves are two case study volumes that chronicle a writing-workshop approach to literacy and seeing the classroom as a community for literacy development.

Graves, Donald H. *The Reading/Writing Teacher's Companion: Experiment with Fiction*. Portsmouth, N.H.: Heinemann, 1989.

Hoge, John D. "Improving the Use of Elementary Social Studies Textbooks." *ERIC Digest* 33 (1986): 2–3. Lists ways to get more meaning from text reading.

Humes, Ann. "Putting Writing Research into Practice." *Elementary School Journal* 84 (September 1983): 3–15. Suggests writing process steps from research for classroom application.

Kornfeld, John. "Using Fiction to Teach History: Multicultural and Global Perspectives of World War II." *Social Education* 58 (September 1994): 281–286. Author describes and analyzes personal experience of teaching sixth-grade literature-based unit including student bibliography.

Langer, Judith A. "A Response-Based Approach to Reading Literature." *Language Arts* 71 (March 1994): 203–211. Overview of research on teaching and learning of response-centered approaches, from a constructivist perspective to literature highlighting differences in student reading purposes, distinguishes reading for exploring horizon of literary possibilities from reading for discursive purposes of maintaining a point of reference common in social studies that includes provocative integrative framework of teaching strategies.

O'Day, Kim. "Using Formal and Informal Writing in Middle School Social Studies." *Social Education* 58 (January 1994): 39–40. Examples of using writing to learn in middle grades.

Spirit, Diana L. *Introducing Bookplots 3*. New York: R. R. Bowker, 1988. Reference work for children's librarians; provides quick access to children's trade books under categories of getting along in family, making friends, developing values, understanding physical and emotional problems, forming a view of the world, understanding social problems, and identifying adult roles.

Yokota, Junko. "Books That Represent More than One Culture." *Language Arts* 71 (March 1994): 212–219. By presenting categories of multiple cultures, presented separately; multiple cultures, comparisons/contrasts, multiple cultures, interactions between/among cultures, advances multicultural curriculum thinking with annotated discussion of children's trade books that deal with more than one culture.

Zarnowski, Myra, and Gallagher, Arlene F., eds. *Children's Literature and Social Studies: Selecting and Using Notable Books in the Classroom.* Washington, D.C.: National Council for the Social Studies, 1993. Each chapter provides sources and suggests how they can be used in literature-based instruction.

Chapter 9

TEACHING SOCIAL STUDIES SKILLS: TIME, SPACE, TECHNOLOGIES

An information explosion of verbal, pictorial, and numeric facts is here. Information is a valuable and strategic resource, and students need the skills that will alow them to access and to understand it. Teachers need to teach specific social studies skills—chronological time, and map and global skills—as well as to use newer technologies, both as a teaching method and as skills for students to use. This chapter focuses on the following topics:

1/ Learning about Chronological Time

2/ Map and Global Skills

3/ Technologies for the Social Studies

LEARNING ABOUT CHRONOLOGICAL TIME

You already know that one of the important goals in teaching history is to help children develop a sense of time and chronology. We all operate in a time-space dimension and constantly view social phenomena in a time-space orientation. We describe events this way: For example, "Throughout the whole fifty states, the United States celebrated the bicentennial of the Constitution on September 17, 1987," or "Yesterday I attended the meeting of the local teachers' organization at Washington School." Time and space are interrelated. For our purposes, however, we will consider them separately—first time (history) and then space (geography).

How do children acquire the concept of *time*? Most children gradually recognize that events fall into patterns. From their home life, children learn that typically there is a time to get up, to eat, to play, and to sleep. Through the use of language and experience, they begin to distinguish among past, present, and future. In the Western model of time, the present is now, and it becomes past almost as soon as we think about it. The future is what will happen. Yesterday and tomorrow are early and important concepts.

A more mature time sense, *chronology*, allows us to move away from personal experience and to extend our understanding of time backward and forward. Dates become orientation points, and events fall into chronological order. We start to visualize how events a hundred or even a million years ago are related to the present. This perspective obviously involves more than simply memorizing dates. We begin to understand the concepts of cause and effect and of continuity. We learn that history is constantly changing. Individuals change, families change, social institutions change, nations change; the whole world changes. Most changes occur gradually; a child grows older, and the dynamics of her or his family shift a little each year.

You know that when you are enjoying yourself, time seems to pass quickly. On the other hand, when you are waiting in the post office line or for a medical appointment, time seems to go slowly. We as adults know that these are *subjective* conceptions of time. However, children do not necessarily understand that the differences they experience in time are an illusion. They do not comprehend the uniform motion or velocity of a clock. They believe that the clock works more quickly or slowly depending on how they experience the time. Some children have reported that school time really seems to drag.

To make time more *objective*, humans use mathematics and astronomy. In our modern technological society we measure time not only in years, months, and days but in smaller periods of specified length such as minutes and seconds. Computer-calculated time is measured in milliseconds and microseconds. The trend toward use of even smaller units of objective time will probably continue.

This section on time and chronology is organized in the order that material is usually taught in the primary grades and then in the upper grades, as shown in the list below.

1. Learn meaning of day, week, month, year.	Primary grades
2. Use calendar to find dates.	Primary grades
3. Understand today, yesterday, tomorrow.	Primary grades
4. Distinguish between A.M. and P.M.	Primary grades
5. Learn to tell time by the clock.	Primary grades
6. Understand timelines.	Fourth–sixth grades
7. Learn to translate dates into centuries.	Middle-school grades
8. Comprehend the Christian system of chronology—A.D. and B.C.	Middle-school grades

However, there are no firm rules about when to introduce time and chronology. In addition, teachers often must reteach to maintain some of these skills.

The History Center (Chapter 5) went beyond these recommendations on what students should be able to do to demonstrate chronological thinking. Examples of student achievement included the following:

In Grades K–2

On listening to or reading historical stories, myths, and narratives, students should be able to reconstruct the basic organization of the narrative: its beginning, middle, and end.

In creating historical narratives of their own, students should be able to establish a chronology for the story, providing a beginning, middle, and end.

In Grades 3–4

Students should be able to group historical events for broadly defined eras in the history of their local community and state.

Students should be able to construct time lines of significant historical developments in their community and state.

In Grades 5–6

Students should be able to construct multiple-tier timelines (important social, economic, and political developments).

Students should be able to interpret data presented in timelines.

Some teachers might think these chronological thinking goals are very ambitious for the age groups shown. What do you think?

From words such as the "Christian system of chronology," you can also see that different cultures have had different calendars for counting time. Probably the earliest ancient complete calendars were based on lunar observations. The moon's phases occur over an easily observed interval, a month. From this, the religious authorities, who were the educated people of their time, declared a month to have begun when they first saw the new crescent moon, with a calendar month containing either twenty-nine or thirty days. Twelve lunar months form a lunar year, almost eleven days shorter than a solar year. This meant that a lunar year was not suitable for agricultural purposes, especially when irrigation decisions had to be made each year. To keep in step with the sun, people created lunar-solar calendars. Hundreds of such calendars, with variations, were developed at various times in such areas as Mesopotamia, Greece, Rome, India, and China. The month was not always based on the phases of the moon. The Mayan calendar divided the year into eighteen months, each of which had twenty days; the year ended with a period of five extra days.

But on what date does a New Year actually begin? Many children are vaguely aware that the Chinese New Year and the Jewish New Year start at different times from January 1. Children may watch a Chinese New Year parade on television. They may observe that the U.S. Postal Service puts out a new commemorative stamp each year stating "Happy New Year, the Year of the Dog" or the appropriate symbol for the Chinese zodiac. Their classmates may miss school because of religious holidays that use a different calendar.

There are alternative systems of recording calendar time: those based on a solar year (such as the Christian Gregorian calendar), those based on a lunar calendar (the Islamic calendar), or those based on a semi-lunar calendar, adjusting the lunar calendar periodically to a solar year (the Jewish calendar). Most children do not realize that the date on which the new year starts is arbitrarily decided, as is the number of days in a month or in a week, and that one culture may not have made the same decisions about calendars as another culture. Different cultures have different name for months, and sometimes the months in one group's calendar will not have the same number of days as months in the calendar of another culture. Is Sunday the first or last day of the week? Why does the date for Easter vary from one year to another? Collecting calendars from a number of cultures and pointing out the different ways that various nationalities have counted time can be a good multicultural lesson, for the divisions of time are culturally based although the scientific measurement of the solar year becomes more and more exact. Finding out how others across the ocean or even within the classroom have organized their time provides an opportunity for children to look at the puzzles as "Who are we?" and "How do we organize time in our lives?" Some cultures may be more influenced by past events in terms of what they think and talk about than are those of us in American mainstream culture.

Most children learn to tell time at home and in school, although the increased use of digital watches and clocks means that they are less familiar with the so-called face of the clock. Almost all children eventually learn to tell objective time through the use of clocks, calendars, and time-zone maps in their mathematics and science work. What is unique about the social studies is the addition of the *cultural* aspect of time. Students learn the distinction between B.C. and A.D. and the meaning of the terms *decade, century,* and *millennium.* Teachers frequently use terms such as *ancient times, the Dark Ages, the colonial period, prehistoric time, several centuries ago,* and *the beginnings of modern times.* We need to make sure that our students know what these terms mean.

Like all abstract concepts, time must be personalized and related to a child's experience if it is to be understood. One way to organize and understand time is through a *timeline.* A timeline is one of the simplest ways to organize historical information. Draw a line. It should be drawn to consistent scale; each inch might equal ten years, one year, or a hundred years, depending on what information you wish to include. Then write in significant events at the appropriate places. A timeline reads from left to right, with earlier events on the left and more recent ones on the right, so children are using a reading convention like that of English with which they are already familiar. Use events that are meaningful to the students, such as occurrences in the life of an ordinary, contemporaneous person (see Figure 9.1). Software for producing timelines on computers also is available.

In the primary grades you can also make timelines for a week or even a month. Put up the days of the week. Then have children draw pictures or symbols for what happened during the week such as special programs or holidays. Be careful not to have so much clutter that the concept of time is not obvious.

Students can begin to understand a timeline by looking at a simple example such as the one in Figure 9.1. Ask your students when Dolores started first grade or what happened to Dolores in 1980. Students an also make timelines of their own lives or those of their families, noting important dates such as marriages, births of children, and graduations. Many teachers post several timelines around their classrooms and ask their students to add the dates of the events they study. Symbols (such as a train for the completion of the transcontinental railroad) make the meaning of the dates clearer.

Continue to introduce more and more complex timelines to students throughout the year. Vary the format by moving the earlier events to the top of the page, and the more recent ones to the bottom, as shown in Figure 9.2.

Ask your students to identify the year in which frozen orange juice was introduced. Then ask them how many years ago that was. But make sure that they are not simply calculating dates from the timeline. Use timeline exercises to introduce critical thinking about the data shown. For example, can students hypothesize

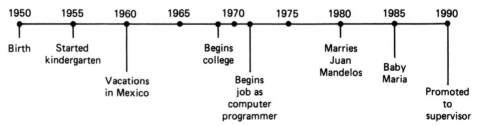

Figure 9.1 Dolores's life

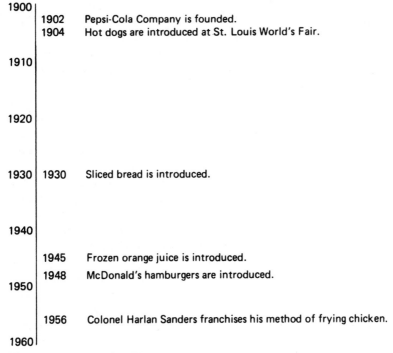

Figure 9.2 American food history

from looking at the American foods timeline what kinds of new foods might be introduced in the coming years? Also, you might ask them to talk about the impact that nationally available frozen orange juice has had on our society in terms of family roles or its impact on the orange industry or on our relationship with Brazil, the world's largest exporter of oranges.

Timelines can be used to teach about historical themes (a timeline showing revolutions through the centuries) or about specific regions or nations. Children's encyclopedias such as the *World Book* often provide timelines about important countries under headings like "Important Dates in Mexico." Consider, for example, the dates in the following list.

Important Dates in Mexico

1325	The Aztecs found Tenochtitlán (Mexico City)
1519–21	Aztec Empire is conquered by Spain
1846–48	Mexico is defeated in war with the United States; Mexico loses much territory
1910–11	Francisco Madero leads a revolution that overthrows the dictator, Díaz

The events above are listed in chronological order rather than scaled as they are on a timeline. What difference does this make in our reading of them? How does consistent scale teach historical lessons? You might provide students with a list like this and then ask them to make a timeline. How long did the Aztec Empire exist compared to the Spanish occupation? Timelines can provide *visual* reinforcement of historical concepts.

Timelines are excellent aids in teaching American history or the history of specific states, as the periods involved in American history lend themselves to detailed timelines. A timeline covering two hundred or three hundred years—or even beginning in 1620, with the landing of the Pilgrims—enables you to include specifics about transportation, communication, and the development of industry as well as important dates in political history. Try having students find or draw pictures of citizens in typical dress for each century or half-century, and paste them to the appropriate parts of the timeline. Many students can calculate how many years ago the Pilgrims landed but have no real understanding of what life was like then or how long ago it was relative to the Civil War or the invention of the airplane. Why, they may ask, was setting out for the New World so frightening? After all, we now travel back and forth to and from Europe all the time. A timeline can help them understand.

After using simple timelines, students may be more ready to tackle concepts like *century*, a period of a hundred years. A new century begins every one hundred years. In the year 2001, a new century will begin. Provide your students with a Western history chronology by centuries, such as the following:

Historical Events Classified by Century

1700	
	American Revolution
	French Revolution
1800	
	Industrial Revolution
	spreads
1900	
	World Wars I and II
	Computers
	Space exploration
2000	

Ask students to place specific events within the centuries. You can give them a random list of dates, including times such as 1776 (Thomas Jefferson writes the Declaration of Independence) or 1861 (American Civil War begins) or 1911 (Mexican Revolution). Don't use the dates of an individual's life, since these often overlap century boundaries. Now ask students what events happened in each century. In upper grades, you might ask whether two historical figures might have talked to each other. Students should get a sense that James Madison could (and did) talk to

Thomas Jefferson but could not have spoken to Woodrow Wilson or Franklin Roosevelt.

When they understand centuries, students may be ready to tackle the difficult concept of A.D. and B.C. in the Gregorian calendar (the Christian calendar) and the contemporary secular designation for these same dates, B.C.E. (Before the Common Era) and C.E. (in the Common Era). Students may also see these abbreviations written as AD, BC, BCE, and CE without periods or space between the letters. In addition, students might encounter the use of B.P. (before the present) rather than B.C. (before Christ) when they study the beginnings of early society. B.P. is used by archaeologists and paleontologists when referring to dates earlier than 1000 B.C. The P is usually defined at 1950. The reason for this is that the techniques used to date ancient objects and fossils are based on analyzing substances found in those objects today. These scientists feel that they introduce the risk of introducing errors if they try to conform to B.C. terminology.

Students need to be told that about 1,500 years ago a Christian pope, Pope Gregory XIII, wanted to date important events in Christian history as well as keep the calendar matching the solar year. A monk decided to start with what he believed was the year of Jesus Christ's birth—*Anno Domini* or A.D. 1. (*Anno Domini* is Latin for "the year of our Lord.") (See Figure 9.3.) The notation A.D. precedes the year (A.D. 1988) whereas B.C. follows the year (673 B.C.). We are now living in A.D. 19 _____. Give students a list of A.D. dates such as 1492 (Columbus encounters America) and 1812 (the War of 1812 begins); ask them to calculate how long ago these events occurred.

The History Center recommended that students should be able to calculate calendar time BC or BCE and AD or CE by the seventh or eighth grades. Comparing two alternative systems of recording calendar time, such as the Chinese and the Christian, is expected in grades 9–12.

When student are comfortable with figuring out A.D. dates, explain that people lived before Jesus was born as well—before A.D. 1, that is. In fact, much of what elementary students consider "history"—dinosaurs, cave people, the Ice Age—occurred before A.D. 1 (see Figure 9.4). The year immediately before A.D. 1 is B.C. 1; there is no zero year (B.C. means simply before Christ); B.C. dates are like negative numbers, a concept your students may not be familiar with. To calculate how many years ago something happened, students must add the A.D. and B.C. figures together. Ask them to calculate, for example, how long ago Rome was founded (753 B.C.) or Athens was defeated by Sparta (404 B.C.).

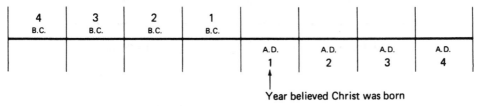

Figure 9.3 Measuring centuries B.C. and A.D.

A.D. 1 to A.D. 100	A.D. 101 to A.D. 200	A.D. 201 to A.D. 300
1st Century A.D.	2nd Century A.D.	3rd Century A.D.

Figure 9.4 Measuring centuries A.D.

Students should also begin to learn how to use reference terms like the *second* century or the *twenty-first* century. Why, they may ask, do we call the century we now live in, 1901–2000, the twentieth century and not the nineteenth century? All years, after all, begin with nineteen. This confusion occurs because there was no *zero* century. A.D. 1 through A.D. 100 was the *first* century; therefore, A.D. 101 through A.D. 200 was the *second* century. Soon we will live in the *twenty-first* century, although the years will all begin with twenty.

Using simply A.D. dates, have students calculate both how many years ago an event took place and what century it was in.

A.D. 1451   First African slaves to Europe.
             Years ago _____   Century _____
A.D. 1534   Cartier claims the St. Lawrence.
             Years ago _____   Century _____
A.D. 1664   English capture New Amsterdam.
             Years ago _____   Century _____

To personalize this activity, ask students in which century they would have preferred to live.

Finally, the most difficult concept for most students is calculating centuries B.C. (see Figure 9.5). Explain that centuries can also be counted in the period be-

300 B.C. to 201 B.C.	200 B.C. to 101 B.C.	100 B.C. to 1 B.C.
3rd Century B.C.	2nd Century B.C.	1st Century B.C.

Figure 9.5 Measuring centuries B.C.

fore Christ. Just as the A.D. 200s are called the third century, the 200s B.C. are the *third century* B.C. The complication is, once again, that there is no zero century B.C. You can repeat the same kind of exercise for B.C. that you did for A.D. Ask students to calculate how many years ago the event occurred and what century it took place in. To do this, students must add the A.D. years (our present year) and the B.C. date together.

4000 B.C.	Agricultural communities appear in ancient China.		
	Years ago _____	Century _____	
1122 B.C.	Feudal states in China increase.		
	Years ago _____	Century _____	
221 B.C.	China achieves unity.		
	Years ago _____	Century _____	
202 B.C.	Han dynasty begins.		
	Years ago _____	Century _____	

As you can see, students often need explicit exercises to understand time concepts. In addition, you need to proceed slowly, one step at a time, making sure they understand dates, first A.D. and then B.C. You cannot assume that everyone understands how to read timelines and can interpret the meaning of A.D. and B.C. or determine the century an event took place. Always examine the timelines in textbooks carefully and explain them to the class.

In this discussion, we have used the time frame or calendar of Western European civilization. Other calendars, as mentioned before, have been used by different groups. Jewish and Muslim calendars are different, as they use starting points other than the birth of Christ when counting the years: the Jewish calendar dates from the beginning of creation, and the Muslim calendar counts from Mohammed's flight to Medina. Use these and other calendars with more advanced students, asking the students to try to figure out dates using different calendars.

You could have a discussion about our own muddled calendar in which different months have different days—28, 29, 30, 31. Critics since the time of the French Revolution, when the metric system of measure was introduced, have advocated a new world calendar; but until this reform takes place, students need to understand our present system of time measurement.

9.1   *ON YOUR OWN: TIME CONFUSION*

Do you recall any confusion you had in your youth about time concepts? Do you think that elementary teachers should use terms such as the *nineteenth century* or the *twentieth century* while teaching? Or do you think it is better to say that in the 1800s the railroad was invented or in the 1900s the airplane was invented?

MAP AND GLOBE SKILLS

Maps, like graphs and charts, are specialized ways of presenting information. However, too frequently, maps remain a mystery to adults. They have not benefited much from their experiences in elementary school learning map skills. Map and globe skills are often taught for a few weeks at the beginning of the year, isolated from the rest of the social studies program. This practice has been encouraged by publishers, many of whom have traditionally started textbooks with a concentration of map skills in the first unit. That situation is changing. More publishers now provide a well-thought-out sequence of map skills in their elementary social studies series. In fact, of all the skills of the social studies—listening, small group work, problem solving, and so on—map skills are probably receiving the most attention from textbook authors. In addition, of all the areas of elementary social studies, more computer software programs have been designed for teaching geography and map skills than for any other area. Much of the computer software in the past, however, has focused on learning the state capitals and other similar low-level factual information.

9.2   ON YOUR OWN: MAP SKILLS AND TEXTBOOKS

> Check the map skills program in an elementary textbook series. If attention is being given in textbooks to map skills, why do you think so many children and adults have trouble using maps?

Although geography and map skills have been taught for generations, the research in this area is still inconclusive, especially regarding the appropriate time to introduce students to specific skills. In other words, although fancy charts on scope and sequence may state that children in grades four to six should use scale and compute distances or compare maps and make inferences, we are not really certain that all children are cognitively ready at these grade levels to learn map skills. Research has shown, however, that when teachers are well prepared and materials are carefully sequenced, most elementary students can indeed learn the basics of "map literacy."

In teaching map-reading skills, you need to be aware of the differing levels of ability among your students. Map reading may be too difficult for some students, especially if the maps contain too much data. Some evidence exists that girls at the elementary level might not perform as well as boys in map-reading skills and geography, though this evidence has been disputed by some experts. You should be aware of your own teaching methods and make sure that you give girls at least as much time and attention in reading maps as you give boys.

If there is one "magic" guideline in teaching map skills, it is to make the concept concrete. Relate what you are teaching to student experiences. Students in the primary grades, especially after exposure to globes, should be provided with the widest possible acquaintance with landscape features. Every town has a landscape that includes some of the geographic, geologic, and cultural features that students find symbolized on maps. But simply taking students outside for a walk is not necessarily productive. To make effective use of outdoor time, you need to plan activities before and after the trip, as well as planning the trip itself. If you do not plan carefully, you run the risk that students will think your walk is simply free time outside the classroom.

First, know what you want to achieve. This means visiting ahead of time the sites your class will see and identifying the major features; it also means communicating the purpose of your trip to your students.

There are administrative considerations to any field trip, even a short walk to local sites. Make sure you inform your principal so that issues of legal liability and safety can be checked. To avoid trespassing, ask property owners for permission, even in the case of an apparently abandoned cemetery. For longer trips, your school will certainly have a policy about permission slips and number of chaperons.

During the trip, try to focus students' attention on what to observe. Students must understand concepts like *swamp* or *treeline* to understand the meaning of these symbols on a map. Symbols for cultural features (buildings, ruins, canals, dams, or even battle sites) must be explained; show students how the buildings they are seeing appear on maps. Finally, water and weather features are sometimes observable: dry salt lakes, tide pools, channels, coral reefs, ponds, warm and cold currents, and prevailing winds. You may want to have students take pictures or fill out worksheets. Anything students can touch (e.g.., rubbing their hands against rock formations, dipping fingers into ponds) will make the trip more memorable.

Finally, plan post-trip activities and use the experience in future classroom activities. Ask students their impressions and observations; review your major objectives with them. Continue to discuss the field trip as a reference in future lessons. Students can make three-dimensional maps of the area they visited. Tabletop maps, clay or sandbox constructions, or paper maps on the floor can also help students demonstrate graphically what they have seen. You might want to have them use blocks or boxes to show miniature buildings, schools, or neighborhoods. The more effectively children can use their experiences, the better they are able to understand the basic ideas and concepts of any field.

In learning map and globe skills, primary-grade students begin with a realization that their local area is only a tiny part of the whole world and move to a broader conception of the world. Use students' trips to help them become more careful observers, as emphasized in the tips on having successful field trips. It is easy to pass through an environment without appreciating or noticing much about it, but all children can develop skills in observing cultural and physical features through short walks, field trips, and trips with their families. Learning to observe is especially important in the primary grades. (See Chapter 3 on observation skills.)

Because of the limitations of the local area, media—videos, television programs, and so on—are usually needed to supplement students' understanding. But the importance of the local environment should never be forgotten at the elementary grade level. Frequently, teachers concentrate on a national commercial textbook and ignore what is right outside the windows of their classrooms. Given a map worksheet with directions on it, students can usually determine location of key items. But many of these same students do not know the directions in their own community. Ideally, children should learn the cardinal directions (north, south, east, and west) by the position of the sun (or shadow). Out-of-door exercises can be most helpful when they are introduced about the third grade.

We also recommend classroom signs or maps indicating north, south, east, and west. But what if you aren't sure where north is? This is not at all unusual. Many people drive freeways without any sense of direction; highway signs indicating east or west exit points mean little to them. Children who get perfect scores on map exercises in the classroom cannot walk or ride their bikes to a specific location using local maps because they cannot orient themselves to where they are. If you are not sure, ask or use a compass. Whenever you take students outside on walks or on field trips in a bus, indicate in what general direction you are all going. Using a compass can often be fun; let students pass it around. Just as students now often know more about computers than their teachers, students sometimes have better senses of direction than their teachers. Identify these potentially helpful students as soon as possible. Often they are children who score extremely high on nonverbal and spatial areas of intelligence tests.

Along with labeling and identifying aspects of the local environment, map teaching involves systematic, step-by-step presentation of a series of questions to help a student learn specific skills.

1. Locate places on a map and globe
   a. Identify continents by shape
   b. Identify hemispheres
2. Orient a map and note directions
   a. Find compass points
   b. Use scale and compute distances
3. Interpret maps and symbols
   a. Use a map key
   b. Visualize what the map symbols mean
4. Compare maps and make inferences

Each one of these skills may have to be explicitly taught. Although brighter students will absorb the concepts without much direct teaching, many others will need as much assistance as you are able to give. Working in pairs may be helpful for many students when they are doing activities or worksheets on map skills; it also makes these activities more fun. Because there is often a sense of accomplishment in completing a map exercise, students frequently report that they like geography and map work at the elementary level; unfortunately, this affection seems to fade in later grades.

What can be done specifically to teach these map skills? Look at the silhouettes of the continents in Figure 9.6. Ask students to label the continents. Once you are confident that students really know the shapes of the continents, move on to identifying hemispheres and locating continents within them. Typically, students see maps only of the Western and Eastern Hemispheres. Occasionally, they are shown maps of the Northern Hemisphere (see Figure 9.7) but very rarely the Southern Hemisphere.

Yet it is important to be able to recognize continents from different perspectives. In effect, this is what happens to the astronauts. Try to show your students maps that were produced in other nations. Maps printed in Germany or Great Britain, for example, have the prime meridian in the absolute center of the map. World maps made in China or Japan show those nations in the center with the American continents squeezed into the right-hand edge. (Good sources for these maps are the offices of consuls of different nations.) At first, students may say that something is wrong with these maps. This is a good lesson to show that people have different perspectives on what the world looks like.

The issue of perspective is important. Young children need to be shown that an object looks different if you view it from the top or from the foot of a moun-

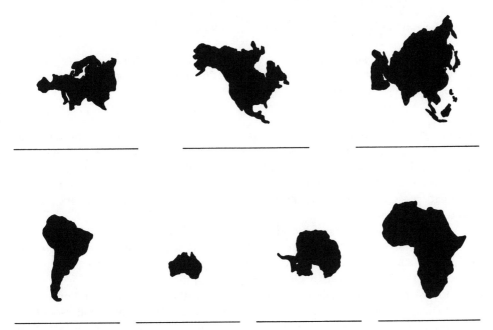

Figure 9.6 Outlines of continents

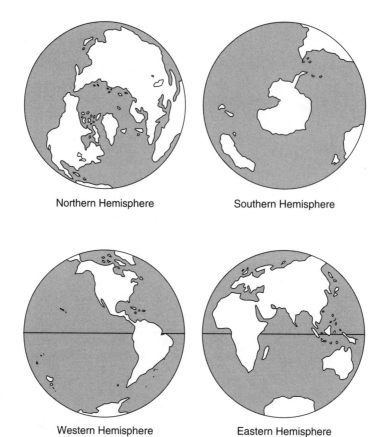

Northern Hemisphere

Southern Hemisphere

Western Hemisphere

Eastern Hemisphere

Figure 9.7 Maps of the hemispheres. *Source:* "Teacher's Resource Binder-Level 3," *Communities Large and Small.* (Lexington, Mass: D.C. Heath, 1985).

tain. In classrooms, a toy doll can be put on top of a miniature mountain and children can be asked to imagine they are seeing through the doll's eyes. Ask the children what they would see if the position of the doll changes. This is similar to exercises asking students to draw their own desks or their shoes as seen from a overhead position. Often students put in heels or other features that they really could not see from above.

As with chronology, specific map skills have to be taught and retaught, both as separate lessons or exercises and as integrated parts of other subjects. You cannot assume that students will transfer the learning of one map skill to another type of map skill or the use of map skills to "real life" without your help.

Almost every expert in the field has stressed the importance of introducing the globe to primary students and of explaining that globes are small models of the world. Some primary teachers bring in a model car to illustrate what they mean by a model so that students will not get confused and think that the world is the size of the globe shown in the classroom. Globes, and especially those with only water and continental land masses indicated, can help students visualize continents, a sphere, a hemisphere, and the equator. Furthermore, correlation with the science and math programs can help provide students with a general understanding of the rotation of the Earth and seasonal changes. Photographs of the Earth taken from outer space are also helpful in giving a new perspective on how the Earth looks.

Flat maps are usually introduced in the intermediate grades, when students learn about scale, geographic grids, and the use of color and symbols in maps. Each skill must be taught and retaught separately. Students should become aware of the following ideas: (1) A map is flat and cannot show true roundness; (2) all flat maps have some distortion (although the technical reasons for different map distortions need not be explained); (3) the legend or key explains what each symbol means; and (4) the scale of the map controls the degree to which we can generalize.

Emphasize the information that a particular map provides. Intermediate-level students can be exposed to different kinds of maps: Students need to learn to interpret a temperature map, a time-zone map, a telephone area-code map, a historical map (of the Roman Empire, for example, where the boundaries of Europe are different from what they are today), and a political map (of the United States, for instance, showing the number of members each state has in the House of Representatives).

Intermediate students must also learn how to locate places on a map. Most maps use a letter-number index to give the location of smaller cities or streets. Each student should have his or her own map with which to practice finding different places by using such indexes. Some teachers like to start this activity with small groups, but you must take care that each student learns the appropriate skill and that one student does not do all the work for the whole group.

In the upper-grade levels, teachers should continually emphasize the interpretation and critical-thinking aspects of reading a map. How will a map help answer certain questions? Students can use a map and a table to recognize a trend such as the shifting center of population in the United States (see Figure 9.8). Ask specific questions (Where was the center of population in 1860?) and broader ones (What does this map tell use about our country?).

An activity that is fun as well as instructive is comparing maps of Pangaea. Have students look carefully at a world map (top, Figure 9.9), especially the Atlantic coast of Africa. Tell students to think of the continents as pieces in a jigsaw puzzle. Where would Africa fit? This relationship among the continents was first noticed in 1912 by Alfred Wegener, a German scientist. He proposed the continental drift theory: that continents had moved and drifted from one large land mass, which he called Pangaea (center, Figure 9.9). Research has upheld Wegener's basic idea, although scientists have made some changes in his theory. The bottom map (Figure 9.9) shows how present-day scientists think the Earth looked more than 200 million years ago. Ask

No. 5. Center of Population: 1790 to 1980

["Center of population" is that point at which an imaginary flat, weightless, and rigid map of the United States would balance if weights of identical value were placed on it so that each weight represented the location of one person on the date of the census.]

YEAR[1]	North latitude			West longitude			Approximate location
1790 (Aug. 2)........................	39	16	30	76	11	12	23 miles east of Baltimore, MD
1850 (June 1)........................	38	59	0	81	19	0	23 miles southeast of Parkersburg, WV
1900 (June 1)........................	39	9	36	85	48	54	6 miles southeast of Columbus, IN
1950 (Apr. 1)........................	38	50	21	88	9	33	8 miles north-northwest of Olney, Richland County, IL
1960 (Apr. 1)........................	38	35	58	89	12	35	In Clinton Co. about $6\frac{1}{2}$ miles northwest of Centralia, IL
1970 (Apr. 1)........................	38	27	47	89	42	22	5.3 miles east-southeast of the Mascoutah City Hall in St. Clair County, IL
1980 (Apr. 1)........................	38	8	13	90	34	26	$\frac{1}{4}$ mile west of De Soto in Jefferson County, MO

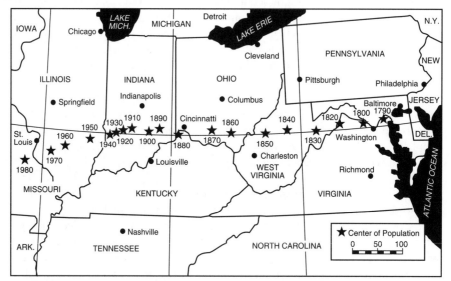

Figure 9.8 Center of population 1790-1980. U.S. Department of Commerce. *Source: Statistical Abstract of the United States 1981* (Washington, D.C.: U.S. Government Printing Office).

students what differences they see among the three maps. Then ask them to explain a bumper sticker on a car reading "Reunite Pangaea!" and why the bumper sticker is really a joke. Students who want to learn more about continental drift can be advised to read about plate tectonics in encyclopedias and other sources.

Notice that we have been emphasizing map-*reading* skills. Map*making* (or making one's own charts, cartoon drawings, etc.) is more difficult than simply reading or interpreting a map or table. Making maps requires visualization abilities. Mapmaking is the supreme test of map understanding; it may be an appropriate activity only for selected students. With proper instruction, however, most students enjoy map production.

The steps in making a map are somewhat similar to steps in making charts and graphs. They usually include (1) collecting or observing data, (2) organizing or sim-

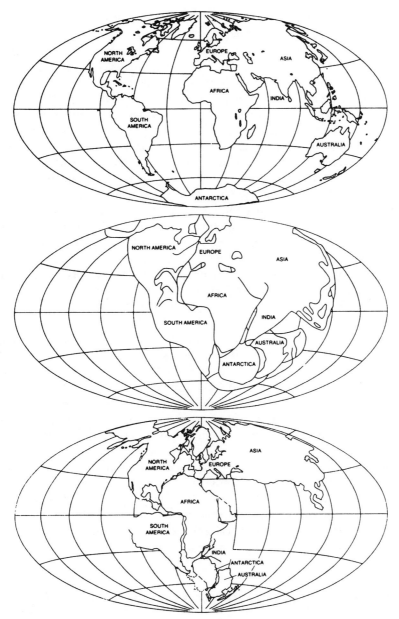

Figure 9.9 Changes in the continents. *Source:* Adapted from "Alfred Wegener and the Hypothesis of Continental Drift" by A. Hallam. Copyright © 1975 by Scientific American, Inc. All rights reserved.

plifying data, (3) planning the map (chart) in terms of scale, and (4) drafting or drawing the map or chart. Of course, computer programs can help students in making charts. Computer programs can eliminate a lot of the drudgery associated with steps 2, 3, and 4. One of the advantages of making maps (or charts) is that students can present what they have learned, especially local data, in a simplified format.

Primary children can make maps. Some teachers start with making a map of their own classroom. Children have to be told that they are looking down from the ceiling as they place desks and other room equipment in the classroom map. After this, children can be asked to make a map of their own bedroom or a room that they wish could be theirs. This activity can be expanded to include a map of their house or a house they would like. Finally a map of the local streets can be made, showing where the children's homes are located. Some teachers have used old shower curtains as the material for the local street map. The advantage of the shower curtain is its large size, making the streets visible in the back of the room. Note in all of these examples that the maps were local and personalized for the class. Usually, students must be taught each separate stage before they can draw the map. One of the advantages of mapmaking is that students can present what they have learned, especially local data, in a simplified format.

Because of the time involved and the visual skills needed to make maps, many teachers ask students to place data on already assembled globes and maps. Unbreakable globes and wall maps that can be marked with crayons and washed off are especially useful. Even inexpensive outline maps (frequently found in teachers' guides for map exercises for students) that have a minimum amount of information on them can be used to real advantage.

We hope that the teaching of map skills will move beyond the rote-memory format that in the past has been typical of many map skills programs. Do you yourself recall the many hours you probably spent on longitude and latitude? How often in real life have you been asked to use these? We should not forget that most adults commonly use road, newspaper, and magazine maps and do not have to compute longitude and latitude. But more important, we should try to teach students that maps and globes are designed to help us think. Maps in textbooks as well as globes should be used throughout the year and not just during a September unit. In this way, teaching children map skills will enhance their critical thinking, an area that needs as much attention as possible in the elementary school.

TECHNOLOGIES FOR THE SOCIAL STUDIES

We have all heard about the "information revolution" or the "information super-highway" that is about to arrive in the schools. The following jargon and phrases are tossed about:

- Classrooms without walls

- Virtual reality in which it is possible that students could "feel" what it is like to live in the cold climate of Antarctica
- E-mail
- Simulations so direct that students feel they are not play-acting
- Small computers on every student's desk
- Using the Internet, the international data superhighway, to link scientists and students
- Getting information instantly from a variety of sources
- High interest as students communicate with other faraway classrooms on social studies projects
- Whole-semester courses, taught by master teachers, from television sources such as the Public Broadcasting System

Testimonials abound from students, teachers, and parents about the usefulness of technology. Teachers have reported that even young kindergarten students can use and love their turn on the computer. Young children can work together in small groups and concentrate on learning tasks far longer than expected. Or using the National Geographic Kids Network, elementary students in one unit can collect data on acid rain, record their findings on a computer, and compare their measurements, via a modem, with research teammates throughout the world. In fact, using electronic mail (commonly referred to as e-mail), students are sending and receiving messages throughout the world with the aid of computers. Linking students in the same age group, e-mail can extend the classroom community beyond the local to national or even international connections. Even a simple telephone can help students complete their assignments, by connecting them to a "homework hot line."

However, the information revolution has stopped at most schoolhouse doors. The potential for both learning and teaching has only minimally been realized by the present use of technology in the schools. There are earnest pleas for more creative and expansive uses of technology. Experts report that computers and other technologies can give students a sense of competence, an awareness that they can do something, as well as the skills to operate in an increasingly global and technologically based economy. But the benefits of technology have not yet to come to most classrooms.

What will be the role of technology in education? The future is uncertain, but presently three challenges must be overcome if we are to reap the learning potential of technology in the schools. The first is money. Many school districts simply lack enough money for the basic costs of education and cannot afford the price of the new technology. School boards may regard the newer technology as frills or extras and may have no organized plans to improve or upgrade existing technology. Too many elementary teachers do not even have a telephone in their own classroom, let alone a computer. To help solve the problem of money, teachers look to other sources to get technology into the schools: partnerships with local businesses and institutions, fund-raising with supermarket chains, and similar strategies.

Second, many teachers lack the training and knowledge to integrate technology into the curriculum. Even when computers are available, they often sit idle in the classroom because teachers don't know how to use them competently, and just learning which buttons to push is not sufficient. To use the new technology effectively, teachers must take on new roles, changing from the omniscient taskmaster to learner, coach, and guide. The teacher is no longer the font of all knowledge.

This shift can be stressful. As students gain proficiency with computers—often at a much faster pace than teachers—the instructor cannot keep up with what every student is doing. In effect, teachers lose some of their control in the classroom, a shift that may bother some. Also, they must commit time to learning new computer programs and functions.

Newer teachers may have an advantage, as many of them used word processing in their undergraduate work and have some familiarity with computers. Often, teachers can learn from their students. Some students are fascinated with computer technology; they have the time and interest to develop real proficiency with programs and functions. Such students should be considered a valuable classroom resource and should be encouraged to share their knowledge with their teachers as well as their classmates.

A third barrier is the available software for the social studies, which is often not of high instructional quality. Many of the tutorials, instructions in new concepts or facts, and drill-and-practice programs (drill and kill for mastery) are in reality only very expensive workbooks. Often they are essentially reading comprehension programs, focused on topics such as capitals of states, which require little thinking from students. Because the quality of these programs is poor, schools seldom buy them; because schools don't buy them, software companies do not invest the money needed to develop better products, setting up a self-defeating cycle. But even with these restraints, there are some interesting and worthwhile programs available. Also, computers and software are not the only technology available to teachers. The following text explores the broader range of technology and how this can be used to enrich the social studies curriculum.

Traditional Noninteractive Media

Technology in the social studies classroom can be divided into two major categories: the first is *noninteractive* media such as films, videos, filmstrips, television, photographs, and records. For these media, the viewer generally cannot change the presentation and is typically a more passive learner. The range of materials in this category is broad, however, and many of them are interesting enough to overcome their noninteractive nature. That makes them useful in teaching social studies. These media can introduce new material, present information by visual means, increase student motivation, or reinforce major ideas in a unit. Often films, television, and videos can contribute an emotional dimension to your objectives. For example, much of our understanding about the Holocaust has come through films and pictures.

The widespread availability of videocassette recorders (VCRs) allows more and more teachers to record programs at home or at school to show in their classes at a later time. This practice offers an increasingly popular way to expand students' horizons. Videos can be shown at timely moments in the classroom. You may have to do some editing, such as skipping portions, for the best results. Presently teachers may record anything, but *permanent* retention and showing of videotaped programs is a violation of the copyright law. Teachers are also renting from commercial outlets classics like *Tom Sawyer* or the *Ox-Bow Incident*, or biographies of such people as Gandhi or Anne Frank. For example, good films for teaching about the Bill of Rights can include *To Kill a Mockingbird* or *Twelve Angry Men*. In addition, public libraries now have classic videos available.

By using noninteractive media in the classroom, you can also help students become critical viewers both inside and outside the classroom walls (see Chapter 5 on the teaching of controversial issues and Chapter 8 on communication skills). Encourage students to listen to certain television programs that may be worthwhile and then discuss them in class. Always encourage students to keep up with current events through television, newspapers, and magazines.

Interactive Media

The second important category of technology is *interactive* media where the student has more control. Under this category we find computers and telecommunication, the images we associate with high technology. Let us examine interactive media, discussing the most common uses first.

Computers.   More and more computers are finding their way into classroom as costs decline. How are they most likely to be used in social studies programs?

Social Studies Software Programs.   Probably the most common use of computers in the social studies is with commercially prepared software. Although in the future there may be whole-year social studies programs available and the teacher will be able to individualize programs for different students within the year's course, presently most teachers will have to select individual elements of software programs that carefully fit into their goals for their own social studies program. In the past, software programs were categorized as simulations, tutorials, or drill and practice, with the software often put in a game format to capture the student's attention and promote competition. Nowadays, it is often difficult to put a particular piece of software in a neat category, as it combines different elements such as a database designed for small group work. Software designed to have students work cooperatively in a small group is known as *groupware*. Sometimes social studies programs that create timelines in an easy format such as Timeliner and Chronos are also included as a special category, timelines. The trend now in local or state curriculum guides is to list all the available software, regardless of type, under such headings as fifth-grade U.S. history.

In making decisions on what software to buy, teachers can start by looking at the catalogues published by the software companies. The best comprehensive educational guide for software in all curriculum areas is *TESS: The Educational Software Directory*, published by EPIE Institute, Hagerstown, MD 21741-1540. In addition, professional social studies organizations review selected software in their journals. Computer journals that cover all subject areas, such as *Learning and Leading with Technology*, also contain reviews of new products and software. The best way to try out the programs is at the exhibit areas of social studies and computer conferences. In general, teachers should buy programs that focus on problem solving, decision making, or the use of databases for student-created projects. These are areas in which the computer can do a better job than traditional formats such as textbook teaching or a simulation not using a computer. Here are a few selected simulations.

Simulations

Cave Girl Clair, elementary grades, Addison-Wesley.
  Cave Girl must ensure her survival by fire-tending, gathering food and medicinal plants.
Choices, Choices: On the Playground, primary, Tom Snyder Productions, Inc.
  Should the new kid, who looks different and talks strangely, be allowed to join your ball game during recess? Kids make difficult choices balancing their own values with expectations of friends, parents, and teachers.
Choices, Choices: Taking Responsibility, primary, Tom Snyder Productions, Inc.
  Should you be a tattletale and tell the truth even though you risk getting into trouble and losing a good friend?
Decisions, Decisions, grades five to ten, Tom Snyder Productions, Inc.
  Series of "You Are There" scenarios on immigration, urbanization, colonization, etc.
Jenny of the Prairie, elementary grades, Addison-Wesley.
  Separated from a wagon train, Jenny must provide food, clothing, and shelter for herself during the winter.
The Market Place, grades three to six, Minnesota Educational Computing Corporation.
  Four programs on selling apples, plants, lemonade, and bicycles.

Oh, Deer, grades five to eight, Minnesota Educational Computing Corporation.

Deer and people are getting in each other's way.

Oregon Trail, grades three to six, Minnesota Educational Computing Corporation.

Students make decisions traveling on the Oregon Trail.

Santa Fe Trail, grades five and up, Educational Activities.

Students make decisions traveling on the Santa Fe Trail.

Bluegrass Bluff, grades five and up, Minnesota Educational Computing Corporation.

Archaeological dig in Bluegrass Bluff, Kentucky, where students excavate artifacts from ancient Native American civilizations.

Lewis and Clark Stayed Home, grades five and up, Minnesota Educational Computing Corporation.

You take over and lead the expedition to explore the Louisiana Purchase.

Run for the Monkey, grades five and up, Scarborough Systems.

Helps students to understand basic economic concepts.

National Inspirer, grades five and up, Tom Snyder Productions.

Groups of students move throughout the United States in search of important resources and commodities; uses state identification, planning, and group cooperation.

Stickybear Town Builder, primary, Social Studies School Service.

Using map symbols, directions, and scale, students design their own town.

SimTown, ages eight through twelve, Maxis.

A CD-ROM based program that allows students to build and manage a small town. Promotes thinking about the environment and cities as the town grows, consumes resources, and produces garbage. Maxis produces a number of other simulations as well that might be worth investigating, some of which are not on CD-ROM.

The next category of software to be considered is what is called drill and practice; in these, students review facts, such as names of continents, oceans, and presidents. Because this content is of little interest to students, most publishers have used a game format to increase children's motivation. This category probably has the widest range of quantity and quality. Geography is frequently used as content. Here are a few examples of drill and practice (games).

Games

The Great Maine-to-California Race, grades five to twelve, Hayden Software.

Children answer questions about each state, playing against each other or the computer.

Where in America's Past Is Carmen Sandiego? grades four to adult, Broderbund.

Students read clues and answer questions about world thief Carmen Sandiego. They use clues plus information from *American History Encyclopedia, Penguin's What Happened When?* and *World Almanac & Book of Facts* for other programs in the series as they play the role of student detectives, traveling far and wide to catch Carmen Sandiego and her gang. Also, **Where in Europe Is Carmen Sandiego?, Where in Time Is Carmen Sandiego,** and **Where in the USA Is Carmen Sandiego?**

Where in the World Is Carmen Sandiego? grades four to adult, Broderbund Software.

Databases. Databases are organized collections of data that permit students to easily retrieve and analyze information on many social studies topics. These databases include a wealth of information and enable students to quickly search through an extensive amount of data to answer questions and to make comparisons. Several software programs provide a database of information and/or enable the students to put in their own data and create their own database (**Bank Street Filer, AppleWorks,** etc.). For example, students can create their own database about the various Native American Indian tribes that lived in their state. After they put in data on each group, they can make comparisons on such topics as food sources or the roles in the family. Here are few selected database programs.

Hometown: A Local Area Study, grade six and up, Active Learning Systems. Students interview people in their local area, input their data, and analyze demographic data in their community.

One World Countries Database, grade five and up, Active Learning Systems. Database on 178 nations.

On-line databases give students access to a wider range of information sources than ever before possible. In the past, only industry and higher education institutions used commercial services such as ERIC and DIALOG, which enabled them to retrieve information from on-line databases such as *Facts on File* or to have access to a large number of magazines or journals. The teacher or librarian does need access to a *modem,* a device that allows the computer to communicate over a telephone line. Current events and topics of personal interest appear to be the most motivating on-line information sources that are both available and written at the appropriate reading levels for elementary students doing social studies projects.

Interactive video systems (Figure 9.10) are another variation using computers. Interactive video systems have the capability of the computer combined with audio and visual data so that the students feel they are part of the experience. Students typically use a commercial multimedia kit. They often can call up informa-

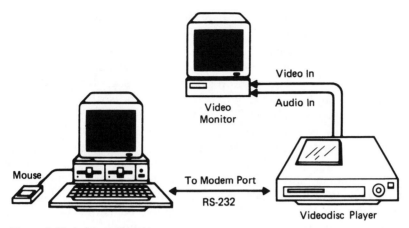

Figure 9.10 An interactive video system

tion from thousands of pages of printed text as well as thousands of images such as photographs, maps, and art work. Videodisc and CD-ROM (compact disc read-only memory) are two of the technologies that hold promise in this area. A videodisc can contain 100,000-plus images. For example, **The First Emperor of China** allows students to examine the life-sized clay warriors from the tombs at Xian and to listen to scholars discuss their discovery and its importance. Resources from art are now available on videodiscs. Many of them are accompanied by hypercard interactive programs that allow students to learn about cross references and construct categories on their own. Currently videodiscs are available on collections from the Louvre and other art museums as well as on particular artists such as Michelangelo. Portraits of famous Americans can personalize history. Instructional Resources Corporation has three history videodiscs: **The American History Videodisc** (2,490 still images and 68 moving sequences), **The Western Civilization Videodisc** (2,100 still images), and **The World History Videodisc** (2,400 images including 71 maps, and 12 sound and image overviews). Presently, many of the videodiscs are better suited for older elementary students. Combinations of computer and other technology are moving toward more *multimedia* instructional tools. Multimedia includes the use of audio, video, graphics, and other technologies and can allow students to create their own projects.

Word Processing.   Computers can be used as word processors. Both students and teachers are more likely to revise and edit what they have written if they use a computer. Written assignments in the social studies, especially longer ones, are promising projects for student word processing. Possible projects using desktop publishing principles might be a pretend historical newspaper such as one written in Boston, 1776, or an event in the students' state's history. Students can produce these if they have enough basic resource material and programs that do newspaper-style columns and heads. They need to learn to use software such as spelling and grammar checks, a boon to all teachers who have to correct written work.

In using word processing, children need to learn to enter information with a keyboard (type). Many families now have computers at home, so more students are familiar with the keyboard than ever before. Most schools that have computer courses introduce students to the keyboard around the sixth grade, or earlier in some schools. Students are often frustrated at "hunting and pecking" until they know how to type with some degree of accuracy. In addition, students need to become familiar with a word processing program that is to be used on the computer. Many students *do* have the skills necessary to use word processing capabilities of a computer at home and in the classroom. To function in our society, however, all students, regardless of their family resources, will need to become skillful in using computers and these experiences should be built into the curriculum.

The future of technologies for use in the social studies looks promising. Think of technology as a help for you as a teacher and not as a burden. Glowing reports abound about teachers who have successfully used computer graphics, on-line research, and on-line town meetings to teach such abstract concepts as the Bill of Rights and school behavior rules. By graphing rights conflicts of students, such as name-calling, students can engage in conflict resolution scenarios and work through multiple potential solutions for each scenario using a computer. They can use word processing to publish a newspaper about rights and responsibilities in their own classroom and their own school. Their newspaper can even be sent out to the community to reach a wider audience.

Teachers soon will be able to tap wide resources that can help to expand the environment of students. Teachers will need to keep up with what is happening in these areas, however, and school districts will need to devote more inservice training to making their staffs familiar with the uses of new technologies.

SUMMARY

Technology can enhance the quality of teaching. Computer usage in the classrooms can increase student-teacher interactions, making for more individualized instruction. Because we cannot give students all the facts they need for a lifetime, we must teach them the skills that will help them in the future. This means that students must learn to understand chronological time, map and global skills, and the ability to use new technologies.

9.3   *ON YOUR OWN: THE BEST USE OF TECHNOLOGY?*

What is the best use of technology that you have seen for the social studies? What features made it effective?

SUGGESTED READINGS

Beaver, John F. *Problem Solving across the Curriculum—Improving Students' Problem-Solving Skills Using Off-Computer & On-Computer Activities.* Eugene, Ore.: International Society for Technology in Education, 1994. Activities to improve students' problem-solving ability. Proven worthwhile activities for both the spur-of-the moment needs and for planned lessons.

Buggey, JoAnne, and Kracht, James. "Geographic Learning." In *Elementary School Social Studies: Research as a Guide to Practice,* Bulletin 79. Washington, D.C.: National Council for the Social Studies, 1986, 55–67. Good for showing that the research base on teaching geography is limited.

Kendall, Diane S., and Buden, Howard, guest eds. *Social Education* 51 (January 1987). Special section with articles on computers in social studies.

Laughlin, Margaret; Hartoonian, H. Michael; and Sanders, Norris, eds. *From Information to Decision Making: New Challenges for Effective Citizenship,* Bulletin 83. Washington, D.C.: National Council for the Social Studies, 1989.

Natoli, Salvatore J., ed. *Strengthening Geography in the Social Studies,* Bulletin 81. Washington, D.C.: National Council for the Social Studies, 1988.

Roberts, Nancy; Friel, Susan; and Ladenburg, Thomas. *Computers and the Social Studies.* Menlo Park, Calif.: Addison-Wesley, 1988. Written for social studies teachers.

Turner, Sandra, and Land, Michael. *Hypercard: A Tool for Learning.* Belmont, Calif.: Wadsworth, 1994. Focus on using applications software in the classroom.

Chapter 10

ASSESSING and EVALUATING CHILDREN'S PROGRESS in the SOCIAL STUDIES

In this chapter we describe the purposes and functions of assessment in the social studies from various perspectives. We discuss techniques for gathering data for the assessment, or evaluation, of learning. We also explore ideas for matching data collection with instructional activities and communicating these data to parents and students. Finally, we present themes for evaluating our instruction. The following topics are used to organize this chapter:

1/ Perceptions of Evaluation

2/ Assessment Alternatives

3/ Assessment Techniques and Tools

4/ Evaluating Learning and Development

PERCEPTIONS OF EVALUATION

Evaluation is something like beauty: Its meaning depends, in part, on who views it. As teachers, we play the pivotal role in this process. We can manipulate its outcome. By examining the motivation of the other actors—the student, the parent, the school system—in the process, we can get a better sense of the power and potential that our own role offers.

The Student

Remembering your own experience or those of your children is a good place to begin when you examine the impact that evaluation can have on a student. How many of us remember report-card day as a positive experience in our lives? Did we have a clue about why we got the reports we did? Was the report itself important, or was the response our parents and friends had about our report what we remember?

From the perspective of a student, evaluation is synonymous with grades and report cards. Unfortunately, the connotation is too often pejorative. Students understand very early that grades represent a mysterious power over their lives. They know when they are grouped for instruction by ability. They are tuned in to any indication that a teacher may, or may not, like them and, seeking confirmation of their suspicions, they connect that indication to the grade they receive.

When questioned, students often do not establish a connection between work habits and grades. They usually do not link final results to a series of smaller steps in preparing for a test, project, or presentation. They see evaluation as something outside their control. For many students, grades have little to do with learning or pride of accomplishment.

The Parent

Parents want their children to succeed. They want you as a teacher representing the school to recognize their child for the special person he or she is. They want assurance that you know their son or daughter. Parents are often amazed to learn about aspects of their child's behavior that they have not seen at home.

Grades and reports worry parents because they represent judgments about their children—the first indications about how the children will do in life outside the home. They want to know whether their children measure up to others of the same age. Most parents see reports and grades as stepping-stones or barriers to "the good life."

Parents want to know what their child is supposed to be learning. Many will want your suggestions about how they can help their daughter or son achieve what is required. Some may use reports as ways either to punish or reward their child at home.

The Teacher

Typically, we see evaluation as a necessary but uncomfortable task. It is a function we are forced to perform as a way to communicate how students are doing to the students, their families, and the school system.

We intend to treat each student fairly as we collect impressions of her or his progress. We are channeled by our school system to work toward instructional objectives according to our grade level and subjects. We realize that these objectives may not be the most appropriate for every student. We are frustrated at our lack of time and energy and our inability to attend more adequately to every child's needs.

We are held accountable by parents to inspire in their children a love of learning and growth in all aspects of their social, cognitive, and physical knowledge and skills. We are expected by the school to produce the best possible test-score results. Sometimes it seems as though no one, not even the student, is accountable to us. We often feel that we are being held responsible by the parents and the school for producing the results they both desire while not being given enough support from either group.

The School System

Evaluation is the principal means of quantifying how students are doing in school. Methods of authentic evaluation that are tied to student performance—checking students' actual work rather than separate or standardized tests against instructional objectives or performance criteria—represent an ideal toward which schools must work. In reality, however, moving systems toward more holistic ways to assess student progress by looking at performance requires expensive teacher training and curriculum revision that few schools can afford. Keeping records of individual student progress is an essential way to communicate with parents and other schools about that student. Reducing the data to grade-level equivalents and numbers or letters is a more efficient way to communicate about individual progress.

The more evaluative data you collect on students, the better your program analysis can become. Decisions about new curricula cannot be made without data on student progress. Other factors are important, but test scores can offer insight to the performance of a school system over a long period. Comparing one district with other districts is difficult without demographic, funding, and standardized test data. Data from standardized achievement tests can also be helpful in evaluation of teacher performance.

The Experts

Broad views about the value of evaluation suggest that it should serve all actors on the school-achievement scene—the student, the parent, the teacher, and the school system. Elliott Eisner listed five functions of evaluation:[1]

1. To diagnose what a child knows and thereby point toward appropriate instruction;
2. To provide data for the revision of curriculum both for the classroom teacher and the system;
3. To compare what children can be before and after instruction and with and without instruction;
4. To anticipate educational needs of children as they progress through a curriculum;
5. To determine if instruction objectives are being met.

Even though we may empathize with the perspective of each of these groups, it is also important to be informed about and take advantage of the potential benefits everyone involved stands to gain from an effective assessment and evaluation process. (By assessment we mean any method of overall evaluations and judgments of understandings, concepts, skills, or competencies that the individual has developed.) All these perspectives are interrelated. Notice that in each perspective, evaluation is a decision-making tool, not an end in itself. No one would object to a process in which evaluation is an integral part of instruction, providing the momentum for instructional effort toward some agreed-on direction.

Experts want to change aspects of each perception described. They want children to participate more in decisions about their learning. They want parents to understand that evaluation is part of a process, not a final judgment about their child or a weight to be held over a child's head. They want teachers to make greater use of assessment results to guide their instructional planning. They want school systems to collect evaluation data in the most unobtrusive, least time-consuming way possible. And they want systems to refuse to test students with instruments inappropriate to the goals the systems have set, or in ways that were not part of the natural activity of learning. And most important, they would urge us first to invest our energies into developing curricula with contemporary, significant content delivered in motivating and meaningful ways.

Everyone wants schools to test students fairly according to the goals the district has established, and ideally in ways that are part of the natural dynamics of classroom learning. What a marvelous idea it would be if students found assessment to be a lively, active, exciting experience! Or if teachers thought standardized tests or those given by the district or state were a fair assessment of their students.

---

[1]Elliott Eisner, *The Educational Imagination*, 2d ed. (New York: Macmillan, 1985), 192.

You will remember from Chapter 1 that the federal government is asking for greater accountability for student learning from the schools. National educational goals and standards in history, geography, civics, and government have been published (see Chapters 1, 4, and 5). With increased attention to standards, it is clear that test methods and test results will continue to be used as arguments in the debate about how to reform education.

Paralleling the growing momentum for national, state, and district testing is the growth of interest and experimentation with alternative forms of assessment. These seek to move away from using only multiple-choice objective test items to judge student achievement. Critics of standardized tests charge that they inadequately and unfairly measure nonwhite, nonmiddle-class students. Further, they argue that the formats of these kinds of tests prompt all students to learn that there is only one right answer to every question or that their job is to get the answer by guessing. The debate about the forms and adequacy of achievement assessment has caused educators to become more critical of how they evaluate student achievement. For all types of assessment, there is general consensus that they should attempt to meet these criteria:

- Encourage high performance standards
- Be gender, ethnic, and class-bias free
- Promote critical thinking and effective citizenship
- Be useful for diagnosis to improve student performance
- Help students apply what they have learned to real-life situations

ASSESSMENT ALTERNATIVES

Alternatives have been developed as a substitute for standardized objective tests with multiple-choice or other fill-in test items. These techniques are known as authentic or performance-based assessment. Performance-based assessment, also called performance assessment or authentic assessment, requires students to create products or to perform, not simply to answer paper-and-pencil tests. The assessment may call for writing or problem solving. Or it may require the students' learning to be measured from the songs or dances or programs they produce as a result of their studies.

Performance-based assessment really is not new. Music teachers always have evaluated students on their performance as they sing or play instruments. Physical education is another example. Teachers typically look at how students perform certain physical skills. In neither music nor physical education have paper-and-pencil tests commonly been used.

Authentic assessment means the assessment tasks are real instances of learning rather than indirect estimates of actual learning goals. Essays or writing assignments are good examples of performance-based or authentic testing. They directly assess a sample of a student's writing instead of using objective tests to assess writing mechanics, spelling, and grammar. If you make an objective test that asks students to indicate which words are spelled correctly, you are only indirectly getting at their spelling ability. In contrast, an essay can directly assess students' spelling as well as their writing ability. We all know students who get perfect scores on spelling tests but do not spell well when they actually have to use the words in a writing effort.

Open-ended problems in math are another example of performance-based assessment. Here the students must show their work and cannot choose a, b, c, or d as a choice for the answer. This format, like evaluating art, music, and oral reading, makes grading subjective.

Probably the most popular form of performance-based assessment in social studies is an assessment of a portfolio of student work. A portfolio is a collection of student work over a period of time that provides evidence of student learning. Student work collected in the portfolio provides a means of judging student achievement and progress in the social studies.

A portfolio contains carefully selected samples of work. Typically, teachers involve their students in selecting their best work to include in the portfolios. Choosing only enough samples to give a representative picture of the student's work keeps the portfolio size manageable. This sampling over time is valuable for examining student growth, especially in writing. Students should be involved in the process of self-evaluation as they select their best work and evaluate their progress toward a goal that they set. Products in social studies might include journal entries based on literature read as part of a unit; timelines integrating data compiled from more than one source about a topic studied, constructed and annotated by the student; or videotaped or audiotaped scripts about a person investigated for a History Day presentation. Portfolios should include an introductory letter or description of the objective(s), or learning goals, a table of contents, and other material that tells the teacher or evaluator what the student is trying to accomplish.

Which is better? Performance-based or authentic assessment, or paper-and-pencil tests? (Look carefully at Table 10.1.) There is no easy answer to this

TABLE 10.1 COMPARISON OF ASSESSMENTS

Authentic Assessments	*Paper-and-Pencil Tests*
Examples: essays, open-ended problems, portfolios, hands-on problems	Examples: short answer, matching, true-false, multiple choice
Subjective evaluation	Objective evaluation
Small sample of tasks	Can tap a large number of content items
Time-consuming evaluation	Easy to grade; can have computer grade
Student directly involved in own learning/ assessment	Tend to separate assessment from learning

question. Partly, it depends on how well either of the approaches is constructed and used. There can be both good and bad performance-based assessment as well as good or poor objective test items. If instruction is poor, the form assessment takes may not be significant. Performance-based assessment can give an actual picture of what the individual can do, but there may be problems in how to rate or evaluate work such as essays or products or performances. Teachers need to devise standard ways or criteria to judge student products. It is probably true that paper-and-pencil tests will be more reliable; this means that different evaluators are more likely to get the same scores when checking a set of student responses on tests than they are when evaluating student products. While paper-and-pencil tests take less time to administer and score and cost less, performance-based approaches have the advantage of being an integral part of instruction and, as such, can be used to engage students in assessing their own progress in terms of what they see in their work rather than in terms of a numerical score or grade.

No one can be sure what direction authentic assessment will take. It is unlikely that the thirty-five states presently using objective tests will replace them entirely with authentic or performance-based assessment. It may be that new tests will combine both approaches to measurement by including writing samples or cooperative learning tasks as well as multiple-choice items. Students may be asked to read a longer historical passage from a primary or secondary source and then answer multiple-choice items that require critical thinking. It may be that more authentic forms of assessment will become a larger part of classroom-level and individual student assessment practice while states and districts continue to require standardized achievement tests as annual or semi-annual global measures.

These diverse perspectives are useful to recall when you examine your thoughts about the purposes of evaluation in children's learning. By focusing on the possible motivations for these various views of evaluation, you can more adequately anticipate where to begin communication about a child's, or a group's, learning. To organize evaluation, however, teachers need more than empathy. Knowledge of a repertoire of evaluation techniques and tools is crucial in instructional planning. The following discussion of assessment techniques and tools should help you in matching instructional purposes in social studies with appropriate assessment methods.

ASSESSMENT TECHNIQUES AND TOOLS

As teachers, we need to be familiar with both the traditional and emerging approaches to evaluating student achievement. Below, we examine first paper-and-pencil tests and then performance-based assessment techniques that might be used by the classroom teacher in evaluating social studies.

Paper-and-Pencil Tests

Paper-and-pencil testing is most suited for assessing social studies goals in the knowledge and thinking skills area. In our test-dominated age, the use of paper-and-pencil testing in the social studies is often taken for granted, almost as a cultural imperative. Furthermore, tests provide a relatively easy means to gather data on what children know and what they are able to do. The data from objective-type test items are easily counted for ranking and averaging. Tests included in textbook-series materials make the chore of preparing tests easier. In addition, tests accompanying texts often have better coverage of textbook content and are written more clearly, especially the multiple-choice questions, than most teacher-made tests because of the time and energy required in test construction.

Most teachers use the commercially prepared tests that accompany textbook series. Feeling compelled to provide numerical evidence of student progress pushes many teachers to rely on textbook-related tests. Thus the content of their instruction tends to be tied to the textbook. You may think this technique for selecting and assessing content is too narrow and limiting. Or you may believe that the content of texts you use is appropriate as a definer of instructional content. Either way, you need to be a critical consumer of prepared commercial tests or tests that accompany a social studies textbook series.

There are several criteria for selecting tests or test items. The principal criterion is to verify that the items are aligned with your instructional objectives. They should be consistent with both the content covered and the level of thinking about the content you have led the students to experience. Choosing the kinds of test items that students have experienced or that you have taught them to work with is another criterion. Providing sufficient items to check individual objectives is still another criterion. That is, we can learn more about a student's mastery of a concept if the student has several opportunities to answer questions about it.

Beyond the general criteria for test and item selection, each type of test brings special considerations.

1. Short Answer. A short answer item is typically a statement with a key word or phrase missing. Which of the following pairs are the better items?

 a. Mexico, Canada, and the United States are _____
 b. The three largest nations of North America are _____, _____ and

 _____ .

 a. _____ invented the _____ in _____ .
 b. The inventor of the cotton gin was _____.

Both "a" examples are inferior. Neither cues the student to the desired content. For short-answer items, the content cue is best presented at the sentence beginning and its completion at the sentence ending. The first example requires students to invent, and they may give semantically correct answers such as "fun" or "big" or "all purple on the map" that have no relation to the content studied.

Short-answer items, and all pencil-paper items, can be criticized as testing reading more than knowledge of the social studies content. Should we give children a grade in the social studies that is really related more to their reading ability than, perhaps, to their social studies knowledge? Most teachers are more concerned with learning what a child knows about the social studies content. They find that poor readers can respond correctly to the items if these items and the possible answers are read aloud.

2. *Matching.* Using the process of elimination is a good thinking strategy. Matching items should prompt students to use this strategy. As with all test-item types, students need practice with this kind of item before they are tested using it.

Which of the following three sets of matching items is best?

    a. You have read about Native Americans, white settlers, and the buffalo. Now, draw lines below connecting the part of the buffalo with the way that part was used by the Plains tribes.

hair	bow strings
hide	food
horns	mattresses
meat	spoons
sinew	

    b. Match the following countries with the continents in which they are located.

Mexico	South America
Chad	Africa
Finland	Europe
Chile	Asia
India	North America

    c. Match the example with the economic category it fits best.

services	skateboard
goods	trip to Disney World
resources	haircut
	gold coins
	farmland
	sleeping
	running a race

The best item is "a," according to testmakers, because it has uneven lists. The student must use the process of elimination as well as either direct recall of what has been studied or analysis of what might be possible. Note that in "a" but not "b" or "c" the choices are listed in alphabetical order. Alphabetical order saves the student time when rereading the list. Other pointers for this type of item include not making the list too long and not mixing categories within the lists. Item "c" commits both of these errors.

3. *True-False.* Items that are true or false invite students to guess and afford them a higher probability of being correct than any other type of test item. For this reason, and because this type of item tends to be written at a low level of cognitive difficulty, most test-construction experts do not favor true-false tests as reliable measures of what children know.

Which of these items is better, a or b, in the following examples?

1. a. _____ Cars are an example of economic goods.
   b. _____ Cars are goods.
2. a. _____ Henry Hudson was a Spanish explorer.
   b. _____ Henry Hudson explored the Caribbean.

Did you choose "a" in 1 and "b" in 2 as better items? (Yes, we know that neither "a" nor "b" is an accurate statement.) 1a and 2b are clearer statements of the content. You could argue, for example, that cars are goods and Henry Hudson was an explorer, albeit not for Spain. Inserting "Spanish" before "explorer" tests the students' care in reading possibly more than their knowledge about Henry Hudson's exploits. If our objective is related to critical reading, "a" in 2 could be counted as a good item.

Writing good true-false items is more difficult than answering them. It is easy to "give away" the answer to this type of item. Even though experts criticize these items, textbooks continue to use them, recognizing that they require less time to check. Below is a list of development rules compiled by researchers that you can refer to when evaluating true-false items.

Checkpoints for True-False Items[2]

1. Avoid using specific determiners (*always, never, only*).
2. Avoid use of negatives or double negatives (*not impossible*).
3. Limit statements to a single idea.
4. State ideas as concisely as possible.
5. Avoid exact wording of the text or source material.
6. Make the statement clearly true or false.
7. Test only important ideas.

To extend true-false items beyond the level of factual recall, you can ask children to rewrite false items to make them true, or to tell one more thing they know about true items.

---

[2]Adapted from a twenty-one-item list developed by David A. Frisbie and Douglas F. Becker, "An Analysis of Textbook Advice about True-False Tests," *Applied Measurement in Education* 4, no. 1 (1990): 69.

4. Multiple Choice.   Testing experts find that multiple-choice items, if well written, are a better test of knowledge than other objective-type items. More answer options lessen a student's chance of getting the correct answer by guessing.

Which of the following two items is better?

1. Traders from Latin America in the late 1500s brought to Europe
   a. cloth
   b. guns
   c. sugar
   d. aluminum
2. Which of the following is a product that traders in the late 1500s brought to Europe from Latin America?
   a. cloth
   b. sugar
   c. both a and b
   d. neither a nor b

The first item is straightforward. Response items that combine answer choices, like options 2c and 2d, are tricky and confusing. Also, it is easier to complete statements than to answer questions.

Combining multiple-choice items with map and chart or graph reading is a valuable application of this type of item. The choices, again, should be plausible and not combinations or negations.

Performance-Based Assessment

Techniques associated with performance-based assessment are integrated in social studies unit plans. The natural flow of unit teaching produces opportunities as the unit evolves to gather data about student progress. Below we highlight several of the ways that authentic or actual work can be organized to provide a picture of student achievement in social studies.

1. Observation.   Teachers continually make judgments based on observations. They move a child so that he or she can do quiet work. They give more practice examples of how to calculate map distances when they see that several children need it. They compliment a child for straightening up the project work area without being reminded. Rarely, however, do they keep records of these observations for purposes of communicating social studies progress.

It would be impossible to record every incident of a child's behavior for evaluation purposes! But for assessment of progress in positive social behaviors, often reported under the rubric of citizenship on primary-level reporting systems, there is a useful middle point between recording nothing and recording everything. Objectives for this goal may be general and year-long, such as "being responsible for myself and my things," or they may be related to a specific unit that involves small group work with an objective of "sharing information for the benefit of the group" (see Chapter 3, Table 3.4, Group Self-Evaluation).

For the first type of objective, teachers can keep a note card file that records the child's name and the date and a sentence reporting the behavior related to the objective (see Figure 10.1). Some teachers like to send these "Super Citizen" cards home with children as they note the child's behavior. Others prefer to accumulate the notes in a folder to be used with parents at conference time. To benefit from this evaluation tool, keep a few specific objectives in mind and focus on them.

Observation by tallies is a convenient technique for gathering data on particular behaviors (see Figure 10.2). Once the form is prepared, you can carry it about on a clipboard during the monitoring of group work and record what individual children do. In a similar fashion, students can observe the on-task behaviors during their small group work and then use the data they collect as an evaluation guide in planning how to improve their individual and group productivity.

Observation as an evaluation technique is best suited to situations of social interaction and independent work habits and group responsibility. Everyone agrees that these skill areas are crucial and must be developed, but student behaviors in these skill areas are not restricted to a part of the school day designed as social studies time.

To use this observational technique, teachers must periodically schedule time and design instruments to focus on these behaviors during a variety of classroom activities.

2. Sampling Work.   Collecting samples of a child's expressive products over time is an important way to amass evaluative data. Drawing and writing efforts are particularly suited to this technique. Dating the samples and accumulating them in individual folders for each child is a management task students can learn and be-

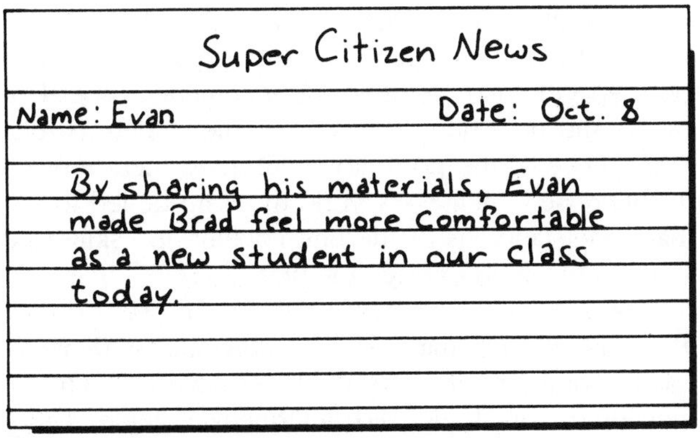

Figure 10.1 Super Citizen News sample card

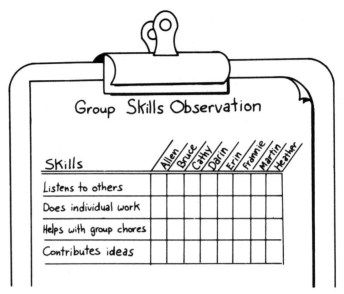

Figure 10.2 Group skills observation

come responsible for. Teachers often have students choose their "best" story or drawing of the week or of the unit to file in their work folders (see Figure 10.3). Other teachers believe that sending all the child's work home in a weekly folder for the parent to examine and return is a more consistent way to maintain communication between the school and the home about student progress. Sending all the work home is not recommended. The teacher loses a cumulative data base that is useful for comparative purposes, and parents and caregivers often have little information with which to measure the significance of these efforts. They look for teacher comments, especially grades, as clues for appreciating the significance of their child's work. By amassing and keeping a collection of each child's work at school, all members of the learning triad—student, teacher, and parent—can see the differences in what a child wrote or drew in September and December. Connecting samples to specific units reinforces the content of social studies. In composing the portfolio and presenting it to others, the student participates in his or her own assessment. Use of the portfolio as an assessment tool promotes critical thinking; as students review their own work, they can be led to discuss, constructively, their initial understandings of the unit content and skills and changes they experienced as they progressed through the unit.

Group products such as murals, scroll movies, and skits do not fit into a single portfolio. Teachers can informally record individual students' contributions to these products as the products are presented and have each child place the notes in his or her individual work folder. For intermediate-grade classes, teachers can ask that individual students write their own file notes about what they contributed to a group product.

Last year my family and I went on a trip to Ohio. It took six hours to get to New Jersey where we stopped for the night. We stayed at the Holiday Inn. When we woke up we could see the Statue of Liberty.

At twelve that afternoon we left to go to Ohio it took one hour to get there.

We stayed there for three weeks.

My greatgrandpa ownstwenty acres of land and fifteen acres of water. When we were going to go into the lake we saw a dead cat fish on the shore.

I took my raft out and jumped into the lake.

There were big cat tailes sticking out of the water. There were at least one thousand sticking out of the water. Me and my dad went through the cat tails. The water was green and it seemed like we were in the jungle.

While we were there me my brother and my sister got to see dad's cousins uncle and aunt. I got to shoot a bow and arrow.

My dad borrowed a motor boat from a friend I got to drive the boat at full speed. My mom was scared when I let go of the stearing wheel and went in circles.

When we came back my grandpa was mowing the lawn with his tractor I got to drive the tractor.

THE END

written by Greg Lanker, September

(a)

THE SUB HUNT

It was the day after Christmas and Mr. Smith got a call from the president saying, "Theres a U.S.S.R. sub in the Persian Gulf and Iwant you to find it and destroy it."

Mr. Smith was surprrised that the president would give him such a order.

The next day Mr. Smith got twenty-five men and they all got in a p3.c orion. They turned on the engiens, taxied down the run way, and took off.

It took three hours to get to the Persian Gulf.

They turned on the radar and started looking for the sub.

One hour went by, two hours went by, three hours went by. Then finaly after three hours and 30 menutes went by they finaly found it.

Then they got a torpedo and droped it from 9 thousand feet in the air.

It was a direct hit the sub was destroyed.

THE END

written by Greg Lanker, January

(b)

Figure 10.3 These writing samples show a student's progress from September to January. The earlier sample (a) recounts a recent experience. The January sample (b) uses fictional elements to elaborate on current events discussed in class and contains plot structure and dialogue. Spelling and usage problems can be worked on through the writing-editing process discussed in Chapter 8. (Samples written by Greg Lanker, Toyon School, fifth grade, Berryessa School District, San Jose, Calif.: Dick Pope, teacher.)

3. Essay.   Essays as a technique for assessing a child's knowledge are emerging from a long period of eclipse. Previously, we were persuaded that a more objective assessment of children's knowledge was one that could be counted and quantified, permitting us to compare individuals and groups. Some teachers welcomed objective tests as a time-saving way to avoid correcting essays. We now recognize the centrality of written expression in all curricular areas for assessing higher levels of thinking. Students who can talk about or write about facts and ideas show that they have structured new information. They not only recall and classify information as an objective-type test item would require, but they also can put the information into a context.

Students need frequent practice and instruction in organizing ideas before this type of testing can legitimately be used. Essays should not be used to test factual recall but to have students relate ideas by combining, differentiating, sequencing, juxtaposing, and extending logically. These thinking tasks should be developed carefully through the year.

Essay items for elementary students need to include an outline for the response. Which one of the following essay items is better?

1. Tell about the Constitutional Convention.
2. List and explain two reasons that the Constitutional Convention was important to Americans in 1787.

Definitely, the second is better than the vague first essay question. But the second item could be further improved by suggesting the kinds of problems—between states and with other nations—the Constitution resolved. Learning to write a response structure in an essay topic takes practice. Look at these items. Both are faulty. How can they be improved?

1. Compare a desert and a woodland forest region in terms of climate and resources.
2. Compare the Sahara and the Appalachian regions.

The first item helps the student begin an answer outline by supplying "climate" and "resources." It does not supply a specific example of the regional types for the student. The result may be that the student spends all of his or her time trying to recall the name of a desert and a woodland forest. Or the student may write in a general way about the two regions, which may not be what the teacher would consider correct given the difficulty of generalizing about regions as disparate as the Gobi, the Sonora, and the Sahara. The second item specifies two regions without giving the student a clue about the criteria on which to compare them. It could be improved by adding ". . . in terms of natural resources, climates, and ways people live."

Table 10.2 is a useful guide for assessing individual portfolio items as it separates the "message," the content of the student's expressive piece, from the

TABLE 10.2   ANALYSIS SCHEME FOR A WRITING SAMPLE

Message Questions	*Medium Questions*
1. In what genre is the child attempting to write? How successful is the child? Are there certain beginnings, endings, sequences used to indicate a certain genre?	1. Does the child show knowledge of the directionality principles of the writing system? How about the spacing principle? Layout features? Paragraphing?
2. Is the text complete according to the genre the child is attempting? If complete, is it sparse, or are relevant details and elaborations included?	2. Does the child show that he or she has a stable concept of letter/word/sentence?
3. Does the child use an interesting vocabulary? Is it appropriate to the genre attempted? Does the child use cohesive ties to knit the text together? Does the child use any words that are unclear or ambiguous—e.g., pronouns with uncertain antecedents?	3. How does the child use punctuation, capitalization?
4. Are there any gaps of information or "missing links" in the text? Does the child order information to make sense?	4. What does the child know about the orthographic system? At what developmental level do you think the child is?
5. Does the child appear to have audience or reader "sense"?	5. How does the child control various grammatical structures—e.g., noun and verb agreement, parallel constructions?

SOURCE: Adapted from Christine C. Pappas, Barbara Z. Kiefeer, and Linda S. Levstik, *An Integrated Language Perspective in the Elementary School: Theory into Action* (White Plains, N.Y.: Longman, 1990), 197.

"medium," the knowledge demonstrated about the form, or process, discernible in the item. One of the positive contributions the whole-language perspective brings to instruction is its focus on the primacy of message over medium in language/literacy assessment. While not negotiating the need for mechanical control over language, assessment of thinking skills and fluency with content requires redirecting our evaluation tradition to issues of "message" when examining student expressive products.

4. Self-Evaluation.   Taking responsibility for their own independent learning is one of the major goals of schooling for students. You can assist them toward this goal by providing frequent occasions for self-evaluation. This technique is appropriate in all the major social studies areas. Ask students to assess their knowledge and skills through questions such as these:

What do you need to spend more time on?
What areas of this topic do you feel you know?
What did you learn today in your research reading?

Continuing self-evaluation can lead students to formulate plans for themselves based on what they see as significant.

Teachers find that self-reports about study habits and citizenship skills are useful data to collect periodically. A sample form that students can use for these reports is shown in Figure 10.4.

Self-evaluation reports can also be tied to specific units in which tasks and choices have been specified. Often known as a "contract," this kind of listing helps some students stay focused on what they need to do (Figure 10.5). Forms such as this give students an overview of a topic and often help to make a unit more coherent and cohesive. The goal of self-evaluation is an increased sense of responsibility. Teachers hope that by lenghtening students' view of school tasks from the period or day to the week or unit, students will begin to take more responsibility for completing their work.

5. Conferences.   Talking individually with children about how they are doing is a powerful assessment and evaluation technique. It enables teachers to bridge the distance between the student and his or her efforts. Initially, many students are timid about discussing their work with teachers in a conference setting, but by the second round of conferences, students usually become accustomed to this kind of scrutiny. Individual conferences should focus on work samples and self-evaluations and any observational data that teachers may have collected. Leading students to see their work in terms of the instructional objectives often sheds a new light on the "why" of school assignments.

My Work Habits and Study Skills				
Name:				
	Poor	Fair	Good	Comment
Turn in work on time				
Plan my work before the last minute				
Seek help when I do not understand				
Use my time to get work done first				
Help others in my work group				
Know where my supplies are				
Help keep the room clean				
Take my turn doing chores				

Figure 10.4 Self-evaluation form

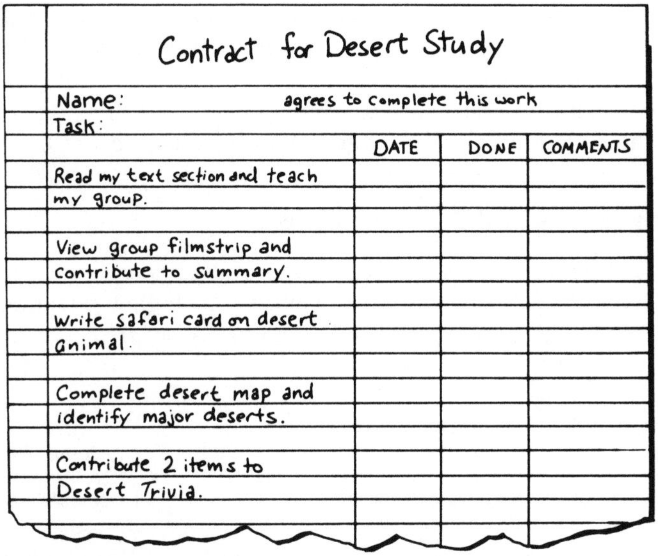
Contract for Desert Study

Name: agrees to complete this work

Task:

	DATE	DONE	COMMENTS
Read my text section and teach my group.			
View group filmstrip and contribute to summary.			
Write safari card on desert animal.			
Complete desert map and identify major deserts.			
Contribute 2 items to Desert Trivia.			

Figure 10.5 Individual contract for social studies

EVALUATING LEARNING AND DEVELOPMENT

For purposes of organizing a clear presentation we have separated our discussion of the kinds of tools and techniques we use to collect learning data from our examination of how we use these data. In actual practice, these activities are not sequential nor separate nor engaged in by the teacher alone. For our expository purpose here, we continue the linear examination of the assessment process by highlighting in this section how the process should be shared and how it can fit into instructional planning.

Instructional Planning and Assessment

In most school districts teachers pay attention to ensuring that what they teach in the classroom is in alignment with the goals and objectives subscribed to by the district. National professional groups and statewide commissions are continually developing standards or levels of performance as a way of further clarifying what teachers are expected to teach and students to learn. Teachers should ask whether their district has adopted performance standards as guides to organizing instructional plans.

Planning for assessment is an integral part of instructional planning at every level of a school system. Assessment requirements at school, district, and state or national levels may set boundaries and standards for instruction at the classroom level. Even with direction from above, much of the planning work of assessment remains for the individual teacher. Once we have instructional objectives selected for a unit topic, or for the year, we must plan how to collect data and what data to collect on individual progress toward these objectives. Categories from the taxonomies of educational goals can help you sharpen your thinking about both the content and the method of your evaluation plans (see Figure 10.6).

Relating Objectives and Process Levels

Checking objectives against a sequence of processes ordered by levels of difficulty will assist teachers in thinking about evaluation. The higher categories of the taxonomies require more practice and greater emphasis on projects that students or-

Knowledge Level	Within Text Example (from "The Little Red Hen")	Curricular Example
Recall: Names, lists, locates, repeats, describes	Names animals in story	Pledge of Allegiance; names 50 states; retells native myth
Comprehension: Tells meaning, interprets, gives examples	Tells why hen ate the bread	Defines family; explains map symbols; tells ways Sojourner Truth showed courage
Application: Explains sequence or process, solves problem, demonstrates	Shows how hen's lesson applies to classroom	Shows how to find east in morning; demonstrates how to make tortillas
Analysis: Outlines, categorizes, relates events or causes	Tells why hen acted as she did	Puts clothes and shelters into climate groups
Synthesis: Revises, investigates, creates, presents	Tells a different ending to story	Presents a play about the beginning of the Revolutionary War
Evaluation: Ranks, judges, compares, using criteria	Discusses whether each animal was treated fairly	After listing basic needs, chooses items for survival in desert
Values		
Receiving: Listens, observes	Attends to story as teacher reads	Attends as teacher explains project
Responding: Participates, complies	Reenacts part of story according to role assigned	Takes turns in cooperative group task
Valuing: Initiates	Repeats hen's line to remind classmate of classroom responsibility	Volunteers to help sort paper for recycling in classroom

Figure 10.6 Taxonomies and instruction. Source: Partial list adapted from Benjamin Bloom (ed.) et al., *Taxonomy of Educational Goals. Handbook I—Cognitive Domain* (New York: McKay, 1956); David R. Krathwohl, ed., *Taxonomy of Educational Objectives: The Classification of Goals, Handbook II—Affective Domain* (New York: McKay, 1964).

ganize and present. Higher levels of thinking need to be supported by instruction and practice on equivalent levels as well as on the cognitive levels that precede them before evaluation at that level is appropriate. For example, asking students to interpret weather information on an outline map of the United States requires that they (1) know the locational geography of the United States and (2) recognize the weather symbols and their meanings.

Cross-checking objectives with these taxonomies can alert you to instructional gaps. In the case of exploring written text or information presented in oral or visual form, the questioning sequence teachers design for children will be more successful if discussions begin at the more basic knowledge level. If the objective is for students to create an ending that shows the animals with different characteristics, then questions need to bring out the basic facts of the original story—such as who the animals were and what characteristic each represented and how the story might have ended if one or all the animals had behaved differently. The whole group needs to hear this information before they are asked to perform a creative task. If the objective requires students to create shoebox dioramas of pioneer life—a synthesis-level task—the children must understand what is involved. For diorama making to be a meaningful, not a copying task, students must first gather information about the activities—for example, the ones that were performed inside a settler's cabin. They must see pictures and hear and read stories about candle making; wood spinning; storing food in the root cellar; conserving food by drying, by soaking in brine, and by larding; cooking at hearthside.

Cross-checking or analyzing what students must know or be able to do before they can complete an activity is known as *task analysis*. Planning for assessment and evaluation should include this step. It is an essential way to examine unit and lesson objectives. Once teachers are aware of the prerequisite knowledge and skills students need to perform an assignment, they can design a more realistic, meaningful, and successful sequence of instruction. A further benefit is that this exercise produces a structure that can be used to make objectives clearer to students.

Relating Objectives and Instructions

Another indication of what kinds of data teachers need to collect comes from the instructional objectives themselves. If students are to learn the names of local landmarks and their locations, they need opportunities to visit the actual sites, view photographs, compose collages that replicate what they have seen or read about, and practice with blank maps, map puzzles, and spelling drills. Pencil-and-paper techniques for mastery may be indicated. If the instructional objective is for children to work productively in a group, they need to be taught appropriate group behaviors and to be given practice working in group situations. Teacher observation complemented by group and self-evaluation and conferences may be necessary. If the objective is for children to be able to distinguish between valid and invalid conclusions, the students must be instructed in supporting conclusions with data and argument and must have guided practice with appropriate reading exercises. Teacher observation of student discussions and writing samples that support or argue against conclusions is appropriate.

Scheduling Data Collection

Deciding when to collect evaluative data is a third element of the organizing task. Benjamin Bloom's ideas are useful for this task as well. He distinguished between formative and summative evaluation.[3] Formative evaluation, the collection of data about how the student is doing as he or she works through an instructional sequence, is crucial if teachers are to strive for mastery learning by every student. Formative evaluation gives teachers information about what they need to reteach for which individuals. This approach to evaluation tends to place the burden of the student's learning progress in the teacher's hands. It suggests that teachers should revise instruction as students proceed according to the progress the children make. A more constructivist view of instructional planning would alter this scenario to engage students in verbal description of what they understand as a way for both teachers and students to go forward based on the student's level of understanding.

Data on what children know about a topic should be collected at the beginning of a unit. For middle grades, this may be done using a pencil-and-paper pretest or an attitudinal technique. For primary students, teacher observation and group discussions are the more preferable tools for collecting these data. These data can be used to select students for cooperative learning groups, placing some of the more informed students with each group, or they may indicate that teachers should spend more direct-teaching time working with students on vocabulary items and providing more concrete and visual experiences.

Data collected during the unit are also useful to formative evaluation. Individual worksheets, student comments, class discussion, and student projects need to be monitored so that reteaching time for individuals or groups can be scheduled as needed. Work habits and cooperation in group efforts need to be evaluated on an almost daily basis.

Formative evaluation benefits both group and individual efforts. By coaching and monitoring group projects, teachers can guarantee better final projects and presentations. The same is true for individual efforts. Formative evaluation of both content and process objectives serves to keep the unit dynamics intact and flowing.

---

[3]Benjamin S. Bloom, George F. Madaus, and Thomas Hastings, *Evaluation to Improve Learning* (New York: McGraw-Hill, 1981).

Summative evaluation is the point in instruction when there is a collective pause to calculate and reflect on what has been learned. It is the moment when projects are presented or when tests are taken. It should be the moment when individual children are asked to assess what they now know or can do or feel and compare it with what they knew or could do or felt at the beginning of the unit. This is the point at which a cumulative grade or assessment is given. In our view, the more deeply each of these assessment moments is integrated into the natural dynamic of unit of instruction, the more authentic the evaluation can be.

We have seen that organizing assessment and evaluation means finding a match between our objectives/instruction and student activity; it also means we must decide on the kinds of student data to collect and when to collect it if we are to determine the additional instructional steps students need to progress toward the objectives. The activity below, "Planning Unit Evaluations," brings these ideas together.

10.1 *ON YOUR OWN: PLANNING UNIT EVALUATIONS*

This is a two-step exercise. First, match each objective with the unit activities that would best help students attain the objective. Second, try to match the assessment techniques to the objectives/activities combinations you have selected. The sequence of the activities follows the order in which objectives are listed. Try working on both samples.

SAMPLE UNIT PLAN 10.1

Putting Food on the Table (primary grades)

OBJECTIVES:

	Step 1: *Activities*	Step 2: *Evaluation Techniques*
1. Student categorizes food items as plant, animal, or both.	_____	_____
2. Student sequences pictures of food production.	_____	_____
3. Student describes jobs related to food production.	_____	_____

---

continued

SAMPLE UNIT PLAN 10.1 (CONT.)

4. Student names ways to preserve food.   _____   _____

5. Student works productively in small group.   _____   _____

6. Student works independently at project centers.   _____   _____

ACTIVITIES:

a. Read story of "The Little Red Hen" and discuss how we take food for granted; have students draw favorite foods.

b. Begin favorite-food research books.

c. Show filmstrips and sequence pictures at classroom centers featuring food production.

d. Use flannel board story to show ways to preserve food.

e. Ask students to do research at home about food sources; add to books.

f. Make a trip to supermarket to watch delivery trucks arrive.

g. Invite local truck farmer to visit class.

h. Do more work on favorite food research books.

i. Have small groups prepare pictures of food histories.

j. Finish favorite food books.

k. Let small groups present pictures to another class.

ASSESSMENT TECHNIQUES:

Think about the activities and the natural opportunities they would present for assessment. There is no need to use every type of technique listed. Use this list for both samples.

pretest	group evaluation
posttest	work sample
individual project	conference
group project	self-evaluation
observation	

SAMPLE UNIT PLAN 10.2

Fifth Grade: "Slavery"

OBJECTIVES:

	Step 1:	Step 2:
	Activities	*Evaluation Techniques*
1. Student describes slave trade of colonial and early republic America and social mentality that fostered it.	_____	_____
2. Student describes how blacks responded to slavery.	_____	_____
3. Student works productively in small group study.	_____	_____
4. Student uses two library sources for individual profile.	_____	_____

ACTIVITIES:

a. Students role-play in small groups using slave-auction documents.

b. Teacher begins reading *Uncle Tom's Cabin* aloud to class.

c. Students choose classmate to research biographical profile.

d. All students read text assignment on plantation life individually.

e. Small groups research and discuss research questions.

f. Teacher shows television segments of "Roots" to class.

g. Small groups discuss and study.

h. Music of slavery period presentation and singing.

i. Small groups edit members' profiles.

Thinking about the Exercise

The second-grade food unit offers several opportunities for collecting data on student progress toward the stated objectives. The students' work on sequencing pictures of food production at the centers could be observed and recorded, or a cut-and-paste worksheet that followed the student session at the center could provide a work sample that would give us some data. Which would be a better measure of what the student knows? Which would be more possible to organize in a busy classroom? For the objectives about categorizing food items and describing jobs and ways of preserving foods, you also have several choices about how to collect data. Most obvious are individual worksheets. As other variations on this theme you could have small groups compose collages from magazine pictures or create a group story about jobs in food production. The story could be recorded with a tape recorder or by an aide. The children could then illustrate the story with a large group picture.

Teacher observation and self-evaluation recommend themselves as techniques for the work-habit and group-skills objectives. The group food-history pictures and presentations will also provide observational data about these objectives. The individual favorite-food research books will tell you about the student's ability to ask questions at home and put his or her information into another form. Through teacher questioning, these books could be used at sharing times to work on the categorizing, food-production jobs, and food-preservation objectives. Again, the data are observational. Perhaps using a clipboard observation form to record social behaviors and thinking skills would help you recall students' oral responses.

Evaluation options for fifth graders are perhaps easier to organize. Completing "I learned . . ." or "What I don't understand . . ." statements could serve as a beginning point following the slave-market role play. The research questions that the small groups discuss should prepare them to respond to the content objectives about the slave trade, the social mentality fostering it, and the African responses to it. But how will you know something about each student's progress in these areas? Clearly, some kind of paper-pencil technique would seem appropriate, perhaps short essays or multiple-choice items.

For the research objective, teachers can easily judge the individual profiles of significant personages of the slavery period. Having students edit the profiles in the small groups would generate observational data the teacher could use to assess productive group study. Small group discussion of the research questions would also provide assessment data.

More mileage could be gained from these projects than is indicated in the activity choices. It would be profitable to form groups to write about people in similar categories—slaves, plantation owners, government leaders, abolitionists, freedmen. You can pool the students' stories and present the compilation to the class, which could then record the data on a retrieval chart and discuss it as a large group, following the Taba strategy. Generalizations could be made as a result of this sharing process, leading students to understand and describe the social mentality fostering slavery and the response to it. Comparing the statements students made after the role play at the beginning of the unit to their feelings and knowledge at the conclusion of the unit would be a powerful self-evaluation technique.

Communicating about Individual Progress

Informing students and parents about instructional objectives helps set expectations for learning. Often, the long-range, or year's, objectives as well as grade-level performance criteria are set by the school or district. These objectives, and additional ones you diagnose as essential for the class or individuals, should be clear to everyone involved. Many of the long-range objectives will have only a tangential relation to the social studies. For parents, seeing the subject matter designation is probably less important than getting a global picture of the year's expectations. You could communicate these objectives through a letter sent home with the students or during the Back to School Night sessions usually held near the beginning of the school year. Unit objectives are best communicated by letter at the beginning of each new unit.

Communication about objectives should happen throughout the year, not just at officially designated report periods. Periodic checklists or work samples can be sent home to keep parents informed. Individual conferences with students are essential means of keeping students focused on where they are and what they need to accomplish.

You should begin conferences with both students and parents by clarifying areas of growth toward the specified objectives. Many teachers find it useful to conduct three-way conferencing among themselves, the student, and the parent(s). Sharing your grade book does little to illuminate the student's work to a parent. Explaining the assessment techniques and evaluation conventions used at the school may also be necessary. The meeting is for student and teacher to show and explain student work samples, such as stories or reports that have been collected over time. Student and parent suggestions on how to plan for further growth should be encouraged. Goal setting is one of the most potent life-molding abilities that teachers can help students develop.

Evaluation of Instruction

Using student data to evaluate instruction should guide what happens next with individual students and the entire class, in addition to providing evidence for future ways of organizing instruction for the teacher. There are several ways to examine student data for the purpose of improving instruction.

Examining the class trends in paper-and-pencil assessments enables teachers to check for their own flaws in instruction or item construction. If the majority of the class misses certain items, several possibilities need to be entertained. Is the item itself ambiguous or tricky? How about the instruction? Was there congruence between the item and variables such as the cognitive level at which instruction about it was presented? Was the amount of time devoted to content sufficient? Did the students have the general readiness necessary to understand the idea or perform the skill?

Another perspective on the appropriateness of instruction is examining the consistency between the amount of work assigned and the amount of work students actually complete. A poor rate of project completion may mean that aspects of the classroom management, such as reward systems and motivation, need to be reconsidered. Social rewards, such as being part of a group that is supportive and sharing results with others in a nonthreatening manner, are relevant considerations. Typically, students will complete a task that has personal significance.

When children do not complete individual projects, a task analysis to find out which skills the students need more instruction on will help teachers carry out similar projects in the future. Report writing from various sources is a classic obstacle for middle-grade students. Consider a fifth-grade assignment in which students are to choose and write about an explorer of the Americas. To do this, a student needs to combine several skills. Each skill listed below requires mastery of the preceding skills. Often we assume that students will figure out how to handle the dynamics of report writing, as most of us did when we were that age, by trial and error and intuition. Commonly, steps two through five are not taught directly to the class, or they are taught for one report and assumed to be mastered for use in all succeeding reports. Looking at the report quality of completed reports and the rate of report completion can indicate which of the skills may need to be emphasized in future instruction.

Task Analysis of Report Writing

1. Locate topic using index and table of contents.
2. Prepare questions or main topics to research.
3. Read for main ideas and supporting details.
4. Take notes in own words to answer research questions.
5. Review notes and organize outline for first draft.
6. Write first draft using outline and notes.
7. Edit first draft for topic flow and organization.
8. Rewrite first draft.
9. Edit for spelling, grammar, and mechanics.
10. Prepare final draft.

10.2 SMALL GROUP WORK: TASK ANALYSIS PRACTICE

Imagine that you teach the third grade and want the class to make a map of the county that shows major landforms and roads. Make a list of what they would have to know about mapmaking and the county before they could do this project. Share your list with a colleague. Do you both agree? Isn't it daunting to become aware of how much we assume when we ask students to do projects? Given this list, discuss how would you prepare the students for this project.

SUMMARY

Classroom teachers must become knowledgeable consumers of prepared assessment instruments and adept designers of procedures and tools for evaluating individual student progress and their own instruction. As modes of assessment evolve and student achievement of subject matter standards is given increasing attention, teachers will be required to focus on assessment more than in the past. With increased attention on assessment, teachers must be clear about the relationship between the kinds of data a particular technique or instrument yields and the questions the data are used to answer. Some techniques and instruments are most appropriate for assessing group achievement and some are more appropriate for the assessment of individual learning. Further, teachers need to understand the limitations of using classroom group averages as data to evaluate their instruction. Assessment of student progress is a continuous process, an integral part of instructional planning.

Good student assessment and evaluation is unobtrusive and instructionally integrated. This kind of assessment is known as authentic. Planning social studies units requires that teachers elaborate ways of collecting evidence about each instructional objective before beginning the unit with students. When assessing student progress, teachers must collect enough evidence to reflect on and communicate about a student's progress toward specified objectives. Evaluation can be made meaningful to students to the degree that they become knowledgeable about what is expected and have opportunities to select, explain, and evaluate their work. Whatever the tools and techniques used, the results of evaluation should be that students recognize their accomplishment and increase their desire to strive for further growth.

SUGGESTED READINGS

Adams, D. M. K., and Hamm, M. E., "Portfolio Assessment and Social Studies: Collecting, Selecting, and Reflecting on What Is Significant." *Social Education* 56 (February 1992): 103–105. Survey of necessary issues to consider when using portfolios as an assessment tool.

Athanases, Steven Z. "Teachers Report of the Effects of Preparing Portfolios of Literacy Instruction." *The Elementary School Journal* 94 (May 1994): 421–439. Participant-observer research probing assessment of teacher quality through teacher's own analysis of response-based literacy instruction.

Cervone, B., and O'Leary, K. "A Conceptual Framework for Parent Involvement." *Educational Leadership* 40 (October 1982): 48–49. Suggestions for involving parents in school learning.

Cramer, Susan R. "Navigating the Assessment Maze with Portfolios." *Clearinghouse* 67 (November–December 1993): 72–74. Presents rudiments of portfolio content design and use as assessment tool stressing importance of previously agreed on criteria for assessing quality.

Doremus, Vivian P. "Forcing Works for Flowers, but Not for Children." *Educational Leadership* 44, no. 3 (November 1986): 32–35. Represents argument against excessive testing of children's achievement and reliance on academic achievements to exclusion of other developmental areas.

Glazer, Susan Mandel. "Assessment: How You Can Use Tests and Portfolios Too" *Teaching K–8* 25 (August–September 1994): 152–154. Brief discussion showing significance for students of portfolios in teacher-student interactive assessment.

McKeon, Denise. "When Meeting 'Common' Standards Is Uncommonly Difficult." *Educational Leadership* 51 (May 1994): 45–49. Brings educational equity concerns to bear on standards movement that shows little consideration of learners from minority cultures and languages.

Simmons, Rebecca. "The Horse before the Cart: Assessing for Understanding." *Educational Leadership* 51 (February 1994): 22–23. Deals with demonstrating how to interpret evolving jargon used to describe assessment ideas when outcome-based education replaces mastery learning.

INDEX